Frieda Lawrence

You think I do not count besides Lawrence, but I take myself, my ideals and life quite as seriously as he does his. This you will not allow, and it is our quarrel, you think I am conceited. I can't help that, but it hurts me very much when you think I do not count as a human being. But you do not think much of women, they are not human beings in your eyes.

LETTER FROM FRIEDA LAWRENCE TO SAMUEL KOTELIANSKY, 9 FEBRUARY 1915

If the day came, which God forbid, that I should see Lawrence as the 'great man', he would be a dead thing to me and it would bore me. Greatness is a thing of the outer world, where I indeed am nothing and don't want to be any more! So I grant you that in the world of men Lawrence *is* and I am *not*! But *that* world is nothing to me, there's a deeper one, where life itself flows, there I am at home! And the *outer* world isn't my affair! All I really want you to admit is the greater importance of the deeper world!

LETTER FROM FRIEDA LAWRENCE TO SAMUEL KOTELIANSKY, 4 DECEMBER 1923

Frieda Lawrence

ROSIE JACKSON

*Including Not I, But the Wind
and other autobiographical writings*

 Pandora
An Imprint of HarperCollins*Publishers*

Pandora
An Imprint of HarperCollins*Publishers*
77–85 Fulham Palace Road,
Hammersmith, London W6 8JB
1160 Battery Street,
San Francisco, California 94111–1213

Published by Pandora 1994
10 9 8 7 6 5 4 3 2 1

Not I, But the Wind first published by
William Heinemann Ltd, 1935

A catalogue record for this book
is available from the British Library

ISBN 0 04 440915 X

Typeset by Harper Phototypesetters Limited
Northampton, England
Printed in Great Britain by
HarperCollins Manufacturing, Glasgow

Contents

List of Illustrations	vii
Acknowledgements	ix

FRIEDA LAWRENCE BY ROSIE JACKSON

The Question of Frieda Lawrence: 'living in greater depth'	3
Mythologies: 'the mother of orgasm'	9
Frieda's Men: 'gratified desire'	17
Frieda and Motherhood: 'the flowers of pain'	53
Frieda, Lawrence and the Feminine: 'beyond an apartheid of gender'	61
The Quest for Frieda Lawrence: 'saying yes'	73
Memoirs and Fictions: 'not I, but the wind'	83
The Outer Life: 'a real destiny'	91

FRIEDA LAWRENCE

Not I, But the Wind	97

'AND THE FULLNESS THEREOF'

Extracts from Frieda's Fictionalized Memoirs	197
Bibliography	231
Notes	235

List of Illustrations

1. 1890s Frieda in Germany (Laurence Pollinger Ltd)
2. *c.*1900 Frieda with Ernest Weekley and his parents (Private Collection)
3. 23 September 1911 Frieda with Weekley and their children on Weekley's parents' Golden Wedding Anniversary (Photography Collection, Harry Ransom Humanities Research Center, The University of Texas at Austin)
4. Early 1900s Frieda with her son Montague (Laurence Pollinger Ltd)
5. 13 July 1914 Lawrence, Katherine Mansfield, Frieda and John Middleton Murry on the Lawrences' wedding day (Nottinghamshire County Library Service)
6. July 1914 Middleton Murry, Frieda and Lawrence at 9 Selwood Terrace, London (Nottinghamshire County Library Service)
7. Else Jaffe, Baroness von Richthofen and Frieda (Dr Marianne von Eckardt)
8. April 1923 Frieda with driver, guide, Spud Johnson and Lawrence, in Mexico (The University of Nottingham)
9. April 1923 Witter Bynner, Frieda and Lawrence en route to Teotihuacan (The University of Nottingham)
10. 11 April 1923 On top of the Temple of the Sun   Temple of Quetzalcoatl, Teotihuacan with Lawrence and Witter Bynner (The University of Nottingham)
11. May 1923 Frieda and Lawrence in Chapala, Mexico (The University of Nottingham)
12. (and front cover photo) May 1923 Lawrence and Frieda at celebrations for Spud Johnson's 26th birthday, Chapala, Mexico (The University of Nottingham)
13. 1923 Frieda with Lawrence at their rented house in Chapala, Mexico (The University of Nottingham)
14. Early 1920s Frieda in embroidered dress in Mexico (The University of Nottingham)

15. Early 1920s Frieda in characteristic hat and cape in Mexico (The University of Nottingham)
16. (and back cover photo) Early 1920s Frieda in Mexico (The University of Nottingham)
17. 22 September 1925 Frieda and Lawrence on the S.S. Resolute leaving America together for the last time (Private Collection)
18. 1927 Frieda and Lawrence at the Villa Mirenda, Italy (Private Collection)
19. Summer 1928 Frieda at Les Diablerets, Switzerland (Lady Huxley)
20. September 1928 Frieda and Lawrence at the Chalet Kesselmatte, Gsteig-bei-Gstaad, Bern, Switzerland (Mrs Margaret Needham)
21. *c.* 1930s Mabel Dodge Luhan, Frieda and Dorothy Brett in Taos (Private Collection)

Acknowledgements

I am grateful to Dr Jan Relf, who gave astute comments on an early manuscript and whose unstinting friendship and feminist insights have been enormously helpful. I would like to thank Dr Keith Sagar for generously sharing photos of Frieda and Lawrence, and Melissa Sagar for her warm hospitality. Frieda's daughter, Barbara Barr, kindly let me stay at Radda, Italy and once again recounted memories of her mother. Chloë Green (née Baynes) allowed me to quote from the memoirs of her mother, Rosalind Thornycroft, and Dr Dorothy Johnston at Nottingham University made it possible for me to reproduce photos from the Lawrence Collection.

The meticulous studies of many devoted Lawrencian scholars and biographers have made more free-wheeling works such as this possible. I am especially indebted to E. W. Tedlock, for his marvellous editing of *Frieda Lawrence: The Memoirs and Correspondence*. Robert Lucas' biography, *Frieda Lawrence*, has been an invaluable source of material. I have also been inspired by *Nora*, Brenda Maddox's exemplary study of Nora Joyce and by Claire Tomalin's excellent biography of Katherine Mansfield.

I am grateful to Sheila Yeger, who first alerted me to the story of Frieda Lawrence, Annie Wilson, who made a vicarious visit to Frieda's home in Taos on my behalf, Ken Mackenzie, whose obstinate faith in Lawrence unwittingly kept alive issues that were to feed into this book, and many students over the years. Also Phoebe Clare Clarke, Mary-Jayne Rust and Kate Saunders for much-valued friendships. Among the staff at Pandora, I am particularly grateful to Karen Holden, for her superb editorial work and endless encouragement and to her successor, Belinda Budge. As ever, deep thanks to John Harlow for unwavering emotional and practical support.

Without the permission of Gerald Pollinger, this book would not have been possible. Copyright material is reproduced with the permission of Laurence Pollinger Ltd and the Estate of Frieda Lawrence Ravagli.

Any errors – whether of fact or judgement – remain fully my own.

Frieda Lawrence

ROSIE JACKSON

The Question of Frieda Lawrence: 'living in greater depth'

I should like to see a full description of her as a whole woman, a real person, instead of this rampant lustful Hun or just somebody who accompanied Lawrence. I don't think she's had a fair deal.

FRIEDA'S DAUGHTER BARBARA BARR, 16 NOVEMBER 1993[1]

*M*y aim in this book is to unsettle the orthodox view of Frieda Lawrence. Frieda spent eighteen of her seventy-seven years with novelist D. H. Lawrence, was the main focus of his erotic and emotional life and provided the model for the most important female characters in his fiction. Yet Lawrencian biographers and literary historians have tended to dismiss her as a stubborn harridan, a woman whose obstinacy and selfishness eventually blocked the full and free flowering of Lawrence's genius. It is true that, far from gratefully accepting the traditional role of writer's muse and mate, Frieda struggled against it and fought, in her own way, for some recognition, autonomy and freedom of self expression. But she was no role model for independent women. Her position was far more complicated and richer than either of these extremes.[2]

Until now, Frieda has not had the reappraisal enjoyed by the wives of other famous men of letters, such as James Joyce's wife, Nora. Apart from Mary Daly's wild attempt to construct Frieda as a battered wife, there has been no female discussion of her life as a woman, nor any unravelling of her relation to Lawrence's work and his ideology of gender.[3] The only full-length study so far has been Robert Lucas' *Frieda Lawrence: The Story of Frieda von Richthofen and D. H. Lawrence* (1973), the subtitle betraying his bias towards the years Frieda shared with Lawrence rather than in her own right.

Women seem not to have known what to do with her. Feminist writers in the 1970s and 1980s made such an unyielding condemnation of Lawrence's sexual politics that it is almost embarrassing to claim serious attention for Frieda, as if her closeness to Lawrence means she must share his worst prejudices, such collusion making her of little value to women now.

However, if we retrace Frieda's life through her own words and reflect on the difficulties of her time with Lawrence, we find someone who refutes many of the myths and fictions about her. She was no feminist, but she fought repeatedly with those aspects of Lawrence and his work that she felt were arrogant or egotistical. She struggled against his theories of male supremacy, and lamented the flaws that they introduced into his art. Unlike later feminists, though, she was not prepared to reject absolutely that imaginative vision she found in Lawrence's work at its best. I shall argue that her defence of this vision is vitally important for us in our current crises around gender, that her insights have bearing on the conflicts that are still taking place, not only between men and women, but between masculine and feminine principles within ourselves and within society.

One of the difficulties facing any discussion of Frieda or Lawrence is the way their lives and characters have been transmuted into myth. They have been in the public sphere for so long that they have become legendary and, with Lawrence especially, the chronicling of the exact minutiae of his history has become as obsessive as the recording of the New Testament. One biography after another claims to be definitive, the multivolumed Cambridge Lawrence biography being the latest and largest of such scholarly enterprises at the time of writing.

This mythologizing process is closely related to the way Lawrence has been seen in the role of prophet and seer. This role was both self-professed and sustained, and promoted by others after his death, Frieda among them. He became known as 'the priest of love' and was elevated by some into an unquestioned genius, whose message would bring life to a dying secular world. His defence of erotic, passionate love and deep relationship as a means of restoring human vitality (though much misunderstood, sentimentalized and misconstrued) has meant that his marriage with Frieda has also been translated into legendary terms. As the woman with whom this new form of intimacy and frankness between the sexes was acted out, she was no longer perceived as Frieda the historical person, but Frieda the incarnation of Womanhood, with all the projections this can imply.

In retellings of the Frieda–Lawrence saga, various degrees of this mythologizing have remained. Like the literary romances of Mary and Percy Shelley a century before, or of Sylvia Plath and Ted Hughes fifty years later, the story of Frieda and D. H. Lawrence has entered history as legend, so that the smallest details of their lives have been inflated and invested with a deep, unconscious charge. It may be that we need to believe in such larger-than-life figures and to see them acting out extraordinary, often tragic, stories on our behalf. Or it may be that our repeated fascination with them stems from their embodying some archetypal drama, which exaggerates and mirrors our own internal conflicts and fantasies.

Some such unconscious attachment is needed to account for the incredible proliferation of biographies, critical studies and hagiographies of Lawrence's life over the last sixty years, as well as for the endless films and film adaptations of his works. At the time of writing this, Lawrence's literary agent, Gerald Pollinger, informed me that there were at least ten further biographies in progress. The 1994 study of Lawrence and Frieda by Brenda Maddox and the biography of Frieda by Janet Byrne, to be published in 1995, are but two further manifestations of this contemporary resurgence of interest.

Frieda's life *was* fascinating and extraordinary, especially by the standards of the time. She left her aristocratic German background to marry an Englishman and live in Nottingham with him for thirteen years; her conventional marriage had interludes of sexual affairs and contact with some radical counter-cultural theory in Germany; at a time when divorce was scandalous, she not only left her respectable husband for a penniless, working-class writer, but had to leave behind her three young children, too; she had a nomadic life with D. H. Lawrence for eighteen years, visiting Europe, Ceylon, Australia, the United States, Mexico; she deeply influenced Lawrence's writing and ideas; she had three marriages; she met some of the most famous literary and artistic names of the time – from Aldous Huxley and Bertrand Russell to Charlie Chaplin, Georgia O'Keefe and Stravinsky.

The itemization of most of these facts of Frieda's life is easy to find in any biography of Lawrence. My own final section here, 'The Outer Life', offers a simple, chronological catalogue of these main external events and dates for easy reference. But my own emphasis is not primarily biographical. It may be time for a reappraisal of the role played by women in the lives of creative men, but I have no wish to add to the already gargantuan critical industry surrounding Lawrence. That is why this present volume is less a traditional biography than a re-presentation of some of the material relating to Frieda. In some sense, biographical subjects will always elude our grasp, and I am less interested in collating empirical 'facts' than in seeing how they are used, how fictions of people and legends of their lives are made. Thus, my focus is not only on the rich and complex emotional and historical realities of Frieda Lawrence's life, but on exploring the ways in which she has been represented and mythologized – processes that affect both our thinking about her as a woman and about wider issues of gender, creativity and genius.

No matter how 'objective' writers or observers may claim or try to be, all are influenced by some personal or ideological persuasion, albeit unconsciously. Because of this, I have made as much room as possible to allow Frieda to speak for herself. She left a number of impressive writings – eloquent letters, memoirs, unfinished fictions – that have received insufficient attention. These allow us to glimpse her from the inside, to share her subjective views of things, to see how she made sense of her experience. Thus, to widen the discussion of Frieda, this book is a partial anthology of the best of her autobiographical writings. It contains *Not I, But the Wind*, Frieda's memoirs of her life with Lawrence, and substantial extracts from her fictionalized autobiography which was called 'And the Fullness Thereof' in Tedlock's edition of her writings. In these introductory pages, I also include many direct quotations from Frieda's letters and memoirs.

I have devoted the next section to a discussion of the mythologies about Frieda Lawrence, which are so extreme and contradictory. What emerges is a telling reflection of the way female sexuality has been constructed in literary history, and how this contrasts with the way Lawrence has been construed as a male genius. Then, using a thematic rather than chronological approach, I explore some of the key issues in Frieda's life. These include Frieda's sexual relationships and views of eroticism; her experience of mothering and the profound effect of losing her three young children; her bonding and battles with Lawrence and their ideas about male–female relationships; her philosophy of life; and, finally, an introduction to her own writings.

'For myself, I find that in her own very different way Frieda is a person as remarkable as Lawrence, and that Lawrence knew it.' This was the verdict of one of their friends, Catherine Carswell, in *The Savage Pilgrimage*. The difference was that Frieda had no ambition to compete in the 'world of men' and no compulsion to write for public recognition. In the letter to Samuel Koteliansky that is one of the epigraphs to this book, she makes it clear that the external world of achievement and competition – that male world in which Lawrence made such an impact – was one where she had no desire to excel: 'But *that* world is nothing to me, there's a deeper one, where life itself flows, there I am at home! And the *outer* world isn't my affair! All I really want you to admit is the greater importance of the deeper world!'

In France, at around the same time, Sonia Delaunay, artist and wife of painter Robert Delaunay, was making a similar disavowal of wanting to compete in male society: 'From the day we started living together, I played second fiddle and I never put myself first. Robert had brilliance, the flare of genius. As for myself, *I lived in greater depth*' (my italics).⁴ Such claims to be living in 'a deeper world' or 'at greater depth' might be read as strategic attempts on the part of strong women to console themselves for secondary roles at the side of extremely successful artistic partners. But in Frieda's case, there was nothing disingenuous about it. She had no longing for worldly success, whether for herself or for Lawrence, and she welcomed the celebration of Lawrence's work only in so far as it genuinely embraced values of the deeper inner life – values that, in Jungian terms, might be called 'feminine' – and that are still anathema to our materialistic and masculine culture.

By focusing on her inner world as well as on the better-known outer events of her life, I hope to present a Frieda rather different from the one promoted by the Lawrence legend. A woman more eloquent and intelligent, more perceptive, sensitive and imaginative, a woman whose compassion was profound and whose commitment to 'living in greater depth' led to a wonderful defiance of all kinds of man-made conventions.

Mythologies:
'the mother of orgasm'

she was Hera and Demeter and Aphrodite gloriously rolled into one . . . ALDOUS HUXLEY, THE GENIUS AND THE GODDESS

One of the most striking aspects of the legend that has been built around D. H. Lawrence over the last sixty years is the repeated way in which the basic facts of Frieda's life have been told and retold to give a particular slant to her character and identity. With these various accretions surrounding her, it has become almost impossible to reach Frieda the historical person with any certainty.

The process of mythologizing began with Lawrence's imaginative transformations of her into, first, goddess, then bitch. His early impressions from 1912 were the enthusiastic and enraptured voice of a man in love: 'You are the most wonderful woman in all England', 'I shall love you all my life', 'She's the finest woman I've ever met – she's splendid, she is really . . . perfectly unconventional . . . Oh, but she is the woman of a lifetime'.

In this positive version of Frieda, she is the embodiment of the feminine as Earth mother and benevolent deity. In *Not I, But the Wind*, Frieda records how Brewster compared her to pictures of Buddhist saints. Her biographer, Robert Lucas, evokes her as being 'Self-confident, generous and kind-hearted . . . radiating warmth and well-being like some pagan goddess of Nature, a mixture of Cybele and Aphrodite Pandemos'.[5]

But the inverse side of this myth is the sudden twisting of the idealized feminine into its opposite. If evidence were needed that Lawrence's early hyperboles were as much to do with his own projected desires as with Frieda herself, by 1918 his praise had switched to insults and he was denouncing her in equally strong terms: 'Frieda is the devouring mother', 'She really is a devil . . . I have been bullied by her long enough. I really could leave her now, without a pang'. Six years of living with Lawrence and, for Lawrence '... the most wonderful woman in all England' had metamorphosed into a man-eater and demon.

These mythologized extremes have shaped the response to Frieda Lawrence ever since. Whether bitch, goddess or elemental nature, no biographical or critical study is free of them. In one of the many early biographies of Lawrence, Catherine Carswell, a personal acquaintance, writes of Frieda:

> He [Lawrence] had chosen . . . a woman from whom he felt he could win the special submission he demanded without thereby defeating her in her womanhood. Sometimes it seemed to us that he had chosen rather a force of nature – a female force – than an individual woman. Frieda was to Lawrence by turns a buffeting and a laughing breeze, a healing rain or a maddening tempest of stupidity, a cheering sun or a stroke of indiscriminate lightning. She was mindless Womanhood, wilful, defiant, disrespectful, argumentative, assertive, vengeful, sly, illogical, treacherous, unscrupulous and self-seeking. At times she hated Lawrence and he her. There were things she jeered at in him and things in her that maddened him – things that neither would consent to subdue. But partly for that reason – how he admired her! . . . In Frieda Lawrence found a magnificent female probity of being, as well as of physical well-being . . .[6]

Aldous Huxley's fanciful version of Frieda in *The Genius and the Goddess* turns her into a variety of maidens and deities, from a 'splendid Valkyrie incongruously dressed in a hobble skirt', to 'a Wagnerian heroine' with 'the body of a strong young matron' and 'the face of a goddess disguised as a healthy peasant girl. Demeter, perhaps . . . [or] Hera playing the part of a milkmaid', 'At nineteen she must have been Hebe and the three Graces and all the nymphs of Diana rolled into one'. Essentially, then, Frieda was seen as 'incarnate maternity', the great Earth mother, 'a kind of feminine Antaeus – invincible while her feet were on the ground, a goddess so long as she was in contact with the greater goddess within her, the universal Mother without' (see Plate 14).

This attribution of earthy physical strength recurs in contemporary descriptions of her. Lady Cynthia Asquith confessed herself attracted to

Frieda's 'health, strength and generosity of nature'. Rhys Davies described her as 'cheerfully alive in her own sunny activity'. Testimonies of her energy, warmheartedness, resilience and healthy physique would recommend her for any promotion of vitamin supplements.

Yet even these qualities provoked a negative backlash. Although Lawrence was doubtless attracted by her strength – when they met, Frieda was in her prime, strong, beautiful, well fed and cared for, with none of the physical or psychological weakness of Lawrence's mother – her health and exuberance came to count against her. At the side of Lawrence's increasing illness from tuberculosis (usually read, like Keats', as a sign of unusual sensibility), Frieda's health has been construed as brutally triumphant, an index of lesser sensitivity.

Her size has contributed to this contrast. There are few compliments about her appearance or weight. Huxley called her 'Rabelaisian', Lucas 'a Cleopatra by Rubens', Miller 'a Renoir with the head of a Greek', but others have been less euphemistic, implying that her large physique was evidence of her lesser moral character. Katherine Mansfield, who had taught herself to eat little after serious weight problems in childhood, insulted Frieda as a 'huge fat pudding'. Mabel Dodge Luhan, who never forgave Frieda for blocking her own amorous approaches to Lawrence, took her revenge by recording their first meeting in Mexico in 1922 in unflattering terms: 'Lawrence and Frieda came hurrying along the platform, she tall and full-fleshed . . . with green unfocused eyes, and her half-open mouth with the lower jaw pulled a little sideways. Frieda always had a mouth rather like a gunman. Lawrence ran with short, quick steps at her side . . . I had an impression of his slim fragility beside Frieda's solidity . . .' Later, Luhan inflates Frieda further into 'the mother of orgasm and of the vast, lively mystery of the flesh'! As late as 1993, Elaine Feinstein invokes current conventions of female slenderness when she judges Frieda as 'not a little overweight'.

The focus on Frieda's powerful physical presence has added to a reading of her as mindless and unintellectual. Many analogies have been made between Frieda and animals, particularly the lion: '[she had a] sturdy body . . . magnificent shoulders . . . Her head and the whole carriage of her body were noble. Her eyes were green, with a lot of tawny yellow in them, the nose straight. She looked one dead in the eyes, fearlessly judging one and, at that moment, she was extraordinarily like a lioness . . .'[8] In 1987, Claire Tomalin referred to Frieda as being 'like a big, bold lioness with her mane of fair hair'.[9]

Thus, when F. R. Leavis came to write his influential study *D. H. Lawrence: Novelist* (1955) – a work that, for the first time, made a careful critical scrutiny of Lawrence's fiction and claimed for it a firm place within a tradition of 'great' English literature – Leavis' slandering of Frieda could both draw on and confirm these various layers of myth, for Frieda was already construed in ways that set up traditional gender stereotypes. She was the Earth mother, the body, coarse matter, in contrast to Lawrence's mind, soul and fine intelligence. Moreover, she had none of his delicate moral discrimination. Unlike Lawrence, she was all crude instinct and blind passion. If Lawrence was in the best tradition of English moral intelligence, Frieda was outside it. She was a foreigner, she didn't belong in this cultured lineage; what was more, in the worst execration Leavis could provide, she was 'amoral':

And when we are taking stock of the disadvantages Lawrence had to contend with . . . we have to consider Frieda herself. *She has, as Lawrence's wife, no home, and, having abandoned her children, no maternal function. She was, in fact, neither maternal in type nor intellectual; she had no place in any community, no social function, and nothing much to do . . .* [my italics] [their union] was hardly one that provided representative experience for pronouncing normatively about marriage. We see the great advantage enjoyed by the author of *Anna Karenina*.[10]

Frieda read these powerful indictments (Leavis' book was published a year before her death) and, with characteristic outrage, wrote to him personally to protest at the injustice of his slander. She strongly rebutted his charges of her bad mothering and her lack of intelligence: 'You say I was not maternal, I think I was, and not intellectual, but I was not dumb either and thought things out for myself'.[11] But she had little chance of making her own voice heard publicly. The problem was not only Leavis and his particular prejudices, but the critical tradition that he represented and the enshrining of male genius it espoused.

More firmly than before, from Leavis onwards, the Frieda Lawrence who entered literary history was a creature of myth. One-dimensional, more of a caricature than a character, she was rewritten as a large, unsubtle, uncreative woman, free of the moral or spiritual agonies that hounded Lawrence to his premature end. Racial and class prejudice etched the negative image deeper. Luhan claimed it was 'the German mind' in Frieda that made it so hard for her to fully understand or appreciate Lawrence and that Lawrence himself complained about the grossness of Frieda's soul. His real empathy, asserted Luhan, was with 'the quick, subtle, Latin spirit – but the north German psyche is inimical to it'.[12] Acton called Frieda 'Lawrence's ferocious German wife, with a red face'. Leavis' transparent contempt for Frieda is in the same xenophobic tradition. He dismissed her as an amoral German aristocrat.

Such racism is not untypical of the British and was fuelled by two wars with Frieda's country of origin, but what is worrying is the way in which such unexamined assumptions have informed virtually all post-Leavisite judgments of Frieda. Her daughter, Barbara Barr, believes this aspect of the prevailing prejudice against Frieda has tended to be overlooked:

> *I feel there's a real antipathy against Frieda among the English, partly because she was German. Dora Carrington wrote of Frieda 'with her German grossness'. But she was not at all gross, anything but. And that line Ottoline Morrell took in her diary, that Lawrence was so sensitive, and Frieda so thick skinned. But she was a very sensitive woman, proud. She sometimes thought that Lawrence turned against her because of her German blood.*

One of the fascinating, if disturbing, elements in the way Frieda has been constructed in Lawrencian criticism is this moral polarity that has been established. The fact that she was from the German aristocracy is made to carry value judgments – of privilege, laziness and grossness – while Lawrence's working-class origins carry opposite ones. Not only is Frieda the healthy, gross female body as opposed to Lawrence's emaciated flesh and tortured male spirit. She is also the Teutonic barbarian, utterly unable to relate to his finer moral scruples and intelligence. Sympathy goes to Lawrence, whose inner torment drives him to death, while Frieda, the healthy survivor, is dismissed as insensitive, if not callous. In Barbara Barr's words:

Some people treated my mother very badly. She was a divorced woman, without her children, so she was vulnerable and people wanted to get at her, especially the women . . . As a young woman, she was beautiful . . . she was also sensitive, she had her pride, she didn't like comments that were detrimental about her appearance, she could be hurt . . . But she shook it off, she would let it go and forgive them. She had this great gusto for life, an elemental quality.

Critics have reproduced Lawrence's own shifting perception of Frieda from woman as goddess to woman as devouring mother and bitch, and have mirrored the Puritanism that permeates Lawrence's thinking. Keith Sagar moves from describing Frieda as 'a handsome and high-spirited girl' of seventeen to a mature woman who was 'amoral, disorderly, wasteful, utterly helpless in the house, lying in bed late, lounging about all day with a cigarette dangling from her mouth, expecting service and deference from everyone as her birthright . . .'; 'Frieda was an extraordinary mixture of openness and prejudice, naivete and low cunning, intelligence and stupidity . . . She was utterly amoral, sexually'.[13] Feinstein's portrait of Frieda in *Lawrence's Women* (1993) shows a marked disdain, as if Frieda's character detracted from Lawrence's moral strengths.

The very language of these versions of Frieda is value-laden. Why should Frieda not choose to smoke or read rather than attend to household chores? Why should such negative attributes be attached to a woman who contradicts Puritan ideals of domestic fastidiousness? The inner world of Frieda, moreover, is completely overlooked. Was this behaviour mere laziness or a mark of deeper, hidden emotions?

Henry Miller's remark, that 'In every biography, Frieda is painted malevolently' is an understatement. From men as different as Koteliansky and Leavis to women as various as Luhan and Feinstein, Frieda has been mythologized as the lazy, aristocratic, German woman to Lawrence's industrious, working-class, English man; he is the hero, she the villain. But Miller's claim that 'Frieda deserves justice too' receives an ironic twist in his own hysterical hagiography of Lawrence.

In Miller's burlesque version, the distortions that are implicit in so many readings of Frieda and Lawrence become overt and reach a graphic climax. Lawrence is now 'a poor and harried man . . . a sick man

. . . misunderstood, ostracised, rejected'. He 'slaved away . . . wrote the furrows into [his] cheeks, begged for a crust of bread so that Frieda would not go without'. She 'really broke his back'. In their 'unhappy marriage', Frieda becomes a Medea-like figure, 'clutching' at Lawrence's 'genitals like a vulture' and threatening to consume his very soul: 'how the hard, whorish beak of the woman you loved carved out your own vulture-like features, made your fine sensitive face twist into a rapacious claw. I know that when your words ripped and clawed it was with the hard whore's beak of her who had eaten into your soul . . .'[14]

Frieda strongly resisted such reductive caricatures of her relationship with Lawrence. As in the letter of protest to Leavis, she spurned the notion that she wasn't 'good enough'. 'Yes, I know they think I was "bad" for L.! From their narrow point of view I was! They would have liked him to be a tame, little writer about nice, well behaved little people! Pah!'[15] She wrote to Koteliansky; 'You tell me I failed him. Your "thought processes" don't do you much good; they take away your sensitivity or you could not make such a heartless or cruel statement to me. It is my riches, my glory, my deepest conviction that I was part of his life and a vital part . . . You can read it in his work everywhere'.

It would be misleading to follow the example of one dust jacket that tries to elevate Frieda into 'one of the most dynamically exciting figures of the twentieth century',[16] or to claim, as her biographer Lucas has done, that 'never before has one single woman, as interpreted by a poet, so radically changed the moral climate of her time',[17] but there has to be some corrective to the wild antipathetic portraits of Frieda Lawrence that have prevailed until now. This is not to say that the facts of her life have been erroneously recorded, but that the way they have been represented needs to be recognized as being inseparable from a cultural process that polarizes men and women in stereotypical ways and invests male creativity with superiority and mystery.

As a woman in close proximity to this creativity, Frieda has been construed as muse, mate and harridan. She has been seen positively in so far as she supported Lawrence's creative enterprise and in negative terms when she opposed, criticized, resisted, failed to give domestic back-up to his writing, or simply moved away and followed her own needs. The more she was her own person, the more accusations of selfishness and amorality have pursued her. Because Lawrence participated in household tasks, Frieda was a lazy bitch. Lawrence was the man writing and Frieda was the slovenly and nagging spouse. If Lawrence crucified himself, Frieda was the one who had condemned him. If she fought back when Lawrence abused her, she was difficult, vicious and bullying.

Any virtues Frieda had have been transformed into their opposites. Her openness, flexibility and generosity to life have been read as lack of discrimination or purpose. Leavis sees her extensive novel reading as a sign that she had nothing to do (though he was doing much the same in a less private domain). Lucas calls her 'inconsistent, erratic and capricious'. Her indifference to social climbing and lack of sophistication have made her vulnerable to charges of being silly and naive. Maria Huxley claimed Lawrence liked Frieda '*because*' she was 'a child'. When she played any more adult role – showed strength of character or determination – she was seen as less attractive and accused of being stubborn and tyrannical. Her refusal to pander to academic intelligence cast her as 'stupid'. Her stoicism and uncomplaining nature were read as lack of profound feeling and superficiality. In the webs of mythology that have been cast around her, Frieda the historical person cannot win.

As Miller summed it up in his one-sided study of Lawrence, 'Frieda was necessary to him, and Frieda was the only woman in the world for him. *She was Woman*, as he himself said, and how necessary woman was to Lawrence it is scarcely necessary to mention. Frieda was the incarnation of Woman . . . the mysterious, unknowable foreign woman whom Lawrence loved, if ever a man loved a woman. . . *As for the living person, Frieda, I do not care a hang*' (my italics).[18]

For more than half a century, Frieda Lawrence has been carrying symbolic projections of archetypal versions of the feminine, from Demeter, Diana and 'mother of orgasm', to Aphrodite, Valkyrie, devil and whore. As we shall see in the next section, it is around Frieda's sexuality that these projections – positive and negative – have been at their most extreme.

Frieda's Men: 'gratified desire'

What is it men in women do require?
The lineaments of Gratified Desire.
What is it women do in men require?
The lineaments of Gratified Desire.

WILLIAM BLAKE, 'THE QUESTIONS ANSWER'D'

Once Frieda had died, Huxley wrote openly about her sexual behaviour as capricious and promiscuous:

Frieda and Lawrence had undoubtedly a profound and passionate lovelife. But this did not prevent Frieda from having every now and then affairs with Prussian cavalry officers and Italian peasants, whom she loved for a season without in any way detracting from her love for Lawrence or from her intense devotion to his genius.[19]

This implication of Frieda's cavalier approach has been the dominant tone in discussions of her sexuality; that she lacked Lawrence's moral integrity and was therefore not entirely worthy of him: 'She was far from a perfect mate – she could be treacherous in love and was to prove capable of betraying Lawrence . . .'[20]

From the malicious rumours, one might believe Frieda had bedded half of Mapperley, Munich and Mexico. Yet, by modern standards, her sexual behaviour was mild and closely related to her emotional needs at the time. The firm evidence shows that her lovers were few, and her three marriages endured some time: fifteen years with Weekley, eighteen with Lawrence, twenty-six with Ravagli.

The depiction of Frieda's female sexuality as rapacious is a perfect example of the perennial turning of powerful or sexual women into monsters.[21] In order to dispel some of these negative impressions, I shall focus here on the most important male figures in Frieda's life – from her

| 17 |

father to her third husband – and discuss the various influences that helped shape her views on love and the meaning of sexual experience. For, far from Lawrence liberating Frieda, as the myth would have it, her own philosophy of personal relations was, in many ways, already established by the time they met and it was her conviction of the importance of intimacy and eroticism that helped concentrate Lawrence's focus on them in his work.

FRIEDRICH VON RICHTHOFEN

I thought him perfection on earth. And I also felt from a small child sorry for him as I felt instinctively sorry for all men.

FRIEDA LAWRENCE, MEMOIRS

Frieda's position within her family gave her a particularly close bonding with her father. Whilst her eldest sister, Else, took on the role of the clever first child and the youngest, Nusch, was cast as the beauty, Frieda became the family tomboy. Her first name, Emma, was quickly supplanted by her third, Frieda – a feminine form of Friedrich – aligning her with her father as if she was the son he never had. Frieda's remarkable indifference to female vanity, as well as her disinterest in many of the games women play, may have stemmed from this early role.

Her father came from the German–Polish aristocracy. His forefathers were in the diplomatic service and lived on Bohemian country estates. At seventeen, Richthofen enlisted in the Prussian army under Bismarck and, from 1870 to 1871, served as an officer in the Franco–Prussian war. Frieda later discovered and translated his war diaries, written in what she called a 'machine gun style', recording a war landscape of brutality, violence and aggression. Richthofen was wounded, captured and imprisoned in the assault on Strasbourg and released only to find the war over and his injuries unfitting him for further military action. At the age of twenty-five he was discharged from the army with the distinction of the Iron Cross and a permanently crippled right hand.

He moved to Metz, joined the Prussian civil service and married Frieda's mother, Anna Marquier, but his ardour for the values of military life remained. At work he was the bureaucrat, imposing the new German order on the French populace; at home he was the autocrat, his authority as the only man in a family of four women unchallengeable. Frieda remembered his values as those of an unyielding and self-righteous patriarch, his image and possessions traditionally masculine: 'On the wall behind him hung a row of guns between boarheads and chamoisheads and deer that he had shot'.[22]

But around this upright persona lay a shadow. Like his father and grandfather, whose rash business investments had lost much of the family's fortunes, Richthofen was a secret gambler. His speculations squandered much of the family's income and destroyed the possibility of a dowry for any of his daughters. For Frieda especially, who had idolized her father, the revelation of this hidden vice must have had a profound effect; behind Richthofen's self-glorification lay a shameful underside.

Interestingly, with this deceptive father figure, none of the Richthofen daughters made a satisfactory first marriage, nor were their relations with men ever straightforward. Else married Edgar Jaffe, a professor of political economy at Heidelberg, but fell tragically in love with sociologist Max Weber, husband of one of her best friends. Frieda's marriage to Weekley failed and ended with the scandal of her elopement with Lawrence. Nusch repeated her parent's misalliance more conspicuously by marrying Max von Schriebershofen, who was later revealed to be an inveterate gambler.

The ambivalence Frieda felt towards her father – with his public success and private failure – informed all her future relationships with men. Like her father, other men aroused her pity as much as her admiration, and her inability to be daunted or intimidated by the opposite sex must have stemmed from this. Photos of her in Mexico in the 1920s show her with male friends in the desert, 'one of the boys' (see Plate 8). She refused to flatter men and was indifferent to their self-advertisement. Her autobiographical fiction reveals how deep the love was between her and her father, but also betrays the feelings of a woman who looks down on a man rather than up to him. Her relations with men, especially in her first marriage with Weekley, reproduced this ambivalence, of love mixed with pity, tenderness with detachment, compassion and adoration with contempt.

Retrospectively, it is possible to see traces of all her future lovers in the person of her father: Weekley, with his adherence to stale conventions and taboos; Lawrence with his shaky masculinity; Ravagli, with his military revels and secret duplicities. It is as if the animus image that Frieda carried inside her from these formative years lay behind all her encounters with the opposite sex, informing them with a profound ambivalence.

ERNEST WEEKLEY

I cannot forget that he had made an image of me and did not know anything about the real me.

LETTER FROM FRIEDA TO MONTY, 1953

There were a few low-key love affairs during Frieda's adolescence. A brief romance with a distant cousin, Ensign Kurt von Richthofen, when she was sixteen, was followed by another with Lieutenant Karl von Marbahr. Marbahr's military ambitions needed the financial support of a rich wife and Frieda's lack of a dowry made their liaison impossible. But he contacted Frieda again in 1944, when he recognized her in the description of Connie in *Lady Chatterley's Lover*:

She is nice, she is genuine, she does not know how nice she is . . . That's how you were long ago, when I was very fond of you; a little bit naive, ingenuous, and yet strong, but very feminine, no bluestocking.[23]

It was in this context of realizing that her marriage prospects were limited, yet under pressure from her mother to marry young, that Frieda met Weekley when he was on a brief vacation in the Black Forest in 1897.

Born in 1863, Weekley came from a lower middle-class family, the second of nine children. When his elder brother died young, Weekley took it on himself to fulfil the family's expectations. His father was a poorly paid local government official in London, but, despite their restricted means, Weekley took advantage of every educational opportunity, from a free place at boarding school onwards. He qualified as a schoolteacher when he was seventeen, took a degree at London

University, studied German at the University of Berne, then Middle English and Modern Languages at Cambridge. A year in Paris at the Sorbonne and a lectureship at Freiburg University were followed by the offer of a professorship at University College, Nottingham. It was prior to taking up this new post that he visited Germany.

His attraction to Frieda – the first woman in his life – who was beautiful, vivacious, warm and intelligent, is easy to understand. Frieda's to Weekley is more puzzling and her elder sister thought their union a great error for Frieda, but Weekley was fifteen years older and had none of the shadow that surrounded her father. She sensed in him a core of fine intelligence that her family lacked – she called it 'moral scrupulousness' – and it impressed her.

From the outset, though, their marriage was profoundly disappointing to Frieda. Weekley's life as a dutiful son and scholar had made him a dull companion, preoccupied with studies and texts. In Frieda's fiction he becomes a Casaubon figure, incapable of meeting his wife's emotional, sexual or psychological needs. His crammed agenda allowed little time for pleasure. As head of modern languages at Nottingham College, he was busy with teaching and administrative duties for five full working days; on three evenings a week he taught modern languages in workers' educational institutes; on Saturdays he lectured in Cambridge; in between times, he produced various textbooks, amongst them volumes on French prose composition, school French grammar, exercises in the French subjunctive.

There was no pre-marital sex, and their first sexual encounter on the marriage night left Frieda disappointed. In contrast to her physical exuberance and vitality, Weekley was hesitant, careful and anxious. But to the twenty-year-old Frieda, his uneasy emotional withdrawal must have felt like rejection. She always felt that her appetite for life was overwhelming for him: 'I remember when we first married and I slithered down those narrow stairs, he rushed out of his study and said: "My God, I am married to an earthquake"'.[24] Any feelings that her sexual desires were excessive must have been compounded by Weekley's later decision to sleep separately. By the time their three children were born, they had individual bedrooms and little or no sex.

health – are moving documents. When the Richthofens were insulted in the family, Weekley made Frieda an exception: 'She was the best'. In his biography of Lawrence, H. T. Moore claims that, after Lawrence's death, Weekley invited Frieda to be his wife again,[28] and, on his death in 1954, his desk drawers were found to contain photos of her, photos of their wedding and early days together.

Frieda paid homage to this love after his death, writing to her son, Monty, in 1954:

> He was a good man in every way according to his lights. You were lucky to have such a good father for such a long time and you were good children to him; that must be a great satisfaction to you. Did he look handsome when he was dead? His generation is nearly gone. Like the wheat crops follow each other.[29]

However, she knew too that, for all her responsibility in wounding him, Weekley's suffering was not simply of her making; it was rooted in his very character: 'I didn't make him into a tragic figure, the tragedy was there before I met him'.[30]

WILL DOWSON

> one great friend had one of the first automobiles in England. He would drive into the forests with her ... then she felt alive again ...
>
> FRIEDA LAWRENCE, MEMOIRS

To relieve her marital boredom, Frieda had a brief love affair with a Nottinghamshire lace manufacturer, Will Dowson, who was also her youngest daughter's godfather. Dowson, married to a suffragette, seems to have made the most of his wife's political absences and – owning one of the few cars in the county – took Frieda on romantic assignations in Sherwood Forest.

This was her first extra-marital affair – more of a friendship to alleviate tedium than a profound bond. Frieda herself only wrote of it by innuendo, but when Dowson heard of her elopement with Lawrence a few years later, he sent her a letter half reproaching her: 'If you had to run away, why did you not do it with me?' By a curious lapse, Frieda (inadvertently?) left this note in the copy of *Anna Karenina* that she and Lawrence had just read and which she then forwarded to Weekley – in the somewhat naive hope that he might learn from it some lessons about showing compassion towards a wife and mother who had left. Hardly surprisingly, Weekley did not respond well to either the novel or the note. With some bitterness, he returned Dowson's letter, not to Frieda, but to Lawrence, without comment, as if to emphasize Frieda's fickleness and depravity.

When Frieda discovered this male correspondence – not addressing her directly, as if she were nothing but an object of exchange between them – her response was typically ironic: 'That's the freemasonry among men'.[31]

OTTO GROSS

> He made me believe in love – in the sacredness of love. He made me see that marriage and all those things are based on fear. How can love be wrong?
>
> D. H. LAWRENCE, MR NOON

Between 1899 and 1912, whilst her deepest life was suspended, Frieda made several visits alone to her family in Germany, often staying with her elder sister Else, then married to Edgar Jaffe.

Unlike Frieda, Else was deeply committed to intellectual emancipation for women and to raising awareness of social conditions. She was one of the first female undergraduates at Heidelberg University, protegée and impossible love object of Max Weber, who supervised her doctoral dissertation, and one of the first woman factory inspectors in Germany. With Jaffe, Else lived first in Heidelberg, then Munich and was in touch with some of Europe's most radical cultural theorists. Profoundly influenced by Weber and secretly in love with him, Else shared his resistance to Bismarck's Germany and supported his ideas of widespread social reform.

For Frieda, trapped in the suburbs of Mapperley with a spouse more aroused by theories of semantics than politics, her time abroad meant immense liberation. Even more so in 1907, when many of these radical ideas were given a dramatic personal impact. This was the year she met Otto Gross, a German doctor who had been a student of Freud and was author of *The Secondary Function of the Brain* (1902), a work seen by some as anticipating Jung's *Psychological Types* (1920). Gross was the son of a criminologist father and his life was a series of reactions against an extraordinarily severe upbringing. By the time Frieda met him, Gross was estranged from Freud and was increasingly pursuing his own idiosyncratic and rebellious theories.

Frieda's short but intense love affair with Gross was her first experience of the possibility of a meeting between minds as well as bodies, and gave her a sexual fulfilment she had not known before. She always recalled it as a major turning point in her life. In the second paragraph of *Not I, But the Wind*, it is Gross who is the anonymous 'remarkable disciple of Freud' awakening her to a 'consciousness of my own proper self', without which she senses she would not have been able to relate so fully to Lawrence. The lasting effect of Gross on Frieda appears almost as a manifesto in Lawrence's *Mr Noon*, where the woman (Frieda) tells Gilbert (Lawrence) about her affair with Eberhard (Gross):

He made me believe in love – in the sacredness of love . . . there can't be love without sex. And it is so true. Love is sex. But you can't have all your love in your head . . . Sex is sex, and ought to find its expression in the proper way . . . And there is no strong feeling aroused in anybody that doesn't have an element of sex in it . . .

On a personal level, the relationship between Frieda and Gross was deep and reciprocal. Their continued correspondence bears witness to a mutually deep impact and appreciation. Gross' letters, in particular, show evidence of his gratitude and emotional generosity, as he reassures Frieda of her worth – an affirmation she must have found especially valuable in the midst of the most barren and depressing years of her first marriage when she was walking 'like a somnambulist in a conventional set life'. 'I am grateful', he wrote, ' that you exist . . . You give me the wonderful strength to make me a genuine human being, and at the same time live for an idea'.

Her experiences with Gross convinced Frieda of the importance of sexual passion as an expression of love, of her right to claim it and of the power of the unconscious. Although Frieda never explored Freud's ideas as fully as she might have done, through Gross she had an introduction to some of the basic tenets of psychoanalysis, and these were as great a gift to her as the sexual and emotional fulfilment she found with him.[32] They confirmed intuitions she already had about the deeper life of the psyche.

What Frieda took from Freud, triggered by this encounter with Gross, was a more explicit and theorized version of what she felt intuitively to be true: that the human being is driven by deeply unconscious forces, particularly psycho-sexual ones. She knew instinctively the rightness of Freud's ideas about the artificiality of a strict demarcation between so called 'normal' and 'abnormal' minds, that there is no innate difference between the 'deviant, or criminal' and the law-abiding, nor between the 'moral' and so called 'immoral'. She was able to identify imaginatively with all these positions, and so was able to see that ethics, rules of morality, notions of what constitutes 'good' or 'bad' behaviour are less absolute judgments than relative human constructions imposed on our actions. She wrote that there is, in all our unconscious lives, another self, a shadow side (as she had witnessed in her father) – a dark double that might 'steal, lie, murder, love another man when he was married'. Like Lawrence, Frieda could move imaginatively out of her own life and was not restricted to a narrow sense of self. A crucial but neglected feature of Frieda's affair – one mostly glossed over by biographers as if it were of little interest – is the fact that Gross had also been her elder sister's lover. Else went to stay with Gross and his wife (also called Frieda) in 1906 and had a sexual affair with him then. Else, too, had found the experience liberating: a diary entry claims that she had found her true nature for the first time (though by then she already had two children). Interestingly, having a lover in common does not seem to have been a source of jealousy or antagonism between the two Richthofen sisters. It would have been relatively easy for Else to prevent rather than encourage a meeting between Gross and Frieda, but there was more of a sense of complicity, as if she wanted Frieda to share the pleasure of her own erotic and emotional awakening.

The brief contact with psychoanalysis also helped sustain Frieda through her own traumas. After the separation from her children, although her emotional suffering was intense, guilt – moral agony – was not its primary feature.

Gross, however, became a sad monument to his libertine ideals, which is doubtless why Frieda fails to mention him by name in *Not I, But the Wind* and gives no hint of his later years and decline. Like many professional medics, Freud included, Gross experimented with cocaine, but, unlike Freud, did not avoid dependency. His drug addiction led to various forms of delinquency and violence and his sexual behaviour became increasingly anarchic. His wife, pregnant at the time of his affair with Frieda, was later abandoned for a younger woman artist and sent to live with a Swiss anarchist, who was also to abandon her. Gross' own life of increasing squalor resulted in his premature death in a Berlin hospital in 1920.

But the shadows of this future addiction and delinquency were not visible when Frieda and Gross had their passionate affair, nor were his more extreme ideas and actions. In theory and practice he came to oppose monogamy, argue for individual hedonism and sexual fulfilment at any price and to defend homosexuality. What Frieda took from him was an earlier and more restrained version of sexual permissiveness, closer to Lawrence's own caution and Puritanism. Yet, however much Gross' dramatic decline made Frieda play down their personal association, his influence on her inner development should not be underestimated. She never lost sight of his ideas and remained committed to her own (perhaps idealized) version of the free love that she had found with him.

It would be hard to imagine any greater contrast to Weekley's moral scrupulousness than the wilfully amoral Gross. The two men were living in different dimensions, and the result of this passionate encounter was to further alienate Frieda from Weekley and all he embodied. The worlds of Munich and Mapperley, of free love and marital chastity, were worlds in collision, and, although Frieda was to suppress her desires for another five years, she was now aware that her dissatisfactions and frustration had a reason and a name.

Without the episode with Gross, and the vindication and understanding it offered her, it is possible that Frieda might not have found the means to release herself from the moral and social codes binding her to convention. As it was, by the time Lawrence appeared in her life in 1912, the ground for her rebellion had been prepared. All the dormant sexuality and longing for life and love that Gross had helped coax into being were now desperate to find fulfilment.

D. H. LAWRENCE

I believe my deepest feeling for L. was a profound compassion.

LETTER FROM FRIEDA TO JOHN MIDDLETON MURRY, 1951

Nobody seems to have an idea of the quality of Lawrence's and my relationship, the essence of it.

LETTER FROM FRIEDA TO F. R. LEAVIS, 1956

Lawrence was the central male figure in Frieda's emotional life. Although they both had other sexual relations, it was with one another that they felt most deeply loved, challenged and alive. It was through their relationship – at its best – that they felt at one with themselves and with the world. This state of 'at-one-ment' was described by Lawrence in *Phoenix* as akin to mystical devotion: 'If I take my whole, passionate, spiritual and physical love to the woman who in return loves me, that is how I serve God'. Such love was their version of religion.

The facts of Lawrence's early life have been extensively documented. He was born David Herbert Lawrence on 11 September 1885, the fourth of five children, in Eastwood, Nottinghamshire. His father, Arthur Lawrence, was a coal miner, his mother, Lydia Beardsall, was a schoolteacher before her marriage. At twelve, Lawrence won a county scholarship to Nottingham High School, then worked as a clerk and, after being seriously ill with pneumonia, became a schoolteacher, first at Eastwood, then at Ilkeston, Derbyshire. From 1906 to 1908, with the help of another scholarship, he went to University College, Nottingham, where one of his tutors was Professor Ernest Weekley. He was not to encounter Weekley's wife, however, until he had spent a further three and a half years teaching in Croydon, South London.

Before Lawrence met Frieda in the spring of 1912, he had experienced intense emotional relationships with Jessie Chambers, Alice Dax, Agnes Holt, Helen Corke and Louisa Burrows. Biographers have traced his probable sexual initiation to 1909, the year of his affair with Alice Dax, a suffragette and socialist who was estranged from her husband. Scandalous though it was, their affair lasted for many months and Alice was still close to Lawrence in 1912 – indeed, she was one of the first he told about Frieda. It also ran alongside Lawrence's love affair with Jessie Chambers, which finally became sexual on a few occasions late in 1909 and early in 1910.[33]

When they met at the Weekley's home, Frieda was thirty-one and Lawrence twenty-six; there was an immediate rapport between them. Yet, surprisingly for a man who had repeatedly declared his distaste for marriage and desire for free love, Lawrence declined Frieda's suggestion that they sleep together. She made this offer within a couple of weeks of their meeting, inviting him to spend the night with her while Weekley was away from home. But although the stakes were so much greater for her than for him, Lawrence insisted she choose between him and Weekley. He effectively forced her hand, making their love for one another known to Weekley, so that compromise or dissimulation were impossible.

Frieda felt that there was only one decision to make and, within a few weeks, had left Nottingham, her marriage, home and children to wander round Europe and Switzerland with Lawrence – a dramatic elopement mirroring that of Mary and Percy Shelley a century before, or Elizabeth Barrett and Robert Browning in 1845. Lawrence affectionately became Lorenzo to her, and, from then on – apart from Frieda's solitary visits to her mother in Germany, or the famous rift of 1923 – she and Lawrence were virtually inseparable for the next eighteen years.

After her etiolated and repressed existence with Weekley, Frieda found Lawrence vital and alert. He enabled her to live life more fully, and her youthful exuberance returned. She captured the tone of their early years in a letter to David Garnett in January 1913: 'we are *really* happy; though we fight like blazes, we shall bring it off'. There is no denying the strength of their mutual attraction and love. The positive side of their relationship is told in glowing terms in *Not I, But the Wind* so I will not dwell at length on this aspect of it here. Frieda distils the best of their time together, relishing the gift of her years with Lawrence: his tenderness, his love of the natural world, his awakening her to the miracle of everyday life. Lawrence did what Nabokov urged we all do –

'caress the divine details' – the specifics that make up our earthly existence, and in this sense, every moment with him was, claimed Frieda, a miracle. Helen Dunmore's novel *Zennor in Darkness* (1993), gives an exquisite portrait of this side of the Lawrence's marriage. Set in North Cornwall in 1917, when they were living at Higher Tregerthen until their expulsion on suspicion of spying, it shows both Frieda and Lawrence as rich, complex, sensitive characters and offers a hauntingly sympathetic view of their relationship.

Yet, from the start, it was a union full of contradictions, if not total opposites. Frieda was married with children, Lawrence was single and childless. She was German, aristocratic, used to servants doing domestic labour; he was English, working class and knew the personal cost of hard work. These vastly different backgrounds determined the nature of much of their life together. There was a frequent struggle between Frieda's prodigality, generosity and excess, as opposed to Lawrence's frugality, orderliness and industry. Such difficult, complex individuals as they were could not but have a fraught, if deeply passionate, relationship. Biographers have charted it as a dramatic rise and fall, moving from initial bliss, though violent conflict, to mutual misery, but it more probably had elements of all these all along.

Both were committed to the idea of a relationship that opened on to the more than personal, but neither found self-effacement easy and their conflicts for attention led to physical as well as verbal confrontation. Witnessing one of their infamous domestic dramas, during some of their hardest years in Cornwall during World War I, Katherine Mansfield was shocked by the level of violence between them. This particular battle was triggered by Lawrence insulting Frieda's intelligence.

> Frieda said Shelley's *Ode to a Skylark* was false. Lawrence said 'You are showing off; you don't know anything about it'. Then she began, '*Now* I have had enough. Out of my house. You little God Almighty you. I've had enough of you'.

Frieda walked out into the garden, saying she would never go back; it was all over.

Suddenly Lawrence appeared and made a kind of horrible blind rush at her and they began to scream, and scuffle. He beat her – he beat her to death – her heart and face and breast and pulled out her hair. All the while she screamed for Murry to help her. Finally they dashed into the kitchen and round and round the table. I shall never forget how L. looked. He was so white – almost green and he just hit, thumped the soft woman. Then he fell into one chair and she into another. No one said a word.

Yet, friendly talk soon resumed, as if nothing had happened. 'And next day,' Mansfield continues, Lawrence 'whipped himself, far more thoroughly than he had ever beaten Frieda, [and] he was running about taking her up her breakfast to her bed and trimming her a hat'.[34]

Later, Frieda admitted that it was during this stressful time in Cornwall that she was most frightened of Lawrence. There are claims that he beat her on occasions – she had bruises to prove it – and she wrote: 'A few times I was really scared of him . . .'[35] Her daughter testifies that Lawrence hit Frieda and that, as his illness developed, until he was too weak to act, his behaviour and words could be cruel. Barbara also describes an incident in which she saw Lawrence pour hot tea over Frieda, but Frieda's spirit was never destroyed:

She believed in a woman sticking up for herself and not letting a man bully her. Lawrence would never have stayed with her if she hadn't had that fighting spirit. Lawrence was abusive to her, he was awful, dreadful, he made her suffer a lot. But much of his cruelty was because he was a very sick man.

It would be as absurd, though to try to construct Frieda as a victimized battered wife as it would be to turn her into the fishwife of some male commentators, such as Anthony West, who claims she regarded good rows as part of her marriage ritual: 'Frieda – one suspects – had come to rather enjoy a good paroxysm', or Miller's caricature, 'Lawrence the man gets plates smashed over his head by an irate spouse'.[36] Frieda commented wryly on this kind of exaggeration: 'So much crockery I must have smashed through the years!! I did it only once! When L. told me women had no souls and couldn't love!'[37]

It seems that, in the early years, even their most vicious rows were quickly mended and Frieda could easily tolerate the strain of their battles: 'Lawrence *is* wear and tear. I am cross with him just at present, he chases my emotions till they drop like panting hares . . . But still it's worth it . . .' Knowing Lawrence's need for another to believe in him and his work, Frieda at first generously answered it, but it was increasingly at a cost to herself.

In *Aaron's Rod*, the character based on Frieda (Tanny) says to the Lawrence figure (Lilly): 'Because I hold you safe all the time, you like to pretend you're doing it all yourself'. Lawrence knew how deeply dependent he was on Frieda, but, because he came to resent this dependence and the impotence it implied, he denied Frieda her full importance. Lawrence's resentment of his dependence lay behind his loathing of Frieda as 'the devouring mother'. It may be, too, that because she was such an essential part of his creative process, Lawrence was uneasy about owning the debt. It was this reluctance to give her due acknowledgment that was one of the things that most angered Frieda.

In what must be one of the most colourful of all metaphors for Frieda, Huxley described Lawrence's 'organic dependence' on her in dramatically visceral terms. To Lawrence, he claimed, Frieda 'wasn't a person; she was his food, she was a vital organ of his own body. When she was absent, he was like a cow deprived of grass, like a man with jaundice struggling to exist without a liver . . . Lawrence was, in some strange way dependent on her presence, physically dependent . . . I have seen him on two occasions rise from what I thought was his death-bed, when Frieda, who had been away, came back after a short absence. The mysteries of human relationships are impenetrable'.[30] Lucas has elaborated on the same image: 'He felt towards her as a man might feel towards his own liver: the liver may give trouble from time to time, but it remains one of the vital organs absolutely necessary to survival'.[39]

In the early euphoria of their relationship, Lawrence did admit his debt to her. At their closest, he described their 'wonderful naked intimacy, all kindled with warmth' and wrote to Murry, 'There isn't a soul cares a damn for me, except Frieda . . .' Barbara Barr reports Lawrence as saying to Frieda once, 'You're the only person who's mattered to me'. But as the years passed, his resentment at his dependence made it harder for him to make any acknowledgement, and Frieda's inner reserves began to run dry. He took from her in many ways.

He repeatedly drew on her character, experience, ideas and feelings as raw material for his fiction – 'he sucked her dry,' writes Miller, 'used her as an instrument' – but with little sense that this might have been at a cost to her.

> *She resented that she gave so much and it wasn't recognized. I've heard her say to Lawrence that she sweated her guts out for him and she got nothing back but lip.*

Lawrence confessed that he was heavily reliant on women in general and Frieda in particular: 'It is hopeless for me to try to do anything without I have a woman at the back of me . . . I daren't sit in the world without a woman behind me'.[40] This was part of Lawrence's initial attraction to Frieda. He was deeply excited to find, at last, a woman without the repressions and neuroses of his mother and many of the women he had met. Frieda lived wholeheartedly in the present tense, untrammelled by fears of past or future and undaunted by social judgments and taboos. They lived in the moment, refusing to worry about the future, their faith that they would be provided for less arrogance than profound trust.

But in poetry written soon after their meeting, Lawrence admits his terror of Frieda abandoning him and invokes demons and gods to keep her. Fearing that she might leave him to return to her biological children, he passes a general curse on women as mothers, women who 'fortify themselves in motherhood, devastating the vision'. His poems are full of reproach to Frieda for looking back towards her children: 'the curse against you is still in my heart/Like a deep, deep burn./The curse against all mothers'.

The least expression of Frieda's love for her children provoked in Lawrence a range of negative emotions that he could not contain. 'Don't forget how jealous he was of you children!' Frieda wrote later to Barbara. It was a jealousy that never really abated. Whenever it was an issue of her trying to see the children or of them visiting or writing, Lawrence would sulk, rage, or explode in bitterness. Frieda would be driven to writing for news of her children in secret, so as not to provoke him. He also resented friendships or activities that Frieda had independently of him: 'Lawrence was often jealous and would sneer at the few friends she did have'.[41] It was her three children, though, who were his main rivals and it was over her love for them that Lawrence's hostility was at its most extreme.

In Frieda's fictionalized account of the impact and aftermath of her meeting with Lawrence, she draws attention to the immense personal cost of the elopement to her. In some painful, haunting passages, she records her suffering in losing her children and Lawrence's insensitivity towards it, but, in *Mr Noon*, Lawrence makes his own position disturbingly, if honestly, clear. He tells how Johanna Keighley (Frieda), a German-born aristocrat, has left her husband and children to live with the working-class, but well-educated, Gilbert Noon (Lawrence), but that Noon expects her not to mind the children's loss. Even his awareness of Johanna lying awake at night, bereft and aghast at Noon's indifference, does not alter his feelings.

This conflict over her children was never fully resolved between them. It opened a vein of suffering and resentment in Frieda, and of guilt and jealousy in Lawrence, that was never entirely closed. Neither could have foreseen that Weekley's vengeance would be so severe, and Frieda has to take responsibility for having such little foresight of the effects of long-term separation on herself and her children – naively, she thought that their relationship would not be seriously harmed. Yet, Lawrence's response suggests a disturbing lack of emotional maturity. For all his love for Frieda and his early attempts to be sympathetic, he simply could not deal with the pain or guilt her suffering caused him. It was impossible for him to manage or contain his own feelings, let alone Frieda's; instead of a full or complex response to the situation, there was a simple eruption of rage. According to one friend in Mexico, Witter Bynner, as late as 1923, when Frieda was leafing through a box of photos of her children, Lawrence leapt 'out of his chair like a rattlesnake', took the photos from her and tore them to pieces.

Frieda regarded this as one of the major causes of contention in their marriage:

Over the children I thought he was beastly; he hated me for being miserable, not a moment of misery did he put up with; he denied all the suffering and suffered all the more, like his mother before him; how we fought over this. In revenge I did not care about his writing. If he denies my life and suffering I deny his art . . .[42]

| 35 |

The worst abuse came in later years, in some of Lawrence's verbal insults and attacks on Frieda's behaviour, appearance and intelligence. On occasions, he humiliated and insulted her, both privately and in public. The benevolent reading is to see Lawrence's aggression as having been aggravated by his tuberculosis (dormant for a long time before it was finally diagnosed), but, whatever it was, there were episodes of immense unkindness between them. His assertions of male dominance appear both absurd and empty, given the power Frieda had in their relationship, but the two of them were caught in a vicious circle. Had he properly honoured her strength, she may not have needed to become so dominant; had she not been felt such a threat, he may not have needed to further provoke her by his own declarations of men's supremacy. Provoked by her strength, though, he responded with a nasty invective that attacked Frieda as the overpowerful and overwhelming mother figure, the 'Magna Mater'.

Lawrence must have hurt her extremely. Mostly because of his illness, he was irritable, he struck her fairly frequently. She would take it all in good part and then she would turn and rend him.

I admired him greatly as an artist, but I wasn't terribly fond of him. Like Frieda, I felt compassion for him . . . in the last year or two of his life, he was frail. He was a very sick man.

It is in the context of this immense physical and emotional strain that Frieda's reaching out for intimacy with another man needs to be understood.

Their attitudes to sexuality and marriage never completely converged; Frieda was far less conventional. Lawrence refused to sleep with her until she had already committed herself to leaving Weekley and it was at Lawrence's instigation that they married. For all his philosophies, Lawrence was more deeply conventional than Frieda in every way. Paradoxically, even his attitude to sex could be called puritanical. He resented any equation of his work with pornography, resisted his own homosexuality and largely misrepresented lesbianism; he hated promiscuity, dirty jokes and vulgarity of any kind. Frieda's physicality and sensuality were far less restrained. She found Lawrence's tight puritanism annoying and at times seems to have deliberately courted a more extreme, even 'vulgar' position to try to shock him out of it. Yet, until the early 1920s, Frieda's emotional loyalty (if not her strict sexual fidelity), to Lawrence are not seriously in question. It has been implied that at Gargnano in 1912, she had a trivial amorous adventure with Harold Hobson while Lawrence was away on a botanic expedition with David Garnett, and that, on another afternoon, she capriciously made love with a woodcutter she didn't know. However, these episodes are based only on Garnett's anecdotal evidence and from some far-fetched incidents in Lawrence's fictionalized *Mr Noon*. According to Barbara Barr, '*David Garnett's story that she went and had an affair across the lake with a woodman is all fiction*'. It would seem likely that claims Frieda had an affair with Cecil Grey in 1917 are equally legendary.[43]

For a woman supposedly so casual in her favours, Frieda was surprisingly possessive of Lawrence sexually – far too much so for a woman who does not care. She was fiercely jealous if her territory was threatened and if female friends trespassed too close, she made the boundaries clear. Indeed, Ivy Low, Mabel Dodge Luhan and Dorothy Brett were all pushed away when they tried to be too intimate with Lawrence.

It is not impossible that Frieda did have some sexual involvements outside her relationship with Lawrence, before the 1920s. However, these particular incidents from 1912, especially given her closeness to Lawrence at the time, fit too conveniently into the dominant mythologizing of Frieda as unpredictable and amoral. Moreover, by overlooking Lawrence's parallel indulgences, they make their relationship – and morality – appear very one-sided.

It is usually assumed that, once he had met Frieda, Lawrence's own sexual life was restricted to their marriage, but Rosalind Thornycroft's memoirs, *Time Which Spaces us Apart*, suggest otherwise. Rosalind Thornycroft (1891–1973) met Lawrence in the summer of 1919 through Eleanor Farjeon, whose brother was married to Rosalind's sister. Later that year, Lawrence and Frieda were Rosalind's guests at Pangbourne and they all spent time together on walks and picnics. Rosalind also devoted time to copying out some of Lawrence's manuscripts.

Rosalind was the daughter of Sir Hamo Thornycroft, who was a Royal Academy sculptor of some standing – friend of Edmund Gosse and recipient of a knighthood in 1917. She attended the London School of Economics and the Slade and, in 1913, married Godwin Baynes, a physician who was later to be a Jungian analyst of high repute, but the marriage did not survive. Godwin had various love affairs, and Rosalind finally succumbed to a brief one of her own, with Kenneth Hooper, in 1918. Although both Rosalind and Godwin had committed adultery, it was hers that was cited as cause for the divorce, largely to save Godwin's reputation and promising medical career. It was during this tumultuous time, with the scandal of her divorce breaking, that Rosalind met the Lawrences in 1919. The apparent immorality of her behaviour, plus her family's high social profile, led to a wild outbreak of hostile publicity and, like Frieda a few years before, Rosalind fled the country. Unlike Frieda, though, she was able to take her three young children with her (the youngest was not Godwin's) and settled with them in Italy, in a rented villa in Fiesole.

Throughout the following months, she and Lawrence corresponded – letters of his that have survived show great concern for her health and position – and by the time they met again the following summer, a warm mutual friendship had been firmly established. According to Rosalind's own memoirs (compiled by her daughter and published in 1991 as *Time Which Spaces Us Apart*), it was when Lawrence visited her in Fiesole in September 1920 that their attraction to each other was acknowledged and their relationship became explicitly sexual. Frieda, meanwhile, on one of her regular trips to Germany to see her mother, was conveniently absent. Rosalind wrote of the event in her notebooks, where she recorded the details of Lawrence's visit to the villa La Canovaia on his birthday. Her memoirs read:

September 11th, 1920. D. H. Lawrence's birthday – Fiesole
After supper on the terrace of the Villino Belvedere . . . we walked towards Monte Ceceri and got out beyond the cypress woods where there were the scents from thyme and marjoram, and the nightjar birds of the hillside. We talked still of the lights of the citta Firenze which were displayed down below us in the valley; but he wanted to say something about ourselves. We . . . sat down at last . . . We talked of stones and gems and their essential qualities and temper. Then he switched away and said:

'How do you feel about yourself now without sex in your life?'

I said I wanted it of course.

'Well, why don't you have it?' says he.

'Yes, why not? But one is so damned fastidious.'

'Yes, damned fastidious! Yes, most people one can hardly bear to come near, far less make love with', says he.

'Yes', say I, 'and it's no good just making love; there must be more to it than a few pretty words and then off to bed.'

'Yes there must be more in it than that, but God save us from the so-called Love – that most indecent kind of egoism and self-spreading. Let us think of love as a force outside and getting us. It is a force; a god. The Ancients had it and for them there were no personalisms, and they were men and still had pride. I don't see why you and I should not have a sex time together. Or is it all too complicated? What about the babies and your husband and Clive? You have your choice to make.'

This was all very off-hand and I liked that. I can't answer for a while. I am so astounded at my happiness.

'Yes, indeed I want it', I say at last.

Firenze and her lights twirled around me and I felt off the world. He so wonderful; my source of acceptable and exciting wisdom of a kind unheard of until he came. I said:

'I had no idea you thought about me so.' . . . then went on somehow:

' . . . but nevertheless how do you account for the fastidiousness we have been talking about if there is no personalism in love?'

'Oh yes', says he 'there must be understanding of the god together.' . . . In half an hour we are home, laughing on the way; and in the bright, ugly little hall passage we embrace and kiss our promise. Then he off down the hill to San Gervasio . . .[44]

It was a few nights before their promise was fulfilled. Rosalind's record continues:

The next day I spent in the greatest elation, and the next day Saturday he came again. Was this our day? But no. I tidied everything in my room to make it sweet for him; but not then. Sunday he came to lunch. We made the dinner together, quite an English Sunday one, beef and batter; and everything was fun. He laughed and played with my Nan and understood her – as he did with children – with delicate, amused perception. We walked out after the heat was over, up behind Fiesole town through the trees . . . and home with things to cook for our supper on the terrace, three hundred feet above Firenze.

'How good it is here. It is something quite special and lovely, the time, the place, the beloved.'

My heart jumps with joy. We sit there until it is quite dark, our hands held together in union. And so to bed.

It is a restrained, yet romantic, account. Like the remainder of Rosalind's memoirs, it shows no attempt at self-glorification, nor any sign of self-deception and the fact that she did not allow the incident to become public until after her death only adds to its authenticity. The way it is presented, it is an episode more likely to enhance than sully Lawrence's reputation.

Yet the recording of Frieda's sexual infidelities has been rather different. No matter what the facts, Lawrence's sexuality manages to remain curiously chaste, while Frieda's has been tinged with suggestions of promiscuity: in marked contrast to his, her behaviour has been presented as dirty, treacherous and demeaning. These double standards are particularly evident in the representation of Frieda's sexual relationship with Ravagli in the early 1920s. This affair undoubtedly took place, but, while Lawrence's advocacy of greater sexual freedom and emotional openness in personal relationships has made of him (for some) a hero, Frieda's *living through* of such a philosophy has made her vulnerable to charges of selfishness and promiscuity. The partisanship towards Lawrence in biographical reconstructions invariably makes Frieda the guilty party. It is she, the monstrous Prussian, who cheated and betrayed Lawrence in his last years, and so intensified his tragedy.

Yet in *Kangaroo* – Lawrence's most explicit fictional version of their marriage – he defends Frieda's unorthodox position. For Harriet, based upon Frieda, 'honour did not consist in a pledged word kept according to pledge, but in a genuine feeling faithfully followed'. Frieda was acting out what Lawrence articulated here, what he called an honouring of an inner flame, 'the right to mate freely . . . irrespective of any other claim than that of life-necessity'. True to these values, Lawrence seems not to have tried to stop Frieda in her supposed infidelities.

Her adultery with Ravagli, moreover, must be seen in the context of the years leading up to it. Frieda had been under the strain of Lawrence's illness for some time, enduring the emotional battering it sometimes caused, and sex between them had ceased. This contrasted with their early years together, when their sexual life had been active and mutually fulfilling. Frieda wrote in 1951, 'It is just absurd to call L. a sexual weakling, anything but: with his intensity'. However, probably due to Lawrence's illness, their sexual life receded and, by 1926, he was impotent.[45] Emotionally and sexually, Frieda was thrown back on her own resources.

Her exact motives, feelings and inner loyalties during this period are hard to fathom and whether she had any qualms of conscience about her sexual infidelity with Ravagli is hard to say. The closest we can come to her state of mind is to recognize that, from the early to mid 1920s, she was increasingly exhausted on a physical and moral level and desperate for some comfort and affection for herself. As Huxley put it, 'even the most stoical fortitude has its limits'. Frieda needed some replenishment.

This was the context of her unsuccessful pass at Murry in 1923 and her affair with Ravagli from 1926 onwards. Lawrence must have known of this affair, but seems to have feigned ignorance for some time. Yet it was not a case of Frieda abandoning Lawrence; when he needed her, she was still there. In 1929, when he summoned her to return from the exhibition of his paintings in London to him in Florence, she immediately returned. She nursed him throughout his final illness, slept in his room and did her best to relieve his suffering. No matter what her unconventional behaviour, it is presumptuous for outsiders to doubt her devotion and love for Lawrence. Many photos capture the poignancy of their relationship (see Plates 12 and 18), especially those showing Lawrence's painfully visible decline (see Plate 20), and it is easy to imagine Frieda's feelings of helplessness and compassion.

Whatever their differences and battles, Frieda believed she and Lawrence were linked deeply together in an inscrutable way: 'Destinies are not mathematics', she wrote, 'and they don't come out like two and two make four'. In 1950, she wrote to Richard Aldington that our closest relationships are, ultimately, beyond reason: 'Anyhow what do we know about each others' relationships always a mystery!' [46]

Long after Lawrence died, Frieda felt they were still united and that his love was making claims on her from beyond the grave. She admitted that her feelings towards such a bond were ambivalent. As she wrote in 1953, 'Part of me likes it, part of me doesn't', but she never tried to undo it or leave it behind. Her relationship with Ravagli never had the quality of her time with Lawrence and was not a full replacement for their deeper union.

Whether we read it psychologically, as a fusion of his need and her compassion, or more romantically, the bond between Frieda and Lawrence was enduring and Lawrence's early death only intensified Frieda's compassion: 'That awful pity I felt for him, that I shall always feel, that he had to die and did not want to die. He still holds me, as if he said grimly, "You are mine"'.[47] If anything, Frieda was more in love with Lawrence *after* his death than *before* it and, despite her critics arguing otherwise, the fact that she was buried close to Lawrence on the hillside at Taos feels entirely appropriate.

JOHN MIDDLETON MURRY

One has to surrender oneself entirely and absolutely to love – at any rate with a woman like you. And I dimly felt this, and was scared: not of you, but of the new world, the new life.

LETTER FROM MURRY TO FRIEDA, 1946

Murry and Katherine Mansfield were among Frieda and Lawrence's closest friends, especially in the difficult years that followed their elopement. Frieda referred to it as their 'only spontaneous and gay friendship'. She and Mansfield were immediately attracted when they met in 1914 and, as a mark of their intimacy, on her way to the marriage ceremony with Lawrence, Frieda gave Mansfield her first wedding ring as a keepsake. This was a symbolic gesture of friendship that meant much to Mansfield and it endured, despite the deep rifts and differences that later came between them. Mansfield always wore Frieda's ring and it was buried with her when she died at Fontainebleau in January 1923.

Any closer emotional bond between Frieda and Mansfield never materialized, any more than did the latent relationship between Lawrence and Murry. Instead, the complicated feelings and desires hovering between the four of them surfaced in classically heterosexual ways, so that it was between Frieda and Murry that an affair later occurred. This was almost immediately after Lawrence's death, in 1930, was short-lived and took place while Frieda's daughter, Barbara, was staying in the same house.

Murry came in one morning and said 'Last night I slept with your mother'.

There is no record of excitement or euphoria on Frieda's side at this experience, nor any evidence that she tried to prolong or repeat it. It seemed, more than anything, a reaction to the strain and trauma of Lawrence's death, with the handsome and familiar figure of Murry offering an obvious source of immediate comfort.

Murry, however, drew repeatedly on the episode. More than twenty years later, he was still writing nostalgic letters to Frieda, referring to their affair in tones that echo Lawrence's spiritualizing of the erotic:

it was from you I learned what a woman's tenderness could be. And you can't say that's a tenderness of the body only . . . it's a tenderness *of the soul* as well . . . You gave me something then that I needed terribly: as it were opened a new world to me.

The affair was also a fulfilment of a sexual attraction between them that had been on hold since 1923. For it was then, when Frieda was at the height of her frustration and anger with Lawrence, that she had invited Murry to be her lover. In the name of loyalty to Lawrence, Murry had resisted: 'What held me back from claiming you as my own in 1923? Nothing else but loyalty to Lorenzo. Precisely the kind of loyalty he despised in me. If I had acted by his philosophy, I should not have let you go'.

As Claire Tomalin suggests in her excellent biography of Mansfield: 'Frieda and Katherine were both more defiant of convention than Lawrence and Murry, and in both women the same streak of sexual anarchy that had first attracted the men later disconcerted them'.[48] Murry later admitted it was cowardice rather than moral principle that had kept him chaste:

> looking back, I think that my shrinking from letting Lorenzo down, though it was a genuine feeling, was merely an excuse. I didn't take what you had to give because I was afraid of love itself . . . It's like taking a tremendous plunge – into a strange, new world.[49]

As if haunted by it, Murry kept coming back, time and again, to this lost experience from 1923. When Frieda was well into her seventies, Murry was still corresponding with her about their illicit and frustrated passion:

> And I sometimes wonder, when I think of that journey of ours to Germany together, and we wanted each other so badly, whether I was not a fool in feeling (or rather thinking) that it would have been disloyal to Lorenzo. Looking back, it seems only an 'idea' – something in my *head* – and that the right and true thing would have been to stay with you, if only for a day or two. Anyway, I felt horribly sad when I left you . . .[50]

It was as if he wanted to give their relationship – and thus himself – a greater importance than they actually had. By this time, though, in 1955, Frieda's own version of the 1923 temptation was reassuringly moral:

> No, you did the right thing, Lawrence was already very ill. I think you averted an ugly tragedy . . . I also owed him loyalty, and had to see him through his life span and you helped me to do it.[51]

She may have been remembering that Lawrence's own patience with Murry had run out long before. He called Murry an 'incorrigible worm', words that were to prove prophetic after his death, when Murry not only promptly bedded his friend's widow, but rushed his own dubious memoirs into print. Exploiting the demand for Lawrencian biography, Murry published *Son of Woman* in 1931, its reverential surface blurring a spiteful attack. When Frieda read it, she was livid at Murry's betrayal and threw her copy on to the fire, sending him the charred ash as a sign of her disgust.

However, her anger was characteristically short-lived and their friendship soon repaired. By the time of the court case over Lawrence's will in 1932, Murry was speaking strongly in Frieda's defence and it was his crucial testimony that turned the judgment in Frieda's favour. Lawrence had died intestate and her claim to inherit was based solely on Murry's assertion that he had been with Lawrence when he had made a previous will that left his estate to Frieda. Some of Frieda's detractors have made aspersions that no such document ever existed and that the claim was totally spurious – a convenient fiction concocted between Murry and Frieda to enable her to inherit the estate.

Frieda's behaviour in this period does show her at her least scrupulous. She alienated Lawrence's family, especially his sister, Ada, and Aldous Huxley thought her strategies none too subtle: 'The stupid woman is embarking on enormously expensive legal proceedings against L's brother . . . Her diplomatic methods consist in calling everyone a liar, a swine and a lousy swindler, and then in the next letter being charming . . .'[52]

The exact truth of the status of Lawrence's supposed testament, however, is now beyond knowing, and, although Frieda's behaviour may not have been exemplary (she was understandably exasperated at the lack of recognition Lawrence had received in his lifetime and wanted some recompense for their years of hardship and poverty), the accusation that she and Murry were conspirators feeds, yet again, into the dominant mythology about her. There is no evidence that Murry made any gain – financial or sexual – from the settlement, and his relationship with Frieda betrayed no tension of conspiracy.

Their correspondence over the next twenty-five years is redolent of nothing more sinister than a friendship sustained for old time's sake. Frieda's letters to Murry are warm and kind, but casual, and never reciprocate his attempt to revive romantic intensity between them. Thus, in 1951, she replies to one of his urgent memories of the 1923 episode:

Yes, indeed, I often think of our friendship first and later of our intimacy with great satisfaction . . . On that journey to Germany I also felt sad but without bitterness because I had a hunch you were fond of me too. There was a lot of goodwill and understanding between us . . . Maybe it was right that way, after all it was my job to see L. through to the bitter end.

It was Murry who kept picking at the memory of their brief passion, trying to inflate their intimacy into something far greater than it had been:

Tell me, Frieda . . . did you love me as much as I loved you in those queer days? It drove me crazy – really crazy, I think – wanting you so badly: the comfort and delight of you, and then feeling Oh God, but Lorenzo will never get over it. I mustn't, I must not . . . And all the while he was pitching in, telling me to 'untwist myself'. Oh Lord, if I had untwisted myself![53]

It was as if he kept returning to their earlier un-realized affair to give him an importance he felt he lacked, an importance not only in her life, but in Lawrence's, too. In retrospect, he was trying to make himself dramatically central in both their lives, to convince himself of a role he had wanted, but never had.

Murry was a bit of a creep, a womanizer. He was nervous in case Lawrence was homosexually inclined towards him. After Lawrence's death he said to Frieda, 'If I could have held him in my arms just once . . .'

If Murry was nostalgic for a life he had never lived, he was also, by taking his place and being his wife's lover, trying to put himself in the much-envied position of Lawrence. Thus, the man who, during World War I, had hated Frieda for her closeness to Lawrence, now dwelt obsessively on his brief affair with her so he would not sink into obscurity.[54] In one of the entries in his journal this self-elevation becomes very clear: 'If I had gone with Lawrence and Frieda [to Mexico], Frieda would have become my woman'.[55] Frieda, one suspects, had different ideas.

ANGELO RAVAGLI

She found it hard that she could have no mental contact with him, she who had enjoyed the fierce arguments . . . and the brilliant talk with the clever men she had known. But this man did not want to hear what she had to say.

FRIEDA LAWRENCE, MEMOIRS

Frieda's relationship with Ravagli, her third husband, was her most enigmatic. Ravagli was the Italian owner of the Villa Bernada, which she and Lawrence rented in the early 1920s. Their affair seems to have begun in 1926, possibly immediately prompted by Lawrence's behaviour, which Frieda found hurtful. When his sister, Ada, came to stay, Frieda was excluded from caring for him and the bedroom door was locked against her. However, as I suggested earlier, there were also other deeper issues. Lawrence was too ill and dependent on Frieda, too aware of her own exhausted devotion and his own impotence, to protest. When he did speak of the affair, it was with a mixture of weariness, sadness and equanimity: 'Every heart has a right to its own secrets'.[56]

They became lovers when Ravagli was thirty-seven, ten years Frieda's junior. Like her father and early suitors, he was a military man, a Lieutenant in the Italian Bersaglieri, of peasant origin. She first saw him in full regalia, with plumed helmet, sword, sash and epaulettes, as if a reincarnation of her father at his most glamorous. In another mirror image of her earlier life, Ravagli too, was married to a teacher, and had three children. Their affair has been seen as Frieda's greatest moral lapse: her biographer calls it 'erotic laxity', while Lawrence's indignant biographers make it the hallmark of her lack of integrity.

People say a lot about Frieda and her amorality, but it's not very significant with her. They make such a fuss about all this, the sex; the English think it's all so terribly important. She was no prude, but she had her own values and her own moral code. She was rather infatuated and foolish about Ravagli, but it's important to remember she'd been under immense strain with Lawrence by then, so long with this virtually dying man who clung to her and was so irritable and difficult. It was very hard for her. She couldn't stand the strain any more.

It must have added to Lawrence's humiliation to know that Ravagli was not only not his equal, but that he was not Frieda's either. Few comments about Ravagli are flattering; most are unequivocal insults:

Ravagli was not a remarkable person, rather uninteresting, there was not much to him at all. Ida Eastman called him 'the ice cream man'.

Yet it may have been because Ravagli lacked Lawrence's intensity and depth that Frieda was first attracted to him. As if drawn to the opposite extreme, Frieda found in Ravagli everything that Lawrence was not. He was simple, able, healthy, not blessed with excessive intelligence or sensitivity, undemanding of her and of life. This simplicity would later pall and she would lament being with a man so blatantly without qualities. She wrote of their fictional counterparts: 'when she was dissatisfied she grumbled to herself about him. "He is so terre à terre, he has no intellect, no imagination"'. Initially, though, Ravagli's normality and mundanity were exactly what Frieda needed.

Ravagli offered her a much-needed reprieve from the inexorable strain of Lawrence's illness. He gave her the affection and sexual fulfilment that were now lacking in her marriage and that she needed to sustain her in the final years of supporting Lawrence. Frieda, though, never showed any intention of leaving Lawrence for Ravagli and their contact seems to have been rare and intermittent.

After Lawrence's death, she once more turned to Ravagli for comfort. She called him 'the soldier – He is so human and nice with me and *real*, no high falute, but such a genuine warmth – I shall be alright'.[57] He seemed to offer her a security that fed into a nostalgia for her childhood days. On these grounds, worried about the wisdom of Frieda's choice, friends and relatives tried to dissuade her from continuing the affair once Lawrence was gone.

Orioli told her Ravagli wasn't worth bothering about, he did his best to dissuade her. He said it was the uniform she went for, it was her father.

Frieda was deaf to their advice. She and Ravagli returned to Mexico, where he set up a small pottery and gave Frieda support and companionship on a day-to-day level. Her demands became very modest. In 1937, Maria Huxley wrote, 'Frieda's life is extraordinary. She lives in such a primitive way that we can hardly understand it. Angelino built her a concrete house . . . and the sitting room is hung by all Lawrence's pictures . . . How much they care for one another, or rather in what way they care for one another I don't know'.[58]

He was practical, he was a help to her on the ranch, and there was probably some kind of relief in that simple, uncomplicated life, but there was no challenge.

The impression of Frieda in her many years with Ravagli – she spent longer with him than with any other man – is of a woman who has opted for a limited relationship. Frieda said simply that they were 'fond of each other'.

He did become rather fond of Frieda, too, for she had something. As Lawrence said, 'Only the loving are loved'.

As if her emotional history had made her too exhausted to seek for more and the intense struggle with Lawrence had worn her out, Frieda accepted a companionship that was much less challenging. She once described herself to Barbara as 'masochistic' and although this was probably with tongue-in-cheek, it also contains some truth. Her relationship with Ravagli was not, ultimately, fulfilling for her. She lamented his lack of intellectual strength and missed the dialogues, however violent they might have been, with Lawrence. Her years with Ravagli had the virtues of ordinariness and comfort, but they were also relatively dull and, as time passed, Frieda's own inner reservations about him grew.

She had originally been close to Ravagli's family, was godmother to his son – named Federico for her – she even spent a few days with them after Lawrence's death and had some correspondence with Ravagli's wife once she was in Mexico. But she came to suspect his family of exploiting the association with her to make money. When he returned to Italy for a visit in 1937, she wrote to him: 'You know I feel what is mine is yours. I don't feel like that about your family. For that you must forgive me, it is only human'. Nor could she blind herself, in the end, to Ravagli's numerous sexual infidelities. Barbara remembers his conspicuous flirtations:

When I stayed there in 1956, I could see that she was bored with him, she was tired of him. He made passes at both me and Elsa, he wrote a letter to Frieda about how if he'd not been a married man, Barby would have been his choice. Yet it didn't put her off. She needed somebody and she felt that her children had grown completely apart from her. At one time, Frieda wrote me that Ravagli was in love with someone else, and that she would be glad to be free of the responsibility of him. But of course he didn't go off, he was looking after himself. My husband called him 'a crook' but Frieda thought it was his wife and children after the money, not he . . . She simply married him to do him a good turn.

The marriage itself was Frieda's decision as much as Ravagli's, but it seems to have been a typically rash act of generosity, to prevent his deportation. Frieda was notoriously naive about money, and it is doubtful whether she considered the full financial repercussions of this union for her children. Certainly, the results have led to suspicions as to Ravagli's motives for staying with and marrying Frieda. For, when she died, Mexican law decreed that her estate be divided equally between her husband and children. By this simple twist of fate, Ravagli's family's endurance of his absence was strangely rewarded (Ravagli is also rumoured to have forged paintings after Frieda's death and asserted they were hers).

In a bizarre postscript, Ravagli returned to Italy to the wife and children he had deserted to be with Frieda, and he remained there until his death in 1975. Under Italian law, he had never been divorced; Frieda had, in a way, been living with a bigamist. Ironically, the descendants of the man who had cuckolded Lawrence were the beneficiaries of half of Lawrence's considerable literary estate and, over the next few decades, became one of the richest landowning families in their region of Italy.

Frieda, though, would not have survived well alone. Ravagli had the pragmatism she lacked, helped her with running the home and took the edge off her isolation. At its best, their companionship was mutually supportive and Frieda described her final years as relatively happy ones. In 1950, aged seventy-one, she expressed her contentment: 'I have the life I want'. Indeed, she had all the visitors she wanted, friends in Hollywood including Charlie Chaplin and Igor Stravinsky, knew artist protegés of Luhan's, like Georgia O'Keefe. Yet, in contrast to her time with Lawrence, these final years seem somewhat bland. At its worst, the relationship with Ravagli represented the kind of dullness that emotional exhaustion and spiritual compromise can drag in their wake.

And, of course, Lawrence thought Ravagli was just a cheap nothing.

Frieda and Motherhood: 'the flowers of pain'

It was wonderful to have the old bond with the children again, I had given up hope, thought it was the price I had to pay for being L.'s wife.   FRIEDA LAWRENCE, LETTER TO MURRY, 1952

*L*eavis' verdict that Frieda was 'unmaternal' is not borne out by the evidence. Her letters and writings, the testaments of friends, Lawrence's intense jealousy, memories from her children – all attest to Frieda's motherly love. Her early delight in them spills over in her correspondence: 'the boy is our great joy', '[he] is really dear, and it is wonderful for me that to him no one is above his "Momamo" . . . It is touching how attached he is to me'. (see Plate 4) Barbara recalls that, as children, they relished their mother's company:

My father was a more distanced figure. We were very fond of him, but she was the one who counted. It was fun when she was around. Frieda enjoyed life, she made the best of it, you never knew that she was secretly dissatisfied and bored in Nottingham. Life was wonderful, magical with her.

Frieda's renunciation of motherhood was not a carefully considered decision, but a quick response to dramatic emotional events. She knew she must escape the slow suicide of her suburban marriage and that she and Lawrence had neither money nor a home that would let them have the children. Moreover, British divorce laws of the time meant that Frieda, as the guilty party, had to relinquish the children to their father.

The opprobrium of leaving her children has been made primarily Frieda's alone. Whereas disciples of Lawrence read the episode as showing his refusal to compromise and his rejection of a shallow sexual affair, for Frieda's critics, it is further proof of her selfishness and amorality. But the pain she felt at being severed from her young children

so full of love . . . that when she was suffering she was as painful to watch as an animal in a trap . . . She could no more forget and abandon her children than a lioness or puma can forget the cubs which the hunter has taken away, and her unhappiness in being separated from them was something simple and elemental'.[64] At times she was paralysed with grief, but witnessing her agony only added to Lawrence's self-recriminations and he resented the shadow cast by Frieda's mothering.

Initially, Lawrence was kind, sharing her shock at Weekley's barbaric retaliation. His poem, 'Ballad of a Wilful Woman', likens Frieda to Mary in the flight from Egypt, only this Mary has left her child with Joseph to follow the 'restless wanderings' of a saviour figure. And at night, 'by the fire's red stain / Her face is bent, in the bitter stream / That comes from the flowers of pain . . .'[65] But, as we have seen, such compassion was not sustained. Through a complex combination of jealousy and guilt, Lawrence could not tolerate Frieda's grief.

When they were in London to try to see the children, Lawrence offered no assistance. It was Garnett and Mansfield who were Frieda's allies, waiting around at the children's school to catch sight of them, or delivering them secret letters: 'Katherine saw a tragically deprived mother who had lost her children for love'.[66] On their first successful encounter with Elsa and Barbara, the two girls were delighted, thinking Frieda might be coming back, but, on the next occasion, a few days later, their responses were frozen and they ran away as if she were a leper. They had been ordered not to speak to her: 'only little white faces looked at me as if I were an evil ghost'.[67]

Frieda always had a rash optimism that insisted on seeing the best in people. Her sister Else said it was a form of naiveté, that Frieda refused to give up a conviction of innate goodness in mankind. Certainly, with Weekley, she never anticipated he could be so cruel over the children. In December 1914, as a last resort, she went alone to visit Weekley in Nottingham and used an alias to get by his landlady. However, he rejected her pleas for legitimate access and subjected her to verbal abuse, saying she was no better than a prostitute and threatening her with arrest if she made further attempts to see her children. Lawrence, who wrote down the episode when Frieda related it, said it was almost farcical: 'funny . . . if weren't too painful . . . but poor Frieda can't see her children'.

Lawrence transformed his perception of the Weekley family into *The Virgin and The Gypsy*, where a vicar's wife runs off 'with a young and penniless man', Weekley being the obvious model for the man of God, with his 'furtive self-righteousness', his 'wild-eyed, tragic look' and overbearing relatives who bring up the children in an 'atmosphere of cunning self-sanctification and of unmentionability', so that they have to 'accept the family verdict' on their errant mother. Elsewhere, he called the children 'duds' and condemned the whole 'maggoty Weekley household – curse the etiolated lot of them, maggots'. [68] Significantly, many of Lawrence's central fictional couples are childless, like he and Frieda and, where children do appear (as with the daughter of Mellors' wife in *Lady Chatterley's Lover*), they are nasty creatures, symbolic extensions of their mother's badness. 'Lawrence said that children should live their lives apart from the grown-ups. He had no patience with the middle-class subservience to the young'.[69]

Predictably, Frieda's three children absorbed the moral judgments passed on to them by their father and his family: 'To the Weekleys, Frieda was the delinquent wife and always belittled to her children'.[70] Frieda's pain of physical separation was intensified by this knowledge that her children were being taught to reject her, as Barbara recalls the episode of her mother's leaving and its aftermath:

Frieda took Elsa and me to Hampstead, then she left. She said nothing. My father came from Nottingham with Monty, who'd stayed with him. I was about seven, at breakfast, with Granny and all the Weekleys sitting around and I said to him 'Where's Mama?' and he got up and walked out of the room. Granny said 'Don't ask about Mama just now'. So we were sad and bewildered but we didn't ask about her. We missed her, my sister and I would cry in bed, but as we grew older, both Elsa and Monty turned against Frieda and took a moral stance. At first we hadn't felt anything like that, we were just confused and wondered where she was. It was all so mysterious, she mustn't be mentioned. I thought she must be in a lunatic asylum. And the Weekleys were always having a smack at her, we were taught to dislike her and disapprove of her. But I loved her and my brother did, too, really. Elsa was the more indifferent, perhaps because Frieda wasn't so nice to her, she used to call her 'my slum child'.

Frieda had to struggle against constant misrepresentation and fight to maintain contact. She never relinquished hope of renewing her relationship with the children. Her letters contain poignant references to the brevity of their meetings. In February, 1917, she wrote, 'If we go to America I shall be in London . . . I may see the children for a *whole* day – perhaps more'; in September, 1917, 'I shall see the children for half an hour at the dirty lawyer's office: I am very glad'; 'I saw the children at the beastly lawyer's office. They were *so* natural and really just the same. It left me with every hope. The boy is quite beautiful, suddenly a youth, nearly six foot already. They *were* nice, I thought'. In Barbara's recollection of this encounter:

My father called for us in a taxi and drove us back to Chiswick in absolute silence. He never spoke about her. She broke his heart. Frieda knew something was broken in him when she left, she knew how grim life was. But she had a reverence for life.

From 1919 to 1923, Frieda didn't see the children at all, though Barbara was still only in her early teens. By 1923, desperate to return to England to see them, Frieda fought with Lawrence to come with her, but he refused and she went alone. Lawrence wrote to Murry, 'Wrong or not, I can't stomach the chasing of those Weekley children'. Disappointed in him, this was when Frieda was tempted, perhaps in revenge, to have an affair with Murry:

I am glad to be alone and I will *not* go back to him and his eternal hounding me, it's too ignominious! I will *not* stand his bad temper any more if I never see him again – I wrote him so – He can go to blazes, I have had enough – The worm that turns.[71]

She did see the children that summer, and from the mid to late 1920s onwards, as they were more mature and could make their own decisions, there was more regular contact and correspondence. Her letters show immense relief and gratitude at the renewed bonds. In 1926 she wrote, 'yesterday . . . we met Monty . . . It was as if something had broken through in him and there was all friendliness and love – all round . . . Of course this is what I have always longed for . . .'; in 1930, 'My daughter

Barbara will come with me; she is an exquisite creature . . .'. Whether with Lawrence in Italy, or Ravagli in Mexico, Frieda delighted in her children's visits. In the summer of 1939, Monty and his family visited her in Taos; Barbara took her daughter Ursula to see her.

Yet although relationships with all three were eventually resumed, the scars of Frieda's leaving never completely disappeared. The elder children in particular could not lose their father's unforgiving stance. Elsa remained the least conciliatory, aligning herself more with Weekley than the others. Even Barbara, whose relationship with Frieda was the closest, admits it could not be restored into a full mother-daughter bond: the loss was a permanent wound for Frieda as much as for them.

She was an outstanding woman, exceptional, some women would have been utterly crushed. And she suffered greatly. She suffered terribly. She took a child to the circus once, and I remember thinking she took this child when she must have been thinking of her own. When she first left us, she felt fear, that if it went on too long, the bond would be broken. And of course it was. When we saw her again, when she tried to burst into the house, she was a strange woman.

In a way, Frieda and I were close towards the end, but it wasn't quite the normal mother and daughter relationship. All those years had gone, been wasted, the years that the locusts have eaten can't be replaced.

When my husband and I went out to stay, there was still a certain tension between Frieda and me. Only when I went to stay with her by myself later, was it alright and peaceful. In the last letter to me, a few days before her death, she wrote 'We had a cloudless time . . .'

Frieda's leaving of her children was not to do with any reluctance or inability to occupy the mothering position. Her relationship with her own mother was strong and a source of inner strength. Baroness Richthofen was present for at least Monty's birth, and even when travel was difficult, Frieda made repeated visits to Germany to visit her (see Plate 7). She had little in common with Lawrence's much more troubled and problematic mothering, which may be why she was as intolerant of his inner difficulties as he was resentful of her relative lack of them. Her mothering instincts and her initial bonding with her children were profound, but this only this made the severance from them all the more painful.

If any suffering carved out Frieda's soul, it was this. Being absent from her children was the most important and formative tragedy of her life. In her own words:

The price I had to pay was almost more than I could afford with all my strength. To lose those children, those children, that I had given myself to, it was a wrench that tore me to bits. Lawrence suffered tortures too. I believe he often felt: have I really the right to take this woman from her children?

Frieda, Lawrence and the Feminine: 'beyond an apartheid of gender'

Frieda says I am antediluvian in my positive attitude. I do think a woman must yield some sort of precedence to a man, and he must take this precedence. I do think men must go ahead absolutely in front of their women, without turning round to ask for permission or approval from their women. Consequently the women must follow as it were unquestioningly. I can't help it, I believe this. Frieda doesn't. Hence our fight.

LETTER FROM LAWRENCE TO KATHERINE MANSFIELD, 1918

*U*nlike her sister, Else, Frieda did not make women's intellectual or social emancipation a priority. She dismissed Lawrence's early love, Jessie Chambers, as 'a bluestocking' who lacked passion and, although she had a few women friends (Cynthia Asquith, Katherine Mansfield, Maria Huxley), she never identified with women more than with men.

There were several women who admired and liked Frieda. Maria Huxley was perhaps her most loyal friend. But she came from that generation that thought women were helpless and frivolous. Her sister Else was exceptional. Frieda would say how embarrassed she was in the street with her sister, this baron's daughter becoming a sanitary inspector! She seemed to think it was men who counted, that she would be the help of men: she was Lawrence's muse.

During her adolescence, she had a brief lesbian relationship, but this was not repeated and she never entertained the idea of freeing herself from relations with men.

She passed no moral judgments on homosexuality. When she saw the film Madchen in Uniform, *she said 'That's me'. She had a lesbian experience*

| 61 |

as a schoolgirl in Germany, which Lawrence used in The Rainbow *and, in Taos, she was very fond of Spud Johnson, who was gay.*

Frieda never sought a viable alternative to heterosexuality. The challenge she set herself – especially with Lawrence – was to renew the possibility of authentic love and equality of feeling in erotic relations *between* the sexes. Her struggles against male supremacy were far more visceral than intellectual; her life, like that of so many women striving for emotional and sexual fulfilment with men, was full of contradictions, errors and flaws.

Yet Frieda was no cipher nor an advocate of female passivity. Early in her marriage to Weekley she complained how 'mean' it was 'that people try to keep us women away by force from everything "brainy", as if one didn't need it just as much when one is married!'[72] If Leavis was wrong in calling Frieda unmaternal, he was equally mistaken to describe her as unintellectual. To judge from her prolific reading, Frieda remained intellectually alert throughout her life. She was bilingual in German and English, learned Italian and was highly literate. Her range of reading extended from Sophocles and Shakespeare to Goethe and George Eliot, from Dickens to Dostoevsky and Tolstoy, from Ibsen to Koestler, from Freud to T. S. Eliot and Joyce; she read contemporary works voraciously as they appeared. She was certainly no champion of female mindlessness. 'You belittle *him*', she wrote, 'if you think I was just a passionate female to him and rather dumb'.[73]

However, the form of intelligence to which Frieda was committed was different from the one espoused and promoted in our Western tradition. She had little reverence for intellect divorced from feeling and no respect for academia. Indeed, she was highly cynical about the academic industry that grew up around Lawrence's work. In 1949, she noted that one Lawrence bibliography contained more than 600 books and essays (they now number thousands) and she regarded them as parasitic, publications that helped academic promotion and ambition rather than deriving from any passionate engagement with Lawrence's vision. This throws light on her remarkable sentence in the opening of *Not I, But the Wind*: 'I wanted to give Lawrence my silence'. It is not that she thinks women cannot or should not speak, rather that the life to which she wanted writing to lead (and to which she felt some of Lawrence's did lead) could not be put fully into language. It was that deeper life, and not critical commentary for or against it, that Frieda wanted to find and realize.

She described Lawrence as a man who would make a god of himself, but for all Miller's parody of her as one of the 'admiring cows' who clustered around Lawrence, Frieda's support of him was not fanatical. She encouraged his work only in so far as it embodied the vision in which they both believed – that fuller, deeper life, beyond the personal ego – and was outspoken in her criticism when she felt he failed it. She was more interested in what Lawrence's writing might achieve than in flattering him. Thus, she had no qualms in telling him that *Sons and Lovers* was disappointing in its overly transparent working out of his mother fixation. She had introduced him to Freud's ideas – one of their earliest conversations, she recalled, was about Oedipus – and she was angry when Lawrence refused to alter the novel. Frieda said he had 'quite missed the point'. She then wrote her own parody of *Sons and Lovers*, called 'Paul Morel, or His Mother's Darling', but Lawrence – whose work may well have benefited from a lessening of both his self-seriousness and mother-fixation – was not amused.

She continued to offer criticism, ideas, support and stimulus. She constantly read his work and gave vigorous feedback. She encouraged him to extend his imaginative range, to take risks, to move into new areas with his fiction, to be more direct. When Lawrence got impatient with Garnett's reservations, it was to Frieda that he turned for encouragement and empathy. She never disguised her approval or otherwise of Lawrence's work. She much preferred *Tenderness*, the first draft of *Lady Chatterley's Lover*, to the later versions that were made more sensational by their four-letter words. She translated his play *David* into German and it was with her consent and co-operation that Lawrence drew extensively on her own experiences for *The Rainbow*. This was originally called *The Sisters* and it was Frieda who gave him both the new title and much of the content. Indeed, her devotion to the process of this particular novel was such that Keith Sagar has suggested that *The Rainbow* should be jointly credited to both Frieda and Lawrence:

Aldous Huxley said that it was not until he met Frieda that he understood why the Buddha included stupidity in the deadly sins.

But the woman who gave Lawrence the only creative criticism he got in the early years, who helped him to write *The Rainbow* and *Women in Love* (and in all fairness *The Rainbow* should have been published as by D. H. and Frieda Lawrence), and who wrote her own book, memoirs, essays and letters, was far from stupid, though she no doubt lacked the only kind of intelligence Huxley at that time understood and valued, a kind which also prevented him understanding Lawrence.[74]

In these and other ways, Frieda was an essential part of Lawrence's imaginative process. His creative projection went from him to her and back before it entered his writing. She is also one of the most constant features in his imaginative landscape. As if Lawrence were sustaining an inner dialogue with her throughout his fiction, Frieda appears in work after work. In the fictional images of some of his central female protagonists, it is Frieda who is repeatedly refracted and remade: as Ursula Brangwen in *Women in Love*, Tanny Lilly in *Aaron's Rod*, Harriet Somers in *Kangaroo*, Kate Leslie in *The Plumed Serpent*, Connie Chatterley in *Lady Chatterley's Lover*.

Yet, as Lawrence's peculiar sexual politics began to evolve – possibly in reaction against his actual dependency on women – Frieda distanced herself and fought against many of his ideas. His earlier work remained true to some of the specifics and complexities of their relationship, but as he came to abstract women more and more, the kind of imaginative and emotional depth present in *The Rainbow* was sacrificed. Frieda's resistance to Lawrence's theories of supremacy was not bloody-mindedness, nor simply jealousy at being ousted from the centre, it was more to do with her disappointment and rage that Lawrence was failing himself. He was failing her, failing their relationship, but more than that, he was failing his own vision.

Even male critics have agreed that Lawrence's writing is at its most deeply flawed when explicitly didactic on this issue of male power: 'The further Lawrence moves towards wish-fulfilment as dominant male, the thinner his art becomes'.[75] It is Norman Mailer who calls Lawrence 'pathetic in all those places he suggests that men should follow the will of a stronger man, a purer man, a man conceivably not unlike himself', and who regrets Lawrence's lamentable tendencies towards preaching the 'absolute domination of women by men, mystical worship of the male will, detestation of democracy'. He even gives thanks that Lawrence died when he did, preventing any more of his tendencies towards Fascism.

Frieda, far from encouraging or supporting Lawrence's reactionary views on male supremacy, violently opposed them. If Kate Millet was fighting Lawrence on gender issues in the late 1960s, Frieda was doing so throughout their time together. The difference is that Frieda had no feminist framework in and through which to articulate her struggle, nor did she see the need for one. She wanted to find her identity and particular form of female integrity *within* and *through* a heterosexual relationship; separatism was not part of her agenda.

Kangaroo, one of the least reworked of Lawrence's novels, contains some of his rawest pictures of Frieda. Transparently autobiographical and written at a time when Frieda was still representing a positive aspect of womanhood to him, it shows the struggle between Somers, the husband who wants to escape the realm of intimate relationship, and Harriet, the wife who resists this splitting of experience into male and female zones.

> once he had slowly and carefully weighed a course of action, he would not hold it subject to Harriet's approval or disapproval. It would be out of her sphere . . . She emphatically opposed this principle of her externality. She agreed with the necessity for impersonal activity, but oh, she insisted on being identified with the activity, impersonal or not . . . She wanted to share, to join in, not to be left out lonely . . . Harriet was not going to be ignored: no, she was not. She was not going to sink herself to the level of a convenience . . .

In generous self-revelation and self-criticism here, Lawrence points out Harriet's complex perception of the man and his ambitions: 'he was so silly in refusing to be finally disappointed in his efforts with mankind, and yet his silliness was pathetic, in a way beautiful. But then it *was* so silly – she wanted to shake him . . .' He even allows she might be justified in mocking the man's pretensions and ambitions and that these may well be little more than a ploy to escape a full emotional encounter with her. It is a sensitive portrait of complex sensibilities in both characters, one that makes a merely reductive reading of Lawrence's portrayal of heterosexual relations, or of his relation with Frieda, a travesty.

Yet this subtlety is increasingly lost. Lawrence's female characters became more and more subsumed into an apostrophizing of Woman, turned into little more than embodiments of a female principle and, as he went deeper into his contorted metaphysics of sexuality, Frieda's support declined. Her response became a mixture of admiration, frustration, contempt and despair: that he should write so well and so badly; with such insight, yet such stupidity; with such sensitivity to women, yet such blind self-righteousness too.

It is easy to find evidence of misogyny in Lawrence's work. There are statements about female inferiority that would outrage any thinking woman – his casual letter to Catherine Carswell, for example, that 'there is something tragic and displeasing about a woman who writes'. In *Fantasia of the Unconscious*, where he expounds his theories (fantasies) of male-female relationships, he despairs at women's intellectual power: 'The great flow of female consciousness is downwards . . . the moment woman has got man's ideals and tricks drilled into her, the moment she is competent in the manly world – there's an end of it . . . She becomes absolutely perverse . . .'[76]

He hated (or feared) intellectual women, claiming that any strength women had over men was not inherent, but a sign of their having falsely taken over masculine attributes and behaviour. This disturbed the natural order and the rot was to be stopped by men reclaiming their proper manliness. If it was men's abdication of their true role that had stopped men being men and women being women, the first step towards wholeness was the restoration of power to men. Lawrence was not alone in this: the interwar years were characterized by a strong misogyny, as – in the wake of women's suffrage, as well as the decimation of the male population during World War I – fears of female ascendancy grew.[77]

Like Robert Bly and other male writers who have more recently tried to relocate the masculine at centre stage, Lawrence laments the emasculation of men in the modern world and equates a man's awareness of his feminine side as a lack, a wound of feminization that needs major reconstructive surgery.[78] This is the Lawrence who has provoked righteous feminist indignation. The Lawrence who rages against the female will; the Lawrence of *The Plumed Serpent*, urging a woman's sexual submission to a man; the Lawrence who caricatures feminism and lesbianism and despises all 'inferior' blood; the Lawrence who is so fearful of the feminine within himself that he repudiates his own homosexual leanings; the Lawrence who girds up his loins to save the human race.

It is hardly surprising that this Lawrence has been ostracized and condemned. Ever since Simone de Beauvoir launched her famous critique of Lawrence and his 'phallic pride' in *The Second Sex* (1949), it has been mandatory for feminists to deride him. De Beauvoir's rejection was made even more absolute by Kate Millet's scathing attack in *Sexual Politics* (1969), which aligned Lawrence with Norman Mailer and Henry Miller as 'counter-revolutionary' in their offensive treatment of women. From then till now, Lawrence has been firmly excluded from any feminist canon. In what Mailer refers to as the 'totalitarian' ideas of feminism, we have had a Lawrence who is bigoted and bombastic, heavily smeared (in Mailer's terms) with 'cans of ideological lard'.

Thus, Frieda's refusal to relinquish her faith in Lawrence's vision, despite all his errors and all her fighting with him as a man, has been anathema to feminist thinking. Yet she had her own form of resistance and when he insisted on mastery, she was unmoved. In *Not I, But the Wind*, she records his hysterical claims to be master as if they were the tantrums of a child. [79] She was not impressed, nor threatened by his desperate male pontificating – partly because somewhere she felt superior to it and partly because she intuitively understood its unconscious source. In *Not I, But the Wind*, she shares her conviction that Lawrence secretly feared women and that his anger stemmed from women having what he lacked: 'In his heart of hearts I think he always dreaded women, felt that they were in the end more powerful than men'.

One of the best discussions of this aspect of Lawrence and its effect on the complex dynamics of his relationship with Frieda is found, ironically enough, not in any feminist criticism, but in Norman Mailer's *The Prisoner of Sex* (1971). This was his vigorous reply to *Sexual Politics*, but, unlike Millet, Mailer is alert to both the *imaginative* enterprise of Lawrence's writing (which permits him to read the fictions as more than ideological tracts) and to the profoundly *unconscious* roots of his struggles with the masculine.

Mailer reminds us that it was Lawrence's early years that shaped his particular sexual politics, that it was his formative submission to his mother than fostered a frantic need both to free himself and to command women. Hence the knots that tied him to Frieda. She was strong enough to represent his mother, holding enough to let him fight out his resentments and angers at his dependence, yet also compassionate and loving enough to indulge his self-expression and creativity.

Lawrence described himself as not having been weaned until the age of twenty-two, and, in some ways, he never felt completely released. Mabel Dodge Luhan's view was that Lawrence kept trying to be 'the father', but could never finally free himself from the role of son. He evolved from mother's son to man's man, and notions of manliness and masculinity were always crucial to his quest for personal identity. In Mailer's words, Lawrence 'illumines the passion to be masculine as no other writer . . . for he was not much of a man himself, a son despised by his father, beloved of his mother, a boy and young man and prematurely aging writer with the soul of a beautiful woman'.

Mailer detects in Lawrence an essentially homosexual psychology. He was 'of the classic family stuff out of which homosexuals are made' and 'had become a man by an act of will'. Also he sees Lawrence's conflicts with Frieda stemming from a need for constant affirmation of his maleness and her refusal to give it:

> she was a strong woman, she was individual, she loved him but she did not worship him. She was independent. If he had been a stronger man, he could perhaps have enjoyed such personal force . . . [but] Lawrence saw every serious love-affair as fundamental do-or-die . . . Dominance over women was not tyranny to him but equality . . . He was ill, and his wife was literally killing him each time she failed to worship his most proud and delicate cock. Which may be why he wrote on the edge of cliché – we speak in simples as experience approaches the enormous, and Lawrence lived with the monumental gloom that his death was already in him, and sex – some transcendental variety of sex – was his only hope, and his wife was too robust to recognize such tragic facts.[80]

What Mailer elicits so well in this reading is Lawrence's simultaneous love and fear of the feminine. He sees that Lawrence's 'quest for power in the male world' conceals – and is in reaction against – his feminine nature. I use the term 'feminine' throughout this section in its widest Jungian sense, to suggest feminine aspects of the psyche: it is in no way pejorative, socially prescriptive or restricted to women.

Mailer may put it in exaggerated, romantic terms, that Lawrence 'lived with all the sensibility of a female burning with tender love', yet he shares Frieda's sense that Lawrence belonged more in the world of women than of men. When some of the clutter of Lawrence's thinking is cleared away, there is, behind it, a devotion to love and the life of the heart and spirit, a rejection of materialism, that is deeply incompatible with the secular – and masculine – values dominating the modern world.

Frieda played her part in trying to defend and sustain this antipatriarchal vein, both in Lawrence's work and in their lives. She makes explicit her own view of women and the feminine in the first section of her semi-fictionalized autobiography. Male institutions, all the so-called rational 'civilization' that men have created, are of little interest to her. She revels in her own cultural *dispossession,* her enjoyment of a life 'deeper' than the social or political: 'If you are a woman, you have the privilege to think as you please, and you do, but also nobody cares a hoot what you do think'. Far from wanting to push women towards the centre of the cultural arena, Frieda celebrates their freedom from the rules and pressures that govern men. Far from wanting men to invite women into their institutions of power, Frieda wants them to step back over the threshold, to move away from their narrow Western civilization towards all that had been sacrificed in its name.

Hence her hatred of war, which she perceived as a masculine activity. 'Women would never make wars. Any sensible woman who has had a child and brought it up, would not want it killed . . . If women understand their own female selves and don't try to be imitation men, they will hate war. Long ago Electra says: "I am not here for hate, I came for love". Being women we are allowed to love everything. Our business is to make things flourish and flower around us. That is our only satisfaction'.[81]

Hence, too, her dissociation from intellectual feminism. As she had no ambition to adopt male values or enter male institutions, Frieda felt

and feminine principles. The fact that they both frequently failed to embody their larger vision of love, that they did not manage to efface their own egos, and that Lawrence failed to resist an (at times) arrogant masculinity, is a sign not only of their humanity, but of the vast cultural pressures working against such a vision being fully realized.

The Quest for Frieda Lawrence: 'saying yes'

She certainly was not modern. If primitive people felt a unity embracing the whole world, they were the fish, the cow, the stone, always part of the whole, the living universe of which you are part, alive or dead, then she was like them. This background of the universe behind her gave her her strength, her deep contentment. This was not mysticism, but a fact. Like hungry creatures we look for the living splendour of the world to feed us, and the splendour is there.

FRIEDA LAWRENCE, MEMOIRS

*T*here was nothing anorexic about Frieda Lawrence. She had an immense appetite for life and refused to suppress it. Proud and unapologetic of her flesh, her strong physical presence was a sign of her desire to be fully on the earth. Her only religion was the one she and Lawrence shared: a celebration of being in the body, a perpetual wonder at the mystery of incarnation. Even in photos taken during her last years, she radiates an unapologetic presence, a sense of life achieved.

Complaining was not Frieda's style and she never shared Lawrence's misanthropy. There is no evidence that she ever sank into depression or melancholy, no temptation of despair. She had extraordinary reserves of stoicism, determination and humour. When Katherine Mansfield was irritated by Frieda's frequent references to sexual symbolism and sarcastically suggested their cottage in Cornwall be renamed 'The Phallus', Frieda welcomed it cheerfully as 'a very good idea'.[84] Even the taboo on her name in the Weekley household was turned into a joke.

She would say, 'I'm like the WC, that can't be mentioned'.

Frieda's joy in life was irrepressible: 'I am a lucky old woman and love living, every moment a gift'. She had a stoicism that could deal with whatever the world hurled at her, an optimism that was never completely punctured. 'When I was just forced to be miserable, something soon bounced me out of the misery. I wake up in the morning and the sun rises on my bed and I run around the house happy and grateful to be alive'.

Her resilience and vitality enabled her to survive in circumstances that would have defeated many. Caring for Lawrence during his prolonged illness must have been an immense psychological as well as physical strain, and the photos show how heart-breaking his last few years must have been. But Frieda never assumed the role of a martyr. She was stoical without being repressed, concerned and compassionate without self-righteousness.

Frieda's privileged early years – a family where her father gave orders, her mother organized labour and servants carried out all menial duties – freed her from the pressures and burdens that weigh down so many women's lives. It was not mere sloth that let Lawrence (willingly) do many of the household tasks: they were simply not part of her early repertoire.

Nor did she have time for social conventions. She was impatient with mere ceremony – though endorsed deeper rituals – and cared little for formalities or ostentation: 'Pleasure and social stuff left me unsatisfied'. She defined herself as being effectively *outside* the social altogether. 'I was not a social being at all. I don't think I ever understood what society meant'. This gave her an indifference to praise or blame, gossip, reputation and social standing, which stood her in such good stead in the years of slander against her. 'If people hated her, well and good, let them hate, but she would not respond with hate, because it took one's freedom away'.[85] It also, however, made her naive and somewhat gullible.

She was happy to be alone a good deal, she liked to get away from people. Both she and Lawrence were quite unpretentious. It was Dr Housman who said to her 'You're a great woman in your humility and simplicity'. But she was so naive. After Lawrence's death, young men used to turn up, his disciples, to talk about themselves . . . one appeared at breakfast completely naked and asked if Lawrence would have approved. Instead of telling him to go and get some clothes on, Frieda tried to give him a reasonable answer!

Quite as much as Lawrence, Frieda hated hypocrisy and superficiality and loathed the pretensions of the literary establishment, particularly the hothouse atmosphere of the Bloomsbury group. 'There was no flow of the milk of human kindness in that group of Lytton Strachey and Bloomsburies, not even a trickle. They were too busy being witty and clever'.[86] Equally strong was her opposition to art for art's sake. Whatever their personal differences, she shared Lawrence's iconoclasm and anti-aestheticism: 'I hate art, it seems like grammar, wants to make a language all grammar'.[87] She loathed, too, the decadence and dandyism of the fashionable literary world. Frieda's priority was never the word written, but the life lived – Eros over Logos – and she was indifferent to cultural or literary fashion.

This led to powerful judgements of many contemporary writers. She detested Ezra Pound and his Fascism. 'Poor Ezra! How could anybody take those blackshirts to their bosom! He was not very bright!'[88] There was similar disdain for Joyce and Eliot. 'That Eliot for instance is quite good as a sort of professor, but his writing is like decorating skeletons, there is no life . . . no flesh and blood and bones, nor the breath of life . . .' According to Huxley, there was also some contempt for H. G. Wells and Henry James: 'And those ladies and gentlemen in Henry James's novels – could they ever bring themselves, she wondered, to go to the bathroom?'[89]

One mark of Frieda's cultural preferences was her increasing loathing of the Faust myth, in which a man sells his soul to the devil for secular power and wealth. In much modern literature, where spiritual values have been sacrificed for material ones, Faust, far from being a tragic figure, has been more heroic. Frieda, though, hated the myth. Far from sharing the usual veneration for Goethe's version of *Faust*, she saw it as an indulgent piece of male egotism and dismissed it as 'bunk'. She had few illusions about Western culture as a whole, which she saw as little more than a veneer over man's primitive impulses. 'I sometimes feel as if the whole of humanity were a jungle, all the ideals and morals only a camouflage . . .'[90]

Having witnessed the devastation of two World Wars, Frieda was well aware of social and cultural disintegration, but her response was not the fashionable one of focusing on negativity. In the face of widespread confusion and rootlessness, Frieda believed in finding personal values and developing inner resources to get through. Thus, she remained unmoved by the eclecticism of Eliot's *The Waste Land*, with its detritus of civilization, and by other clevernesses of modernism. She was far closer to Lawrence's faith in renascent spiritual values than to the pessimism of more secular art. Like him, she preferred to turn from things dying and imagine them reborn. Her personal life could have been cast in a sad light (the loss of her children, the prolonged fatal illness of her husband), but she was not seduced by tragedy. On the contrary, her vision is close to the redemptive, resurrecting view of the great comedies. One critic has related her optimism to a non-patriarchal way of seeing the world:

> [Lawrence] owed his untragicalness to Frieda . . . In Frieda's world the sun always rose again . . . Nothing was final but recurrence and renewal. Tragedy was the life-form appropriate to the world of men, to the world of lineal progressive moralistic history. But for Lawrence – because of Frieda – the Ship of Death always sees a spot of light growing on the horizon after having driven as far as possible into total night. This is the cyclical world of comedy . . .[91]

Self-imposed exile was a feature of artistic life at the turn of the century, but Lawrence and Frieda would have claimed their own exile less as a reactive political statement than a quest for more enduring values.[92] (It was also a wise move practised by other women at the time who needed to escape the scandal of divorce). In Lawrence's words, 'I very much want to put into the world again the big old pagan vision'. They found their pre-industrial Utopia in Mexico and it was there that Frieda returned after Lawrence's death. Knowing she would not be able to fit any more into 'that crazy old Europe', she settled in Taos, which was her adopted home for the rest of her life: 'it's marvelous [*sic*] to live here in paradisal bliss, the horses, the marvelous free lovely place'; 'America, she knew, had metamorphosed her . . . In America most emotions were burnt away and washed out. A man was no longer a soul but an entity of cells, and you looked at problems with an attempt to solve them out in the open . . . America . . . was tougher, less vulnerable, less scared. It hadn't lost its sense of adventure, it went for things with a will'.[93]

Frieda shared Lawrence's anti-industrialism and preferred being among people of working-class or peasant origins.

She would say to me, 'Barby, marry a common man'. She meant a working-class man, because there was more reality there.

Her form of dress, far from following superficialities of style, mirrored this ideal of primitivism. She hated fashion and favoured peasant clothes, particularly embroidered linen dresses and hats (see Plates 14 and 15). Unlike Nora Joyce, also in exile with her literary husband, Frieda was not seduced by *haute couture* and preferred simplicity and comfort to ostentation. She economized by making her own clothes, even though her loose outfits were at times untidy and mildly eccentric. Vanity was not one of her major faults: 'I am *not* beautiful in the society sense . . .'[94] Huxley admitted himself impressed by her lack of self-consciousness in dress: 'There was nothing fatal or obsessive about [her] femininity, nothing consciously sexy'. Nor was she addicted to perfection. She had no desire to play the literary hostess, no envy of women like Lady Ottoline Morrel. Her own values mattered more to her than convention or public approval.

Frieda claimed for herself what few women have dared to claim. She wanted life at its best and fullest, on her own indomitable terms, even though she might be condemned for it. She did what it was more usual for a man to do – leave a spouse and children for a love affair – reversing the more expected and permissible sexual symmetry. She knew it would be construed maliciously. 'Sex is such a weary word', she wrote. 'It could mean a divine urge or a nasty story, but the nasty story always gets a larger audience'.[95]

Frieda had a healthy self-protection, she thought her life would be miserable so she decided to make a bold move to save herself. She had a lust for life, lustig, which is different from sexual lust – a passion for life and happiness. Instead of doing it all surreptitiously, she made a bold move and went away with Lawrence, flouted the conventions. Lawrence must have had great force, something remarkable, to make her feel she must go, an extraordinary power. Frieda would say her leaving was dreadful for us as children but it also made a bond between us, which was true, but she was also comforting herself. Of course she was selfish in going, but unless someone sometimes goes against the order of things, nothing would ever happen. Life would be completely stagnant. I think she was right to do what she did. If she hadn't left she would have settled down, with perhaps another affair or two, and become a dissatisfied elderly woman.

It was an era of radical experiments in erotic freedom, a time when the influences of Freud and figures such as Edward Carpenter, or Dora and Bertrand Russell's defence of free love, contributed to a new awareness of sexuality. But Frieda's sexual behaviour was not a political statement. Nor was it driven by unconscious need, in the way one may read the frenzied, even neurotic, pattern of Mansfield's numerous affairs. It was simply an extension of that celebration of the flesh and joy in life that were so important to Frieda. Lawrence's feeling that 'the vast marvel is to be alive . . . the supreme triumph is to be most vividly, most perfectly alive. We ought to dance with rapture that we should be alive and in the flesh, and part of the living, incarnate cosmos' was also Frieda's. She wrote to Mansfield in 1916: 'I am so anxious now to *live* without any more soul harassing . . . we won't bother anymore [*sic*] about the *deep* things, they are all right, just let's live like the lilies in the field'.[96]

Reflecting this affinity with the natural world, Frieda's pleasures were simple. She liked being outdoors and enjoyed rural life – walking, swimming, horse riding, picnicking – and ordinary domestic tasks – growing plants and flowers, shopping at markets, sewing, cooking, visiting, being with friends. After Lawrence's death, she renewed her friendships with Luhan and Brett (see Plate 21). She liked smoking – a symbol, perhaps, of her irreverence and liberation. She painted vibrant watercolours and decorated furniture. She loved music. Bessie Smith's 'Empty Bed Blues' sent her into raptures in 1929, though she played it so often that Lawrence – who detested it and gramophones – broke the record over her head.[97] She shared Lawrence's wonder in the natural world, and her writings talk of the rich delight of wildlife. She was averse to any repressive discipline. Her main activities and pleasures were thoroughly unsophisticated.

Her background gave her a confidence she would always be provided for (Else Jaffe may have subsidized her and Lawrence in the early years) and, thus, she felt no pressure to earn her living. Yet, until she inherited Lawrence's literary estate, she was never wealthy: much of her time with Lawrence was spent in relative poverty. They led an essentially nomadic life, untrammelled by property or possessions and settling nowhere for long. Only when she had some money from Lawrence's estate did Frieda buy a house of her own on the Gulf of Mexico.

It would be wrong, though, to claim there was no arrogance in Frieda. She could not totally erase the effects of her class background, and Lawrence reinforced any sense she had of innate worth by revelling in her explicit nobility. His worship of heroic individualism and his contempt for the masses reinforced and, to some extent, mirrored her own. She was proud of her origins as a Richthofen baroness and aware of her sense of difference.

Frieda did have a certain arrogance. She said most people are slaves – and, after Lawrence's death, she remarked rather sadly, 'One never meets one's equals'.

However, to equate this aspect of their thinking with Fascism, actual or embryonic, is misleading.

Bertrand Russell sowed the seeds of this accusation. He compared Lawrence to Hitler and Mussolini, saying his ideas 'led straight to Auschwitz', charging him with developing 'the whole philosophy of Fascism', and holding Frieda to be his conspirator. 'He had the eloquence, but she had the ideas . . . Lawrence was an essentially timid man, who tried to conceal his timidity by bluster. His wife was not timid . . . Under her wing he felt comparatively safe . . .'[98] The discovery of notes for an essay on Hitler's *Mein Kampf* among Frieda's unpublished papers, where she discusses the quality of its writing, has added fuel to the charge.[99]

Frieda felt that Lawrence had been unwise to venture into the political arena at all and was wiser than to follow him. 'The one time I did not believe in Lawrence's activities was when he and Bertrand Russell planned to make some reform in English government . . . I thought they were both off their tracks'. She was astute enough to know that, politically, they were both utterly naive, and she rejected as absurd this notion of Lawrence's Fascism.

He was neither a Fascist nor a Communist nor any other 'ist'. His belief in the blood was a very different affair from the Nazi 'Aryan' theory, for instance. It was the very opposite. It was not a theory, but a living experience with Lawrence – an experience that made him love, not hate. He wanted a new awareness of everything around us . . . we have more ways of knowing than merely through the intellect.[100]

Her own allegiances were very clear. She detested both Fascism and Nazism, called Hitler and Mussolini devils who had 'unholy success', violently opposed Ravagli's verbal support of Mussolini and, throughout World War II, longed for Hitler's defeat. 'I suffered tortures of shame about the Nazis being German, but many of the members of the family were anti-Nazi and did all they could. The trouble was they did not take Hitler seriously till it was too late'.[101] She was further from the political Right than has been credited: Barbara Barr remembers that '*Lenin was one of her heroes*'.

Despite the century's horrors and hostilities, Frieda never relinquished her vision of a new humanity. She was curiously able to look through suffering and transform it, and the vision that lies behind her few writings radiates a certainty of transformation, inner as well as outer, global as well as personal. Even in the midst of World War II, when Nazism was at its height, she was able to proclaim her faith in the future and a new humanity.

> Yes, the world is a chaos, but I feel curiously happy and hopeful, as if out of the chaos something new will be born. Surely humanity has lots of possibilities yet. The Nazis will die of their own horror and then if we are wise and follow the best in us, a wonderful people might come. It is so beautiful, this life, one seems to know the value of it more, with all the horrors going on.[102]

For Frieda as much as for Lawrence, physical death was less an ending than a means of transformation. At Lawrence's funeral, knowing he hated her in black, she refused to wear mourning and lovingly tossed mimosa into his grave, though it earned her the reputation of '*la veuve joyeuse*', the merry widow. Her own death came quickly and she dealt with it with her usual stoicism.

She hated one critic's description of Lawrence's 'historic vitalism' and would have despised other categories of paganism or animism. But she was far from being an atheist. Like Lawrence, she was convinced that the mechanistic society of the West was killing the human spirit, and that only by turning away from it could a rich, pantheistic view return. This would feed the heart, imagination and body, as well as the spirit – a holistic vision as far from the narrow view of secular culture as it was from the arid, life-denying practices of most religions.

She didn't disbelieve in God. She had spurts of being religious, but she didn't go to church. She was very interested in the account Aldous Huxley sent her of Maria's death in California, how he'd helped her to die, and it interested her, preoccupied her when she was older. She had a book called Ars Morandi, *the art of dying.*

In Huxley's perception of Frieda she 'wasn't the praying kind. For her, the supernatural was Nature; the divine was neither spiritual nor specifically human; it was in landscapes and sunshine and animals, it was in flowers . . . it was in kisses . . . [and] in the nocturnal apocalypses of love, in the more diffuse but no less ineffable bliss of just feeling well'.[103]

In the vast Mexican landscape, that meant so much to her, Frieda found her spiritual fulfilment. In her own words:

What was religion? What was belief? . . . it was awareness, awareness of all that the universe holds and means. Belief was the secret and forever unknowable mystery that people called God or many gods or Buddha or Christ or the great spirit. It had many names. It did not matter what it was called, but it was there. It was the prime nourisher of every living entity, the umbilical cord that feeds us and connects us with the whole. Once the connexion is broken, we become loosely floating, meaningless atoms, our pivot gone. Animals and plants never lose it, only to man is given the choice of severing it or keeping it.[104]

This was not an abstract mysticism and had nothing to do with a purified or rarefied spiritual life. Frieda stayed in touch with a sense of the sacred and divine not through formal religious practice, nor through asceticism, but through savouring incarnation in all its fullness and sensuality. 'I am sure the good Lord put us on this earth that we enjoy it to the full'. It was *this* earth that was the only paradise.

Such affirmation of life on earth, of life fully realized and celebrated, was something Frieda never lost. As she wrote joyfully of Lawrence: 'To me his relationship, his bond with everything in creation was so amazing, no preconceived ideas, just a meeting between him and a creature, a tree, a cloud, anything. I called it love, but it was something else – *Bejaung* in German, "saying yes"'.[105]

Memoirs and Fictions:
'not I, but the wind'

If England ever produced a perfect rose, he was it, thorns and perfume and splendour – He has left me his love without a grudge, we had our grudges out; and from that other side, that I did not know before his death, he gives me his strength and his love for life – Don't feel sorry for me, it would be wrong, I am so rich, what woman has had what I have had? and now I have my grief – It's other people I pity, I can tell you, who never knew the glamour and wonder of things.

LETTER FROM FRIEDA TO E. M. FORSTER[106]

When Frieda returned to New Mexico, leaving Lawrence's ashes at Vence, she wrote: 'I can't still believe he is dead! . . . It seems all a dream, that life with him and I see him as such a wonderful thing, only a radiance in spite of all temper and difficulties!'[107] The more she thought about him, the more important he became: 'he grows and grows for me'; 'How sure he was in life, how generous we were with each other, how much he gave me, whatever I gave I got back a thousand-fold . . .'; 'I . . . feel as if for years I had looked into a terribly strong light and now I'm dazed'.[108] This backward view gave Lawrence and their personal life an increasingly legendary status.

Frieda took on a far more central literary and executive role after Lawrence's death. Throughout the 1930s, she dealt with his will, with complicated disputes over contracts, with publishers, agents, royalties, film versions and, as the Lawrence critical industry grew, with biographers, students and academics. In 1931, she had to try to stop a pirated edition of *Lady Chatterley's Lover* – 'What a lot of fighting one has to do' – and struggle to get hold of misplaced money and manuscripts. She had lengthy correspondences with the publisher Edward Titus, husband of Helena Rubinstein, over Lawrence's publications; with Caresse Crosby over ownership of the script of Lawrence's story *The*

| 83 |

Escaped Cock; with Richard Aldington, supporting his works on Lawrence, Laurence of Arabia and his own fiction; with Aldous and Maria Huxley.

She assumed the part of literary widow with some relish and Ada Lawrence, jealous of Frieda's closeness to her brother, thought her guilty of gross self-aggrandisement.

> The homage paid to her, as the widow of D. H. L. [sic], goes to her head, and fills her with a false sense of self-importance . . . She is very happy in her role as the wonderful woman who made Bert what he was, she also has plenty of money, and will never want, and on the whole is getting a much bigger kick out of life than ever she got while he lived.[109]

Frieda was aware of this slander, and some of her letters do betray a preoccupation with money and an anxiety not to be swindled, but neither greed nor personal ambition were her main aims. The temptation to enjoy Lawrence's posthumous fame was countered by her own humility and irony. 'I come in for Lawrence's "glory" and I don't know what to do with it! He has escaped that anyhow!'; 'All this fame is almost too much!'; 'I read *Rainbow* and *Women in Love* again and got puffed up – It's me, It's me, so much is me! – But then I thought, no he sensed it, he turned it into art and I subsided again'.[110] It was not mere egotism that made Frieda claim for Lawrence what she thought was his due.

> *After Lawrence's death, he had been so maligned she felt she had to raise him up out of the mire.*

Ironically, the woman who had written in 1923 that 'If the day came, which God forbid, that I should see Lawrence as the "great man", he would be a dead thing to me and it would bore me', devoted much of the energy of her later years to sustaining and reinforcing that very 'greatness' she had once treated with such marvellous irreverence. But she now sincerely believed Lawrence was a prophet whose time had not yet come. In 1948, she wrote:

> Lately I have seen Lorenzo in a new light. I see him in the tradition of St. Augustine . . . even of Francis of Assisi . . . I could never see

Lawrence in line with english [sic] novelists, it is something different . . . Don't you agree that Lawrence is a descendant of these men?

Not I, But the Wind, Frieda's public testimony of her relationship with Lawrence, was an early part of this process of placing him more and more in a spiritual, rather than exclusively literary, tradition. It appeared in 1934, in the midst of dozens of reminiscences and hagiographies that had been rushed off the press since Lawrence's death, and was Frieda's attempt to redress some of the wilder versions of their life. It was a hurried work, which accounts for both its virtues – it has the immediacy and rawness of unpremeditated writing – and its flaws – sketching in events with little reflection on their meaning. Frieda justified this to herself by promising a longer and fuller work in the future, one that would include a richer portrait of her own life, but this was never completed.

Not I, But the Wind is written from the heart. It distils Frieda's years with Lawrence into an unaffected chronological narrative. There are a few lyrical passages and some reflections, but, on the whole, the focus tends more towards a catalogue of external events and an impressionistic version of their emotional life. Although they are Frieda's memoirs, there is little concentration on her inner world. Their centre is not I, the woman, but he, the man. This deflecting of interest back from Frieda to Lawrence is reflected in the fact that half the original text is taken up by dozens of Lawrence's letters (mostly excluded in the present volume).

Frieda's writing is straightforward and direct. English was not her mother tongue, but she used it with a natural ease and fluency and with no attempts at intellectual complexity. 'I believe I can write simply and beautifully', she claimed in her *Memoirs* and all her work has the same unpretentious and heartfelt quality, strikingly free from self-consciousness. Alice Dax, one of Lawrence's early loves, read *Not I, But the Wind* in 1935, and wrote to Frieda from her home in Shirebrook, Nottinghamshire, to say how it 'nearly broke my heart with sadness and gladness and other conflicting emotions . . . I am so glad that you allowed yourself to be borne upon a wind so fresh, fragrant of simplicity and sincerity. A story moving and so terrible, yet so rich and beautiful, written by the one person so competent to know . . .'.

Unlike Lawrence, Frieda felt no compulsion to write. His own equation of writing with neurosis – as in his famous maxim that 'one sheds one's sicknesses in one's books' – had no mirroring in Frieda. She did not need words for her survival and lacked any real drive to write or complete any of her books. Hence the padding out of *Not I, But the Wind* with Lawrence's own words – hence too her merely half-hearted attempts at writing fiction. Even in twenty-six years of life after Lawrence, Frieda did not put pen to paper in any committed way – an indication that she lacked the motivation, the 'sickness' or neurosis that (Lawrence believed) drives one to write. Frieda's creative impulses were aimed less towards the production of art than the maintenance of life. If Lawrence was the writing 'genius', Frieda was happy with Lawrence's description of her own 'genius in living', as if simply being and cultivating the self were enough.

Interestingly, by keeping the focus of *Not I, But the Wind* sharply on Lawrence, Frieda also manages to withhold some crucial information about herself. Except where she talks about missing her children, she reveals little of her own feelings. There is no mention of the increasing dissatisfaction with Lawrence that drove her to reach towards other men, no reference to her affair with Ravagli. Thus, its candour is somewhat deceptive. *Not I, But the Wind* is a text as telling for what it omits as for what it includes and this unspoken level of the relationship between Frieda and Lawrence needs to be borne in mind while reading. The work presents itself as one of the great love stories of the early twentieth century, but this is made possible only through its many silences and gaps.

The text of *Not I, But the Wind* reprinted in this present volume is slightly changed from the version that was published in 1934, in that it excludes some of the letters and poems by Lawrence that padded out the original. These have been omitted here, partly because they are now readily available elsewhere and partly because they add nothing to our understanding of Frieda herself. Asterisks indicate where such pieces have been removed. I have, however, left in the text some early letters from Lawrence to Frieda that were written at the time of their meeting and elopement. These not only capture the joy of their initial passion and throw light on Lawrence's view of their relationship – as Frieda wrote in 1953, they show 'his attitude, almost religious, to marriage' –

but they were of immense value to Frieda and remained among her most treasured possessions. All of Frieda's own words from her original script are retained.

She took her title from Lawrence's poem 'Song of a Man Who Has Come Through', where he repeats the importance of surrendering to forces larger than the little 'I' of the ego self: 'Not I, not I, but the wind that blows through me'. Lawrence had a stronger sense than Frieda of the urgency of this task – for cultural as well as personal renewal – but they both wanted to be in touch with a lost wholeness. The idea of symbolic death and rebirth of the self was as crucial to Frieda as to Lawrence and his lasting symbol, the phoenix – bird of resurrection and inner transformation – could equally well have been hers.

In 1915, she reproached Russell for not understanding that there is an 'impersonal' self in everyone. In 1916 she wrote to Lady Cynthia Asquith. 'For perfect love you don't only have two people, it must include a bigger, universal connection', later echoing this, 'I think a real relationship only begins where the all too personal leaves off . . .'[111] She saw her quest as being to strip away the personal and egotistical – a quest close to Jung's idea of individuation. 'It's hard work to be a genuine human being such as we were meant to be . . . we have falsified and dramatized all the great simple experiences of our natural existence till life itself knows us no longer. We are so very falsely important'[112]

In a letter to Aldington in 1949, Frieda reintroduced the metaphor of the wind as she found it in Montaigne, one of her favourite writers:

> I think one of the chief points about Lawrence is that he was always aware of the elemental, the unpredictable in people, as Montaigne says: 'We are all wind. And even the wind more wisely than we, loves to make a noise and move about, and is content with its own functions, without wishing for stability and solidity, qualities that do not belong to it.[113]

With Lawrence, Frieda welcomed such 'a force larger than myself', sensing it was akin to a spiritual experience inaccessible to intellect alone. 'We know so much and experience so little'. It accounted for her attraction to the vast natural landscape of Mexico, where the connection with the elements – earth, water, fire and air – was so powerful. 'This country suits my very soul'; 'She loved the stark simplified country. Everything was itself. The earth was the earth and bare, and the sky was a great dome where the clouds had space to travel and meet, and the mountains rose solid and stern from the plains. No trimmings, no disguises, all things stood distinct and defined'.[114]

Even when writing, it was not language itself that was Frieda's priority, but the truths to which it might give access. 'Writers are so beside the point, not *direct* enough'.[115] She was not concerned with trying to write better, nor with making language self-conscious. Hence, once again, the importance of that ambiguous line in *Not I, But the Wind*: 'I wanted to give Lawrence my silence'. It was not the quiescence of a woman stepping down before man, nor any denial of women's right to speech, but the silence that lies before and beyond the babble of language, the silence that passeth understanding, the place where she and Lawrence might finally be one.

Apart from her letters, Frieda's only other significant writings after *Not I, But the Wind*, were fragments of fiction that were intended to be part of a longer, autobiographical novel, provisionally entitled *And the Fullness Thereof* . . . Prompted by the inadequacies of *Not I, But the Wind* in recording her own life, she began to write these in 1935 and worked on them sporadically through the War and over the next decade: 'She was old now and wanted to leave behind some result of her years of living and the satisfaction of it all'. The book was never brought to completion, but papers and fragments were collected and edited soon after her death by E. W. Tedlock. These were published with her letters in one volume, *Frieda Lawrence: The Memoirs and Correspondence* in 1961.

Some extracts from these fragments are reproduced here after the text of *Not I, But the Wind*. They are obviously autobiographical. The female protagonist, Paula, is clearly Frieda, while the names Charles Widmer, Octavio, Andrew and Dario are thin disguises for Ernest Weekley, Otto Gross, Lawrence and Ravagli respectively. Yet their semi-fictional quality allows Frieda to explore and dramatize personal feelings more fully than in the kind of minimal narrative found in *Not I, But the Wind*. Not only do they throw fascinating light on Frieda's perception of her closest relationships with men – and her painful separation from her children – but they also show her to be a potentially talented writer. She is able to convey intense feelings with simplicity and conviction, while lightening the intensity with touches of humour and wit.

The chapters she wrote about Weekley ('English Marriage') and Gross ('Octavio') are reproduced here with little or no editing, while those on Lawrence ('Andrew') and her time after Lawrence's death, have been edited more severely. This is not only because the descriptions of her time with Ravagli are anti-climactic and have little emotional intensity, but because she gave more time and attention to the earlier chapters, reworking them in various ways, and they are far more successful as pieces of writing. I have excluded the obviously unfinished sections on Mexico and Lawrence, except for an extract from 'Last Chapter – Friends', which gives a sense of completion to her time with Lawrence.

Informing all these writings are qualities that filled Frieda's life and which make *Not I, But the Wind* and her letters such gratifying reading: a sensual delight in the natural world, a deep pleasure in the texture of things, a celebration of earthly life and its epiphanies. At her best, Frieda Lawrence was in touch with these moments of grace, when there was no distinction between spirit and matter. Her life was lived in a way that tried to remain open to the unforeseen and elemental, far from the desperate ego control, material and personal possessiveness that characterizes so much of modern life.

The 'lustful Hun' and 'German hausfrau' images of so many biographical and critical studies are travesties of this deeper side of Frieda Lawrence. Despite the myths about her, she was not particularly concerned with self-promotion. 'Greatness is a thing of the outer world, where I indeed am nothing and don't want to be any more!' Her priority was a deeper, inner world, beyond the individual self, and her undaunted vitality and ability to love – what Lawrence called her 'genius in living' – were extraordinary.

Yet behind her remarkable strength, resilience and desire for gratification, lay a rare humility. 'We are so much more than we understand', Frieda wrote. 'Our deepest selves are buried so very deep down . . . We think we know so much and we don't really and maybe about ourselves least of all'.[116]

| 89 |

The Outer Life:
'a real destiny'

I believe I had what few women have, a real destiny.

FRIEDA LAWRENCE, MEMOIRS

1879 11 August, Frieda (Emma Maria Frieda Johanna Freiin von Richthofen) is born in a rural suburb of Metz to Protestant parents: Baron Friedrich von Richthofen (b. 1845 in Silesia) and Anna Marquier (b. 1851, of French descent). One elder sister, Else, was born in 1874 and one younger, Johanna, or 'Nusch', in 1882.

1880s Frieda is educated at a Roman Catholic convent school, then a boarding school, Haus Eichberg, in the Black Forest.

1897 Frieda meets Ernest Weekley.

1899 29 August, they marry in Freiburg and settle in Nottingham, later moving to the city's outskirts in Mapperley. Frieda becomes pregnant within a month of their marriage.

1900 15 June, the birth of Frieda's first child, Charles Montague, 'Monty'.

1902 13 September, the birth of Elsa Agnes Frieda, 'Elsa'.

1904 20 October, the birth of Barbara Joy, 'Barby'.

1907 On a visit to Germany, Frieda has a love affair with Otto Gross.

1912 March, meets Lawrence at her home. 3 May, Frieda and Lawrence elope. They visit Metz to celebrate the fiftieth anniversary of Baron von Richthofen's entry into the army and spend the summer travelling in the Alps and in Gargnano, Italy.

1913 April, leave for Bavaria. June, return to England. Frieda fails to see her children. Spend some months in Kent. August, visit Germany, then go to Italy. From September, they live near Lerici, working together on *The Rainbow*.

1914 May, Frieda's divorce from Weekley is made absolute. She goes alone to visit her family in Germany, remeets Lawrence at Heidelberg and travels with him to London. 13 July, they marry at Kensington Register Office, with Mansfield and Murry as witnesses (see Plates 5 and 6). World War breaks out while they are starting a tour of the Lake District. They live in Buckinghamshire and are gradually introduced to many in the London literary scene, including Catherine Carswell, Richard Aldington, Hilda Doolittle, Amy Lowell, H. G. Wells, David Garnett, Samuel Koteliansky, Compton Mackenzie. In December, Frieda, incognito, visits Weekley in Nottingham. Her plea for access to the children is refused.

1915 January, move to Viola Meynell's house in Greatham, Sussex. Through Lady Ottoline Morrell, they meet Julian and Aldous Huxley, Bertrand Russell, Ford Madox Ford, Ivy Low and the Bloomsbury set. Frieda's father dies in Germany, aged seventy. 30 September, publication of *The Rainbow*, followed, in November, by its seizure by the police and its suppression as obscene. 30 December, move to Zennor, Cornwall. Remain there for two years.

1916 Mansfield and Murry join them, but later move to South Cornwall.

1917 October, Frieda and Lawrence are expelled from Cornwall on suspicion of being German spies. December, they move to a cottage in Berkshire.

1918 May, Frieda and Lawrence rent a cottage in Derbyshire for the rest of the War. 11 November, Armistice.

1919 From July to September, stay in Rosalind Thornycroft's house near Pangbourne. 15 October, Frieda goes alone to Germany. 14 November, Lawrence goes to Italy. 3 December, reunite in Florence and move south to Capri.

1920 March, move to Taormina, Sicily. August to September, Frieda again visits her mother in Germany. Lawrence travels in Italy, spends time with Rosalind Thornycroft in Fiesole. October, Frieda and Lawrence return to Taormina.

1921 January, make a joint excursion to Sardinia. Spring, Frieda goes to Germany to nurse her mother, where Lawrence joins her for May and June. July, they visit Frieda's younger sister in the Tirol. Return to Taormina.

1922 March, they travel to Ceylon, staying with Earl and Achsah Brewster. Then, to Australia, settling for three months in New South Wales. 10 August, sail for America via Tahiti, arriving in San Francisco 4 September and travelling on to Santa Fe to meet Mabel Dodge Luhan. Spend winter near Taos.

1923 March, visit Mexico City. 11 April, visit pyramids at Teotihuacan (see Plates 9 and 10). Rent house at Chapala (see Plate 13). July, travel via New Orleans and Washington to New Jersey and New York. August, Frieda leaves alone to sail to Europe. In London, she meets her children, Koteliansky and friends. Murry accompanies her to Germany, where she visits her mother. November, Lawrence follows Frieda to London, meets her daughters.

1924 January, February, travel together via Paris to Baden-Baden to see Frieda's mother. March, return to America. Spend April in Taos. May, move to Kiowa Ranch in the Sangre de Cristo mountains. October, visit Mexico City. November, settle in Oaxaca, with Dorothy Brett nearby.

1925 February, both Frieda and Lawrence are ill. Lawrence contracts malaria, and subsequent tests in Mexico City diagnose tuberculosis. March, return to Kiowa Ranch. 22 September, leave America together for the last time (see Plate 17). Stay briefly in London, then visit Lawrence's sister, Ada, in Nottinghamshire, and Frieda's mother in Baden-Baden. On to Spotorno Italy, and, in November, rent the Villa Bernarda from the Ravaglis.

1926 Are visited by Frieda's two daughters and, in February, by Ada. Lawrence and Ada depart for Monte Carlo and Nice. Lawrence proceeds alone to Capri. Frieda stays with her daughters in the Villa Bernarda, then rents the Villa Mirenda outside Florence for the next two years. 12 July, Frieda and Lawrence go to Baden-Baden for her mother's seventy-fifth birthday, then on to England. Lawrence meets Monty for the first time since he and Frieda eloped. August, Frieda stays in London while Lawrence visits Eastwood and Scotland. Frieda meets him at

Mablethorpe for a few days. 28 September, they leave England for the last time and return to Villa Mirenda. Over the next few months, are visited there by Richard and Arabella Aldington, Aldous and Maria Huxley and Ravagli. Lawrence begins work on *Lady Chatterley's Lover*.

1927 Based at Villa Mirenda (see Plate 18). Spring, Frieda visits Baden-Baden alone. Lawrence and Earl Brewster go on their Etruscan tour. Barbara visits them at Villa Mirenda. July, Lawrence ill with haemorrhage. 4 August, they leave for Villach, Austria, and stay in the Villa Jaffe, Irschenhausen, which belongs to Frieda's sister, Else. October, go to Baden-Baden for a fortnight.

1928 January, Frieda and Lawrence travel to Les Diablerets, Switzerland, stay at Chalet Beau Site (see Plate 19). Frieda visits Baden-Baden alone. March, they return to Villa Mirenda. April, Barbara stays and Frieda takes her to Alassio, then travels alone to Spotorno to meet Ravagli. June, Frieda and Lawrence leave Villa Mirenda to spend summer in Switzerland. Rent a chalet, Kesselmatte, at Gsteig-bei-Gstaad, high in the Alps (see Plate 20). They visit Baden-Baden together in September. October, Frieda sees Ravagli in Trieste, with Lawrence's knowledge. In November, she and Lawrence settle for the winter at Bandol, on the French coast.

1929 March, Frieda goes alone to visit her mother; meets Lawrence in Paris. They stay with Harry and Caresse Crosby at Ermenonville. 7 April, leave for Majorca. 4 June, Frieda breaks her ankle. Mid June, Lawrence departs for Florence and Frieda for London. Early July, Frieda sees the exhibition of Lawrence's twenty-five paintings at the Warren Gallery: thirteen of the pictures are seized by the police. Lawrence, ill in Florence, telegraphs Frieda to return immediately. They spend from July until September in Germany, including visits to Frieda's mother. 12 August, Frieda celebrates her fiftieth birthday. 25 August, they travel to Bavaria and, in September, return to Bandol to rent the Villa Beau Soleil.

1930 6 February, Lawrence is transferred to a sanatorium in Vence, above Nice. Frieda and Barbara stay in a hotel nearby. 1 March, they all move to Villa Robermond, above Vence. 2 March, Lawrence dies. 4 March, Lawrence's burial. At the end of March, Frieda travels to London to try to settle Lawrence's finances then returns to Italy and the

Villa Robermond. Murry comes to Vence to visit, and he and Frieda have a brief affair. Frieda takes Barbara to see her mother in Germany, then returns to Italy, where Barbara suffers a partial breakdown. Frieda is summoned again to Baden-Baden, where her mother dies on 21 November. Frieda returns to Italy and Barbara to England where she soon recovers. Frieda spends Christmas in Florence.

1931 Frieda returns to Taos with Ravagli.

1932 November, Frieda goes to London for the legal hearing concerning Lawrence's will. She is appointed Lawrence's sole heir.

1933 April, Frieda and Ravagli return to Taos. 30 May, lay the foundation stone of their new ranch. *En route* to visiting Ravagli's brother and sister in Buenos Aires in the winter, an acquaintance attempts to swindle them. Ravagli flees into Colarado to avoid arrest and Frieda meets him at Alamosa. After their visit to Buenos Aires, they return to Taos.

1934 Frieda's memoirs, *Not I, But the Wind*, are published in America. In the autumn, Ravagli builds a chapel for Lawrence's ashes on Kiowa Ranch and travels to Europe to collect them.

1935 After many mishaps *en route*, Lawrence's ashes are finally interred at Taos.

1937 The Huxleys spend the summer with Frieda.

Late 1930s to 1940s Ravagli builds a workshop and pottery at Taos. Frieda buys a house for winter use. They spend their summers at Kiowa Ranch and winters in El Prado. Remain in Mexico throughout World War II.

1950 31 October, to protect Ravagli's immigrant position, Frieda and he marry.

1952 June, Frieda makes her last visit to England, staying in London with her son Monty and his children.

1954 Spring, Frieda meets her elder sister, Else, in Albuquerque. May, Weekley dies in Nottingham.

1956 Summer, Frieda suffers a partial stroke. Barbara comes to stay at Taos Ranch until 15 July. 8 August, a second stroke paralyses Frieda's right side. On her seventy-seventh birthday, 11 August 1956, Frieda dies in a coma. Two days later, in a simple ceremony, her body is buried in front of Lawrence's memorial shrine.

She was buried high on that hill. She had asked for a small, plain, wooden cross, but Angelo was afraid people would think he was being mean, so he had a tombstone made.

PART II

Not I, But the Wind

BY FRIEDA LAWRENCE

Contents

Foreword	100
We Meet	103
Going Away Together	106
Isartal	118
Walking to Italy	127
1913–1914	133
The War	141
Lawrence and My Mother	151
After the War	154
America	164
Going Back to Europe	177
Nearing the End	189
Conclusion	196

Foreword

It was still cold last night, though it is the middle of May.

Here the ranch, with the Sangre de Cristo mountain range behind it to the northeast, slopes to the desert. The big pine trees stand like dark sentinels in the night at the edge of the twenty-acre alfalfa field. Beyond them floats the desert. You can see far. A few lights twinkle at Ranchos de Taos. A shepherd's fire glows. All is covered by an enormous sky full of stars, stars that hang in the pine trees, in Lawrence's big tree with his phoenix on it that the Brett painted, stars that lean on the edge of the mountains, stars twinkling out of the Milky Way. It is so still. Only stars, nothing but stars.

This morning early there was still ice on the edge of the irrigation ditch from the Gallina Canyon. There is such a rush of water. The ice is melting high up in the mountains and the water sings through one's blood.

But now, about midday, it is warm. The desert below circles in rings of shadow and sunshine. The alfalfa field is green, during these last days of sunshine it has turned green.

I am in the little cabin that Lawrence built with the Indians. I sit in the chair that he made with the 'petit point' canvas that we bought in the Rue de la Paix in Paris and that I embroidered. It took me a long time, and when I got bored, he did a bit.

It is a nice chair, although a bit rough, carved as it was with only a penknife.

So I sit and try to write.

I did not want to write this book. I wanted to give Lawrence my silence. Would he have wanted me to write it? Would he have jeered at me as one of those intellectual females whom he disliked so much? Is it any use, my writing?

Do I want to blow my own trumpet? Yes, I do. But will it have a clear rousing sound or will it be a bit wheezy and out of tune? Can I hear the real song of our life, the motifs gay, bold, sad, terrible, or can't I?

After all, this is my book, that I am writing. Do I understand anything at all or am I recording unliving dull facts?

Is it a genuine necessity for me to write or has Lawrence said it all a million times better than I could? Will this, that costs me so much, be of any use, any pleasure to anybody else? Will others who come after learn from our life, take from it the good and avoid our mistakes? . . . I wonder . . ..

Anyhow, I will try to write as honestly as I can. Lies are all very well in their place but the truth seems to me so much more interesting and proud, but truth is not so easily conquered, there is always more of it, like a bottomless pit is truth. It was a long fight for Lawrence and me to get at some truth between us; it was a hard life with him, but a wonderful one. Stark and bare, without trimmings and frills. But a few realities remained, a lasting truth triumphed.

Whatever happened on the surface of everyday life, there blossomed the certainty of the unalterable bond between us, and of the ever-present wonder of all the world around us.

We had so many battles to fight out, so much to get rid of, so much to surpass. We were both good fighters.

There was the ordinary man-and-woman fight between us, to keep the balance, not to trespass, not to topple over. The balance in a human relationship was one of Lawrence's chief themes. He felt that each should keep intact his own integrity and isolation, yet at the same time preserve a mutual bond like the north and south poles which between them enclose the world.

Then there was the class war. We came from different worlds. We both had to reach beyond our class, to be reborn into the essence of our individual beings, the essence that is so much deeper than any class distinction.

Then beyond class there was the difference in race, to cross over to each other. He, the Englishman, Puritan, stern and uncompromising, so highly conscious and responsible; I, the German, with my vagueness and uncertainty, drifting along.

Only the fierce common desire to create a new kind of life, this was all that could make us truly meet.

As for pretending to understand Lawrence or to explain him, I am neither so impertinent nor such a fool. We are so much more than we understand. Understanding is such a little part of us, there is so much in us of unexplored territory that understanding can never grasp. As Lawrence and I were adventurers by nature, we explored.

I only know that I felt the wonder of him always. Sometimes it overwhelmed me, it knocked out all my consciousness, as if a flame had burnt me up. I remained in awe and wonder.

Sometimes I hated him and held him off as if he were the devil himself. At other times I took him as you take the weather. Here's a spring day, glorious sunshine, what a joy! Then another day – alas! all is changed: it is chilly and it rains and I wish, how I wish, it were sunny again.

I learned that a genius contains the whole gamut of human emotions, from highest to lowest. I learned that a man must be himself, bad or good at any price.

Life and emotions change in us. We are not pictures, 'Patiences on monuments'; anyhow Lawrence wasn't, nor I either. Ours was not just a love affair, just as his writing was not just writing as a profession.

His love wiped out all my shames and inhibitions, the failure and the miseries of my past. He made me new and fresh, that I might live freely and lightly as a bird. He fought for the liberty of my being, and won. Just as in his writings he tried, with his fierce and responsible love for his fellow men, to free them of the stale old past, and take the load of all the centuries of dead thought and feeling on himself.

Will the world gain from him as I did? I hope so, in the long run.

We Meet

As I look back now it surprises me that Lawrence could have loved me at first sight as he did. I hardly think I could have been a very lovable woman at the time. I was thirty-one and had three children. My marriage seemed a success. I had all a woman could reasonably ask. Yet there I was, all 'smockravelled', to use one of Lawrence's phrases.

I had just met a remarkable disciple of Freud and was full of undigested theories. This friend did a lot for me. I was living like a somnambulist in a conventional set life and he awakened the consciousness of my own proper self.

Being born and reborn is no joke, and being born into your own intrinsic self, that separates and singles you out from all the rest – it's a painful process.

When people talk about sex, I don't know what they mean – as if sex hopped about by itself like a frog, as if it had no relation to the rest of living, one's growth, one's ripening. What people mean by sex will always remain incomprehensible to me, but I am thankful to say sex is a mystery to me.

Theories applied to life aren't any use. Fanatically I believed that if only sex were 'free' the world would straightaway turn into a paradise. I suffered and struggled at outs with society, and felt absolutely isolated. The process left me unbalanced. I felt alone. What could I do, when there were so many millions who thought differently from me? But I couldn't give in, I couldn't submit. It wasn't that I felt hostile, only different. I could not accept society. And then Lawrence came. It was an April day in 1912. He came for lunch, to see my husband about a lectureship at a German University. Lawrence was also at a critical period of his life just then. The death of his mother had shaken the foundations of his health for a second time. He had given up his post as a schoolmaster at Croydon. He had done with his past life.

I see him before me as he entered the house. A long thin figure, quick straight legs, light, sure movements. He seemed so obviously simple. Yet he arrested my attention. There was something more than met the eye. What kind of a bird was this?

The half-hour before lunch the two of us talked in my room, French windows open, curtains fluttering in the spring wind, my children playing on the lawn.

He said he had finished with his attempts at knowing women. I was amazed at the way he fiercely denounced them. I had never before heard anything like it. I laughed, yet I could tell he had tried very hard, and had cared. We talked about Oedipus and understanding leaped through our words.

After leaving, that night, he walked all the way to his home. It was a walk of at least five hours. Soon afterwards he wrote to me: 'You are the most wonderful woman in all England'.

I wrote back: 'You don't know many women in England, how do you know?' He told me, the second time we met: 'You are quite unaware of your husband, you take no notice of him'. I disliked the directness of this criticism.

He came on Easter Sunday. It was a bright, sunny day. The children were in the garden hunting for Easter eggs.

The maids were out, and I wanted to make some tea. I tried to turn on the gas but I didn't know how. Lawrence became cross at such ignorance. Such a direct critic! It was something my High and Mightiness was very little accustomed to.

Yet Lawrence really understood me. From the first he saw through me like glass, saw how hard I was trying to keep up a cheerful front. I thought it was so despicable and unproud and unclean to be miserable, but he saw through my hard bright shell.

What I cannot understand is how he could have loved me and wanted me at that time. I certainly did have what he called 'sex in the head'; a theory of loving men. My real self was frightened and shrank from contact like a wild thing.

So our relationship developed.

One day we met at a station in Derbyshire. My two small girls were with us. We went for a long walk through the early spring woods and fields. The children were running here and there as young creatures will.

We came to a small brook, a little stone bridge crossed it. Lawrence made the children some paper boats and put matches in them and let them float downstream under the bridge. Then he put daisies in the brook, and they floated down with their upturned faces. Crouched by the brook, playing there with the children, Lawrence forgot about me completely.

Suddenly I knew I loved him. He had touched a new tenderness in me. After that, things happened quickly.

He came to see me one Sunday. My husband was away and I said 'Stay the night with me'. 'No, I will not stay in your husband's house while he is away, but you must tell him the truth and we will go away together, because I love you'.

I was frightened. I knew how terrible such a thing would be for my husband, he had always trusted me. But a force stronger than myself made me deal him the blow. I left the next day. I left my son with his father, my two little girls I took to their grandparents in London. I said goodbye to them on Hampstead Heath, blind and blank with pain, dimly feeling I should never again live with them as I had done.

Lawrence met me at Charing Cross Station, to go away with him, never to leave him again.

He seemed to have lifted me body and soul out of all my past life. This young man of twenty-six had taken all my fate, all my destiny, into his hands. And we had known each other barely for six weeks. There had been nothing else for me to do but submit.

Going Away Together

We met at Charing Cross and crossed the grey Channel sitting on some ropes, full of hope and agony. There was nothing but the grey sea, and the dark sky, and the throbbing of the ship, and ourselves.

We arrived at Metz where my father was having his fifty-years-of-service jubilee. Pre-war Germany: the house was full of grandchildren and relatives, and I stayed in a hotel where Lawrence also stayed. It was a hectic time. Bands were playing in honour of my father, telegrams came flying from England. Lawrence was pulling me on one side, my children on the other. My mother wanted me to stay with her. My father, who loved me, said to me in great distress: 'My child, what are you doing? I always thought you had so much sense. I know the world'. I answered: 'Yes, that may be, but you never knew the best'. I meant to know the best.

There was a fair going on at Metz at the moment. I was walking with my sister Johanna through the booths of Turkish Delight, the serpentmen, the ladies in tights, all the pots and pans.

Johanna, or 'Nusch', as we called her, was at the height of her beauty and elegance, and was the last word in 'chic'. Suddenly Lawrence appeared round a corner, looking odd, in a cap and raincoat. What will she think of him? I thought.

He spoke just a few words to us and went away. To my surprise, Johanna said: 'You can go with him. You can trust him'.

At first nobody knew of Lawrence's presence except my sisters. One afternoon Lawrence and I were walking in the fortifications of Metz when a sentinel touched Lawrence on the shoulder suspecting him of being an English officer. I had to get my father's help to pull us out of the difficulty. Lo, the cat was out of the bag, and I took Lawrence home to tea.

He met my father only once, at our house. They looked at each other fiercely – my father, the pure aristocrat, Lawrence, the miner's son. My father, hostile, offered a cigarette to Lawrence. That night I dreamt that they had a fight, and that Lawrence defeated my father.

The strain of Metz proved too great for Lawrence and he left for the Rhineland. I stayed behind in Metz.

Here are some of Lawrence's letters, which show his side of our story up to that time.

EASTWOOD – TUESDAY

I feel so horrid and helpless. I know it all sickens you, and you are almost at the end of the tether. And what was decent yesterday will perhaps be frightfully indecent today. But it's like being ill: there's nothing to do but shut one's teeth and look at the wall and wait.

You say you're going to G . . . tomorrow. But even that is uncertain. And I must know about the trains. What time are you going to Germany, what day, what hour, which railway, which class? Do tell me as soon as you can, or else what I can do? I will come any time you tell me – but let me know.

You must be in an insane whirl in your mind. I feel helpless and rudderless, a stupid scattered fool. For goodness' sake tell me something and something definite. I would do anything on earth for you, and I can do nothing. Yesterday I knew would be decent, but I don't like my feeling today – presentiment. I am afraid of something low, like an eel which bites out of the mud, and hangs on with its teeth. I feel as if I can't breathe while we're in England. I wish I could come and see you, or else you me.

D. H. LAWRENCE

QUEENS SQUARE
EASTWOOD, NOTTS
2 MAY 1912

I shall get in King's Cross tomorrow at 1.25. Will that do? You see I couldn't come today because I was waiting for the laundry and for some stuff from the tailor's. I had prepared for Friday, but Thursday was impossible. I am sorry if it makes things tiresome.

Will you meet me, or let somebody meet me, at King's Cross? Or else wire me very early, what to do. It is harassing to be as we are.

I have worried endlessly over you. Is that an insult? But I shan't get an easy breath till I see you. This time tomorrow, exactly, I shall be in London.

I hope you've got some money for yourself. I can muster only eleven pounds. A chap owes me twenty-five quid, but is in such a fix himself, I daren't both him. At any rate, eleven pounds will take us to Metz, then I must rack my poor brains.

Oh Lord, I must say 'making history', as Garnett puts it, isn't the most comfortable thing on earth. If I know how things stood with you, I wouldn't care a damn. As it is, I eat my blessed heart out.

Till tomorrow, till tomorrow, till tomorrow (I nearly put à demain).

D. H. LAWRENCE

P.S. I haven't told anything to anybody. Lord, but I wonder how you are.

D.H.L.

METZ

Damn the rain! I suppose you won't go out while it continues heavily. I'll venture forth in a minute – 9.15 already. I don't know where you live exactly – so if I can't find you I shall put this in number 4. That's the nearest I can get; is it right?

If I don't meet you, I suppose I shan't see you today, since this is the festive day. I don't mind. At least, I do, but I understand it can't be helped.

I shall go into the country if it'll keep a bit fine – shall be home here about 2.30 I suppose. I can work as soon as I like.

Let us go away from Metz. Tell Else I'm not cross. How should I be? You are the soul of good intention – how can one be cross with you? But I wish I had the management of our affairs.

Don't love me for things I'm not – but also don't tell me I'm mean. I wondered what had become of you this morning. Were you being wise and good and saving my health? You needn't. I'm not keen on coming to your place to lunch tomorrow – but I am in your hands – 'into thine hand, O Lord I commend', etc. I want you to do as you like, over little things such as my coming to your father's house. In oddments, your will is my will.

I love you – but I always have to bite my tongue before I can say it. It's only my Englishness.

Commend me to your sister. I lodge an appeal with her. I shall say to her – it's no good saying it to you – 'Ayez pitié de moi'.

No, I'm only teasing. It doesn't matter at all what happens – or what doesn't happen, that's more to the point – these few days. But if you put up your fingers, and count your days in Germany, and compare them with the days to follow in Nottingham, then you will see, you – (I don't mean it) – are selling sovereigns at a penny each. No, you are not doing it – but it's being done.

Don't be hurt, or I shall – let me see – go into a monastery – this hotel is precious much like one already.

This is the last day I let you off – so make the most of it and be jolly.

TUESDAY

Now I can't stand it any longer, I can't. For two hours I haven't moved a muscle – just sat and thought. I have written a letter to E . . . You needn't, of course, send it. But you must say to him all I have said. No more dishonour, no more lies. Let them do their – silliest – but no more subterfuge, lying, dirt, fear. I feel as if it would strangle me. What is it all but procrastination? No, I can't bear it, because it's bad. I love you. Let us face anything, do anything, put up with anything. But this crawling under the mud I cannot bear.

I'm afraid I've got a fit of heroics. I've tried so hard to work – but I can't. This situation is round my chest like a cord. It mustn't continue. I will go right away, if you like. I will stop in Metz till you get E . . .'s answer to the truth. But no, I won't utter or act or willingly let you utter or act, another single lie in the business.

I'm not going to joke, I'm not going to laugh, I'm not going to make light of things for you. The situation tortures me too much. It's the situation, the situation I can't stand – no, and I won't. I love you too much.

Don't show this letter to either of your sisters – no. Let us be good. You are clean, but you dirty your feet. I'll sign myself as you call me – Mr. Lawrence.

Don't be miserable – if I didn't love you I wouldn't mind when you lied. But I love you, and Lord, I pay for it.

HOTEL RHEINISCHER HOF, TRIER
8 MAY 1912

I am here – I have dined – it seems rather nice. The hotel is little – the man is proprietor, waiter, bureau, and everything else, apparently – speaks English and French and German quite sweetly – has evidently been in swell restaurants abroad – has an instinct for doing things decently, with just a touch of swank – is cheap – his wife (they're a youngish couple) draws the beer – it's awfully nice. The bedroom is two marks fifty per day, including breakfast – per person. That's no more than my room at the Deutscher Hof, and this is much nicer. It's on the second floor – two beds – rather decent. Now, you ought to be here, you ought to be here. Remember, you are to be my wife – see that they don't send you any letters, or only under cover to me. But you aren't here yet. I shall love Trier – it isn't a ghastly medley like Metz – new town, old town, barracks, barracks, cathedral, Montigny. This is nice, old, with trees down the town. I wish you were here. The valley all along coming is full of apple trees in blossom, pink puffs like the smoke of an explosion, and then bristling vine sticks, so that the hills are angry hedgehogs.

I love you so much. No doubt there'll be another dish of tragedy in the morning, and we've only enough money to run us a fortnight, and we don't know where the next will come from, but still I'm happy, I am happy. But I wish you were here. But you'll come, and it isn't Metz. Curse Metz.

They are all men in this hotel – business men. They are the connoisseurs of comfort and moderate price. Be sure men will get the best for the money. I think it'll be nice for you. You don't mind a masculine atmosphere, I know.

I begin to feel quite a man of the world. I ought, I suppose, with this wickedness of waiting for another man's wife in my heart. Never mind, in heaven there is no marriage nor giving in marriage.

I must hurry to post – it's getting late. Come early on Saturday morning. Ask the Black Hussy at Deutscher Hof if there are any letters for me. I love you – and Else – I do more than thank her. Love.

D. H. LAWRENCE

HOTEL RHEINISCHER HOF
TRIER – THURSDAY

Another day nearly gone – it is just sunset. Trier is a nice town. This is a nice hotel. The man is a cocky little fellow, but good. He's lived in every country and swanks about his languages. He really speaks English nicely. He's about thirty-five, I should think. When I came in just now – it is sunset – he said, 'You are a bit tired?' It goes without saying I laughed. 'A little bit', he added quite gently. That amuses me. He would do what my men friends always want to do, look after me a bit in the trifling, physical matters . . .

* * *

One more day, and you'll be here. Suddenly I see your chin. I love your chin. At this moment, I seem to love you, because you've got such a nice chin. Doesn't it seem ridiculous?

I must go down to supper. I am tired. It was a long walk. And then the strain of these days. I dreamed E . . . was frantically furiously wild with me – I won't tell you the details – and then he calmed down, and I had to comfort him. I am a devil at dreaming. It's because I get up so late. One always dreams after seven a.m.

The day is gone. I'll talk a bit to my waiter fellow, and post this. You will come on Saturday? By jove, if you don't! We shall always have to battle with life, so we'll never fight with each other, always help.

Bis Samstag – ich liebe dich schwer.

D. H. LAWRENCE

* * *

POSTCARD WITH PICTURE OF TRIER, BASILICA

Now, I am in Hennef – my last changing place. It is 8.30 – and still an hour to wait. So I am sitting like a sad swain, beside a nice, twittering little river, waiting for the twilight to drop, and my last train to come. I shan't get to Waldbrol till after 11.00 – nine hours on the way – and that is the quickest it can be done. But it's a nice place, Hennef, nearly like England. It's getting dark. Now for the first time during today, my detachment leaves me, and I know I only love you. The rest is nothing at all. And the promise of life with you is all richness. Now I know.

D. H. LAWRENCE

WALDBRÖL – MITTWOCH

I have had all your three letters quite safely. We are coming on quickly now. Do tell me if you can what is E . . .'s final decision. He will get the divorce, I think, because of his thinking you ought to marry me. That is the result of my letter to him. I will crow my little crow, in opposition to you. And then after six months, we will be married – will you? Soon we will go to Munich. But give us a little time. Let us get solid before we set up together. Waldbrol restores me to my decent sanity. Is Metz still bad for you – not? It will be better for me to stay here – shall I say till the end of next week? We must decide what we are going to do, very definitely. If I am to come to Munich next week, what are we going to live on? Can we scramble enough together to last us till my payments come in? I am not going to tell my people anything till you have the divorce. If we can go decently over the first three or four months – financially – I think I shall be able to keep us going for the rest. Never mind about the infant. If it should come, we will be glad, and stir ourselves to provide for it – and if it should not come, ever – I shall be sorry. I do not believe, when people love each other, in interfering there. It is wicked, according to my feeling. I want you to have children to me – I don't care how soon. I never thought I should have that definite desire. But you see, we must have a more or less stable foundation if we are going to run the risk of the responsibility of children – not the risk of children, but the risk of the responsibility.

I think after a little while, I shall write to E . . . again. Perhaps he would correspond better with me.

Can't you feel how certainly I love you and how certainly we shall be married? Only let us wait just a short time, to get strong again. Two shaken, rather sick people together would be a bad start. A little waiting, let us have, because I love you. Or does the waiting make you worse? – no, not when it is only a time of preparation. Do you know, like the old knights, I seem to want a certain time to prepare myself – a sort of vigil with myself. Because it is a great thing for me to marry you, not a quick, passionate coming together. I know in my heart 'here's my marriage'. It feels rather terrible – because it is a great thing in my life – it is my life – I am a bit awe-inspired – I want to get used to it. If you think it is fear and indecision, you wrong me. It is you who would hurry, who are undecided. It's the very strength and inevitability of the oncoming thing that makes we wait, to get in harmony with it. Dear God, I am marrying you, now, don't you see. It's a far greater thing than ever I knew. Give me till next week-end, at least. If you love me, you will understand.

If I seem merely frightened and reluctant to you – you must forgive me.

I try, I always try, when I write to you, to write the truth as near the mark as I can get it. It frets me, for fear you are disappointed in me, and for fear you are too much hurt. But you are strong when necessary.

You have got all myself – I don't even flirt – it would bore me very much – unless I got tipsy. It's a funny thing, to feel one's passion – sex desire – no longer a sort of wandering thing, but steady, and calm. I think, when one loves, one's very sex passion becomes calm, a steady sort of force, instead of a storm. Passion, that nearly drives one mad, is far away from real love. I am realizing things that I never thought to realize. Look at that poem I sent you – I would never write that to you. I shall love you all my life. That also is a new idea to me. But I believe it.

Auf Wiedersehen

D. H. LAWRENCE

ADR. HERRN KARL KRENKOW
WALDBROL – RHEINPROVINZ
14 MAY 1912

Yes, I got your letter later in the day – and your letter and E . . .'s and yours to Garnett, this morning. In E . . .'s, as in mine to E . . ., see the men combining in their freemasonry against you. It is very strange.

I will send your letter to Garnett. I enclose one of his to me. It will make you laugh.

With correcting proofs, and reading E . . .'s letter, I feel rather detached. Things are coming straight. When you got in London, and had to face that judge, it would make you ill. We are not callous enough to stand against the public, the whole mass of the world's disapprobation, in a sort of criminal dock. It destroys us, though we deny it. We are all off the balance. We are like spring scales that have been knocked about. We had better be still awhile, let ourselves come to rest.

Things are working out to their final state now. I did not do wrong in writing to E. . . . Do not write to my sister yet. When all is a 'fait accompli' then we will tell her, because then it will be useless for her to do other than to accept.

I am very well, but, like you, I feel shaky. Shall we not leave our meeting till we are better? Here, in a little while, I shall be solid again. And if you must go to England, will you go to Munich first – so far? No, I don't want to be left alone in Munich. Let us have firm ground where we next go. Quakiness and uncertainty are the death of us. See, tell me exactly what you are going to do. Is the divorce coming off? Are you going to England at all? Are we going finally to pitch our camp in Munich? Are we going to have enough money to get along with? Have you settled anything definite with E. . . .? – One must be detached, impersonal, cold, and logical, when one is arranging affairs. We do not want another fleet of horrors attacking us when we are on a rather flimsy raft – lodging in a borrowed flat on borrowed money.

Look, my dear, now that the suspense is going over, we can wait even a bit religiously for one another. My next coming to you is solemn, intrinsically – I am solemn over it – not sad, oh no – but it is my marriage, after all, and a great thing – not a thing to be snatched and clumsily handled. I will not come to you unless it is safely, and firmly. When I have come, things shall not put us apart again. So we must wait and watch for the hour. Henceforth, dignity in our movements and our arrangements – no shufflings and underhandedness. And we must settle the money business. I will write to the publishers, if necessary, for a sub. I have got about £30 due in August – £24 due – and £25 more I am owed. Can we wait, or not, for that?

Now I shall do as I like, because you are not certain. Even if I stay in Waldbrol a month, I won't come till our affair is welded firm. I can wait a month – a year almost – for a sure thing. But an unsure thing is a horror to me.

I love you – and I am in earnest about it – and we are going to make a great – or, at least, a good life together. I'm not going to risk fret and harassment, which would spoil our intimacy, because of hasty forcing of affairs.

Don't think I love you less, in being like this. You will think so, but it isn't true. The best man in me loves you. And I dread anything dragging our love down.

Be definite, my dear, be detailed, be business-like. In our marriage, let

us be business-like. The love is there – then let the common-sense match it.
   Auf Wiedersehen

D. H. LAWRENCE

   This poetry will come in next month's English. I'm afraid you won't like it.
   D.H.L.
   And I love you, and I am sorry it is so hard. But it is only a little while – then we will have a dead cert.

WALDBRÖL – THURSDAY

I have worked quite hard at my novel today. This morning we went to see the Ascension Day procession, and it rained like hell on the poor devils. Yesterday, when we were driving home, luckily in a closed carriage, the hail came on in immense stones, as big as walnuts, the largest. The place seemed covered with lumps of sugar.

   You are far more ill than I am, now. Can't you begin to get well? It makes me miserable to think of you so badly off the hooks. No, I am well here. I am always well. But last week made me feel queer – in my soul mostly – and I want to get that well before I start the new enterprise of living with you. Does it seem strange to you? Give me till tomorrow or Saturday week, will you? I think it is better for us both. Till the twenty-fourth or twenty-fifth, give me. Does it seem unloving and unnatural to you? No? See, when the airman fell, I was only a weak spot in your soul. Round the thought of me – all your fear. Don't let it be so. Believe in me enough.

   Perhaps it is a bit of the monk in me. No, it is not. It is simply a desire to start with you, having a strong, healthy soul. The letters seem a long time getting from me to you. Tell me you understand, and you think it is – at least perhaps, best. A good deal depends on the start. You never got over your bad beginning with E. . . .

   If you want H . . ., or anybody, have him. But I don't want anybody, till I see you. But all natures aren't alike. But I don't believe even you are your best, when you are using H . . . as a dose of morphia – he's not much else to you. But sometimes one needs a dose of morphia, I've had many a one. So you know best. Only, my dear, because I love you, don't be sick, do will to be well and sane.

This is also a long wait. I also am a carcass without you. But having a rather sick soul, I'll let it get up and be stronger before I ask it to run and live with you again.

Because, I'm not coming to you now for rest, but to start living. It's a marriage, not a meeting. What an inevitable thing it seems. Only inevitable things – things that feel inevitable – are right. I am still a trifle afraid, but I know we are right. One is afraid to be born, I'm sure.

I have written and written and written. I shall be glad to know you understand. I wonder if you'll be ill. Don't, if you can help it. But if you need me – Frieda!

Vale!

D. H. LAWRENCE

WALDBRÖL – FRIDAY

That was the letter I expected – and I hated it. Never mind. I suppose I deserve it all. I shall register it up, the number of times I leave you in the lurch: that is a historical phrase also. This is the first time. 'Rats' is a bit hard, as a collective name for all your men – and you're the ship. Poor H . . . poor devil! Vous le croquez bien entre les dents. I don't wonder E . . . hates your letters – they would drive any man on earth mad. I have not the faintest intention of dying: I hope you haven't any longer. I am not a tyrant. If I am, you will always have your own way. So my domain of tyranny isn't wide – I am trying to think of some other mildly sarcastic things to say. Oh – the voice of Hannah, my dear, is the voice of a woman who laughs at her newly married husband when he's a bit tipsy and a big fool. You fling H . . . in my teeth. I shall say Hannah is getting fonder and fonder of me. She gives me the best in the house. So there!

I think I've exhausted my shell and shrapnel. You are getting better, thank the Lord. I am quite better. We have both, I think, marvellous recuperative powers.

You really seriously and honestly think I could come to Munich next Saturday, and stay two months, till August? You think we could manage it all right, as far as the business side goes? I begin to feel like rising once more on the wing. Ich komn – je viens – I come – advenio.

We are going to be married, respectable people, later on. If you were my property, I should have to look after you, which God forbid.

I like the way you stick to your guns. It's rather splendid. We won't fight, because you'd win, from sheer lack of sense of danger.

I think you're rather horrid to H. . . . You make him more babified – baby-fied. Or shall you leave him more manly?

You make me think of Maupassant's story. An Italian workman, a young man, was crossing in the train to France, and had no money, and had eaten nothing for a long time. There came a woman with breasts full of milk – she was going into France as a wet nurse. Her breasts full of milk hurt her – the young man was in a bad way with hunger. They relieved each other and went their several ways. Only where is H . . . to get his next feed? – Am I horrid?

Write to me quick from Munich, and I will tell them here. I can return here in August.

Be well, and happy, I charge you (tyranny).

D.H. LAWRENCE

I found these letters by accident in my mother's writing desk after Lawrence's death. At the time he wrote them, I was in such a bewildered state of mind, the depth of their feeling did not touch me, all I wanted was to be with him and have peace. I have not found my letters to him.

Isartal

Last night I looked into the flames that leap in the big adobe fireplace that Lawrence built with the Indians, here at the ranch, in my room. He found an iron hoop to make the large curve of the fireplace. I don't know how he did it but the chimney draws well, the big logs burn fast.

Those leaping flames seemed he himself flickering in the night. This morning I found the wild red columbines that I had first found with him. There they were at my feet, in the hollow where the workmen have been cutting the logs for the new house. A delicate blaze of starling red and yellow, in front of me, the columbines, like gay small flags.

A rabbit stood still behind an oak shrub and watched me. A humming-bird hummed at me in consternation, as startled at me as I was at him. These things are Lawrence to me.

I shrink from remembering and putting down that almost too great intensity of our life together. I resent committing to paper for others to read what was so magic and new, our first being together. I wanted to keep it secret, all to myself, secretly I wanted to exult in the riches he gave me of himself and me and all the world.

But I owe it to him and myself to write the truth as well as I can. I laugh at the claims of others that he might have loved them and that he didn't care for me at all. He cared only too much. I laugh when they write of him as a lonely genius dying alone. It is all my eye. The absolute, simple truth is so very simple.

I laugh when they want to make him out a brutal, ridiculous figure, he who was so tender and generous and fierce.

What does it amount to that he hit out at me in a rage, when I exasperated him, or mostly when the life around him drove him to the end of his patience? I didn't care very much. I hit back or waited till the storm in him subsided. We fought our battles outright to the bitter end. Then there was peace, such peace.

1. 1890s Frieda in Germany

2. 1900 Frieda with Ernest Weekley and his parents

3. 23 September 1911 Frieda at Weekley's parents'
Golden Wedding Anniversary

4. Early 1900s Frieda with her son Montague

5. 13 July 1914 Lawrence, Katherine Mansfield, Frieda and John Middleton Murry on the Lawrences' wedding day

6. July 1914 Middleton Murry, Frieda and Lawrence at 9 Selwood Terrace, London

7. Else Jaffe, Baroness von Richthofen and Frieda

14. Early 1920s Frieda in embroidered dress in Mexico

15. Early 1920s Frieda in characteristic hat and cape in Mexico

16. Early 1920s Frieda in Mexico

17. 22 September 1925 Frieda and Lawrence on the *S.S. Resolute* leaving America together for the last time

18. 1927 Frieda and Lawrence at
the Villa Mirenda, Italy

19. Summer 1928 Frieda at
Les Diablerets, Switzerland

20. Summer 1928 Frieda and Lawrence at the Chalet Kesselmatte,
Gsteig-bei-Gstaad, Bern, Switzerland

21. *c.*1930s Mabel Dodge Luhan, Frieda and Dorothy Brett in Taos

I preferred it that way. Battles must be. If he had sulked or borne me a grudge, how tedious!

What happened, happened out of the deep necessity of our natures. We were out for more than the obvious or 'a little grey home in the West'. Let them jeer at him, those superior people, it will not take away a scrap of his greatness or his genuineness or his love. To understand what happened between us, one must have had the experiences we had, thrown away as much as we did and gained as much, and have known this fulfilment of body and soul. It is not likely that many did.

But here I am far from the little top floor in the Bavarian peasant-house in the Isartal.

Lawrence had met me in Munich.

He had given up the idea of a lectureship at a German University and from now on he lived by his writing. A new phase of life was beginning for both of us. But on me lay still heavily the children I had left behind and could not forget. But we were together, Lawrence and I. A friend had lent us the little top flat with its balcony, three rooms and a little kitchen. The Alps floated above us in palest blue in the early morning. The Isar rushed its glacier waters and hurried the rafts along in the valley below. The great beechwoods stretched for hours behind us, to the Tegernsee.

Here we began our life together. And what a life! We had very little money, about fifteen shillings a week. We lived on black bread that Lawrence loved, fresh eggs, and 'ripple'; later we found strawberries, raspberries, and 'Heidelbeeren'.

We had lost all ordinary sense of time and place. Those flowers that came new to Lawrence, the fireflies at night and the glow-worms, the first beech leaves spreading on the trees like a delicate veil overhead, and our feet buried in last year's brown beech leaves, these were our time and our events.

When Lawrence first found a gentian, a big single blue one, I remember feeling as if he had a strange communion with it, as if the gentian yielded up its blueness, its very essence, to him. Everything he met had the newness of a creation just that moment come into being.

I didn't want people, I didn't want anything, I only wanted to revel in this new world Lawrence had given me. I had found what I needed, I could now flourish like a trout in a stream or a daisy in the sun. His generosity in giving himself: 'Take all you want of me, everything, I am yours'; and I took and gave equally, without thought.

When I asked him: 'What do I give you, that you didn't get from others?' he answered: 'You make me sure of myself, whole.'

And he would say: 'You are so young, so young!' When I remonstrated: 'But I am older than you' – 'Ah, it isn't years, it's something else. You don't understand.'

Anyhow I knew he loved the essence of me as he loved the blueness of the gentians, whatever faults I had. It was life to me.

'You have a genius for living,' he told me.

'Maybe, but you brought it out in me.'

But there were awful nights when he was still ill and feverish and delirious and I was frightened. Death seemed close. But the shadow of sickness soon vanished in the healthy, happy life we lived. He became strong, and full of energy and hope.

He would do nearly all the work of the small flat, bring the breakfast to me with a bunch of flowers that Frau Leitner had left on the milk jug in the early morning.

Frau Leitner had a shop underneath, with shoestrings and sweets, and bacon and brooms and everything under the sun. She gave Lawrence, whom she called 'Herr Doktor', tastes of her 'Heidelbeerschnapps', talking to him in her Bavarian dialect, while I, in a dream of wellbeing, would let time slip by. When I spilt coffee on the pillow I would only turn the pillow over. Nothing mattered except feeling myself live, and him. We talked and argued about everything. Vividly he would present to me all the people he had known in his youth, Walker Street with all its inhabitants, the close intimate life of what, for a better word, I called the common people; his mother, such a queen in her little house, and his father, down at the pit, sharing his lunch with the pit-pony. It all seemed romantic to me. And the colliers being drunk on Friday nights and battles going on inevitably, it seemed, every Friday night in nearly all the houses, like a weekly hysteria. I listened enchanted by the hour. But poverty in his home was grievous. Lawrence would never have been so desperately ill if his mother could have given him all the care he needed and the food she could not afford to buy for him with the little money she had.

Bitter it was to him, when a friend at the high school who took him home to tea, refused to continue the friendship as soon as he heard Lawrence was a miner's son. Then I would tell him about my early life in Lorraine. Mine had been a happy childhood. We had a lovely house and gardens outside Metz. I lived through the flowers, as they came: snowdrops, scyllae and crocuses, the enormous oriental poppies in their vivid green leaves so overwhelmingly near one's small face, the delicate male irises. My father would pick the first asparagus and I would trot behind his bent back. Later in the summer, I lived on the fruit trees: cherry, pear, apple, plum, peach trees. I would even go to sleep on them and fall off, sometimes, trying to do my lessons up in them. I did not like school.

First I went to a convent, where I did not learn very much. 'Toujours doucement, ma petite Frieda', they would say to me as I came dashing into class with my Hessian boots. But it was no use; I was a wild child and they could not tame me, those gentle nuns. I was happiest with the soldiers, who had temporary barracks outside our house for years. They invited my sister Johanna and me to their big Christmas tree hung with sausages, cigars, 'hearts of gingerbread', packages from home, and little dolls they had carved for us. And they sang for us accompanied by their mournful harmonicas: 'Wenn ich zu meinem Kinde geh'. Once my father's old regiment acted the occasion on which he had received his iron cross in the Franco-Prussian War. It was on the Kaiser's birthday. After the ceremony the soldiers lifted my father on their shoulders and carried him through the hall. My heart beat to bursting: 'What a hero my father is!'

But a few days after one of my special friends, a corporal, told me how he hated being a soldier, how bullied you were, how unjust and stupid it all was, that military life. He stood there talking to me in the garden path, in his bright blue uniform, while he tied some roses. He had a mark over his bed for each day he had still to serve, he told me. A hundred and nineteen more there were, he said. I looked up at him and understood his suffering. After that the flags of the dragoons and the splendid bands of the regiments had no longer the same glamour as they passed along the end of the garden to the Exerzierplatz.

When the regiments were filing past, Johanna and I sat on the garden wall, very grandly. Then we would throw pears and apples into the ranks. Great confusion would arise. An irate major turned toward his men and yelled, we popped quickly out of sight behind the wall, only to reappear and begin anew.

What I loved most of all was playing with my boy friends in the fortifications around Metz, among the huts and trenches the soldiers had built. I always liked being with the boys and men. Only they gave me the kind of interest I wanted. Women and girls frightened me. My adolescence and youth puzzled me. Pleasure and social stuff left me unsatisfied. There was something more I wanted, I wanted so much. Where would I get it, and from whom? With Lawrence I found what I wanted. All the exuberance of my childhood came back to me.

One day I bathed in the Isar and a heel came off one of my shoes on the rough shore; so I took both shoes off and threw them into the Isar. Lawrence looked at me in amazement. 'He's shocked, as I must walk home barefoot, but it's a lonely road, it doesn't matter,' I thought. But it wasn't that; he was shocked at my wastefulness.

He lectured me: 'A pair of shoes takes a long time to make and you should respect the labour somebody's put into those shoes.'

To which I answered: 'Things are there for me and not I for them, so when they are a nuisance I throw them away.'

I was very untidy and careless, so he took great pains to make me more orderly. 'Look, put your woollen things in this drawer, in this one your silk clothes, and here your cotton ones.'

It sounded amusing, so I did it.

Then I said: 'But I like to be like the lilies in the field, who do not spin.'

'What! Don't they just work hard, those lilies,' was his reply. 'They have to bring up their sap, produce their leaves, flowers and seeds!' That was that. Later on he aroused my self-respect. 'You can't even make a decent cup of coffee. Any common woman can do lots of things that you can't do.'

'Oh,' I thought, 'I'll show him if I can't.' But that was later on.

One day, in Munich, seeing all the elegant people in the streets I had an aristocratic fit. I bought some handkerchiefs with an F and a little crown on them. When I brought them home he said: 'Now I'll draw my coat-of-arms.' He drew a pickaxe, a school-board, a fountain pen with two lions rampant. 'When they make me a Lord, which they never will,' he said. Then, half jokingly, but I took it seriously: 'Would you like me to become King of England?' I was distressed. 'Isn't he satisfied, the whole universe is ours, does he want to be so dull a thing as a king?' But I never doubted that he might have been a king if he wanted to. Then he would write poems for me, poems I took a little anxiously, seeing he knew me so well.

He would go for walks by himself, and his quick, light feet coming home told me in their footfall how he had enjoyed his adventure.

He would have a large, heroic bunch of flowers, or a tight little posy for me or a bright bird's feather.

Then the story of his adventure, a deer peeping at him inquisitively from the underbrush, a handsome Bavarian peasant he had spoken to, how raspberries were just coming out, soldiers marching along the road.

Then again we would be thrown out of our paradisial state. Letters would come. The harm we had done; my grief for my children would return red hot.

But Lawrence would console me and say: 'Don't be sad, I'll make a new heaven and earth for them, don't cry, you see if I don't.' I would be consoled yet he was furious when I went on. 'You don't care a damn about those brats really, and they don't care about you.' I cried and we quarrelled.

'What kind of an unnatural woman would I be if I could forget my children?' Yet my agony over them was my worst crime in his eyes. He seemed to make that agony more acute in me than it need have been. Perhaps he, who had loved his mother so much, felt, somewhere, it was almost impossible for a mother to leave her children. But I was so sure: 'This bond is for ever, nothing in heaven or earth can break it. I must wait, I must wait!'

My father had written: 'You travel about the world like a barmaid.' It was a grief to him, who loved me, that I was so poor, and socially impossible.

I only felt wonderfully free, 'vogelfrei' indeed. To Lawrence fell the brunt of the fight, and he protected me. 'You don't know how I stand between you and the world,' he said, later on. If I supported him with all my might, the wings of his sure spirit made a shelter for me always.

Now I lie writing by the stream, where it makes a little pool. The bushes all around form an enclosed shelter for bathing; while in front stretches the alfalfa field, then the trees, then the desert, so vast and changing with sun and shadow. Curtains of rain, floating clouds, grey, delicate, thin but to the west today white, large, round, billowing.

It is the end of June. I wonder if the strawberries are ripe, in the hollow by the aqueduct, or if the wild roses are out, the very pink ones, along the stream by the Gallina. Shall I see a wild turkey, if I walk along the path Lawrence took so often, I running behind, to the mouth of the Gallina?

He and Mr Murry laid the big pipes on pillars of wood to bring the water along. Where tall aspens stand and the Gallina waters come tearing down. Often the pipes had to be fixed, after a cloudburst had broken the whole thing down.

Here at the ranch we are alive, and busy, but Lawrence will see it no more.

Last night the coyotes have torn to pieces a young sheep, on the ranch. Poor thing, that looked at me with scared sheep's eyes, when I drew near. How hateful coyotes are. Mr Murry tells me they even play with lambs, whisking their tails among them, to get them away more easily. Nature sweet and pure!

This is one of the perfect moments here. The days are swinging their serene hours across the immense skies, the sun sets splendidly, then a star comes, and the young moon in the old moon's arms. The water sings louder than in the daytime. More and more stars come as the light fades out of the western sky.

But then, in the silence of the beautiful night, the coyotes, a few yards from the house, tore the lamb to pieces. How I wish someone would shoot them all, but they are hard to shoot.

Here I am in the present again, when I want to write of the past. I will go back to Icking, our village in the Isartal, and that young Lawrence who was beginning to spread his wings.

I think of my going into a chapel, in a village near Beuerberg. I looked at the Madonna on the altar: she wasn't a mater dolorosa, nor of the spiritual sort, she was of the placid peasant type, and I said to her: 'Yes, you have a halo round your head, but I feel as if I had a halo around the whole of me, that's how *he* makes me feel. You have nothing but a dead son. It doesn't seem good enough for me. Give me a live man.'

Sitting on a little landing pier, once, by the Kochelsee, dangling our feet in the clear water of the lake, Lawrence was putting the rings of my fingers on my toes to see how they looked in the clear water. Suddenly a shower overtook us. There was a bunch of trees behind, and a road going in both directions. We ran for shelter and must have run in opposite ways. I looked all around but Lawrence was not there. A great fear overcame me, I had lost him, perhaps he was drowned, slipped into the lake. I called, I went to look, somehow he had dissolved into the air, I should never see him again. There was always this 'not of the earth' quality about him.

By the time I saw him coming down the road, an hour later, I was almost in hysterics. 'Brother Moonshine' I called him, as in the German fairytale. He didn't like that.

Then he would sit in a corner, so quietly and absorbedly, to write. The words seemed to pour out of his hand onto the paper, unconsciously, naturally and without effort, as flowers bloom and birds fly past.

His was a strange concentration, he seemed transferred into another world, the world of creation.

He'd have quick changes of mood and thought. This puzzled me. 'But Lawrence, last week you said exactly the opposite of what you are saying now.'

'And why shouldn't I? Last week I felt like that, now like this. Why shouldn't I?'

We talked about style in writing, about the new style Americans had evolved – cinematographic, he called it.

All this idea of style and form puzzled Lawrence.

For my part, I felt certain that a genuine creation would take its own form inevitably, the way every living thing does.

All those phrases 'Art for art's sake', 'Le style c'est l'homme', are all very well but they aren't creation. But Lawrence had to be quite sure in everything.

On some evenings he would be so gay and act a whole revival meeting for me, as in the chapel of his home town.

There was the revivalist parson. He would work his congregation up to a frenzy; then, licking his finger to turn the imaginary pages of the book of Judgment and suddenly darting a finger at some sinner in the congregation: 'Is *your* name written in the book?' he would shout.

A collier's wife in a little sailor straw hat, in a frenzy of repentance, would clatter down the aisle, throw herself on her knees in front of the altar, and pray: 'Oh Lord, our Henry, he would 'ave come too, only he dursn't, O Lord, so I come as well for him, O Lord!' It was a marvellous scene! First as the parson then as the collier's wife Lawrence made me shake with laughter. He told me how desperately ill he had been at sixteen, with inflammation of the lungs, how he was almost dead but fought his way back to life with the fierce courage and vitality that was his. It made me long to make him strong and healthy.

Healthy in soul he always was. He may have been cross and irritable sometimes but he was never sorry for himself and all he suffered.

*　*　*

Walking to Italy

It is five o'clock in the morning. The air is fresh after last night's heavy rain. There is a slight mist, but the sun from the desert is driving it away.

Suddenly it comes over me so strongly that Lawrence is dead, really dead. The grief for his loss will be my steady companion for the rest of my life. Sometimes it will be a friend, consoling me, putting everything in proper proportion. And sometimes this grief will follow me, dogging my footsteps like a hyena, not wanting me to live. Never will anything matter so desperately any more.

I remember Lawrence saying to me: 'You always identify yourself with life, why do you?'

I answered: 'Because I feel like it.'

I know now how completely he trusted his life to me, he in whom death was always so near.

I hated that death and I fought against it like a demon, unconsciously on my own. I did not know he was consumptive till years later when the doctor in Mexico told me. All my life with him there was this secret fear that I could not share with him. I had to bear it alone. Then in the end I knew, and it was an awful knowledge, that I could do no more. Death was stronger than I. His life hung by a thread and one day that thread would break. He would die before his time.

This true mountain morning takes me back to our journey across the Alps.

It was in the middle of August that we set out gaily. Neither of us knew Italy at the time, it was a great adventure for both. We packed up our few possessions, three trunks went ahead of us to the Lago di Garda. We set off on foot, with a rucksack each and a Burberry. In the rucksack was a little spirit lamp; we were going to cook our food by the roadside for cheapness.

We started on a misty morning very thrilled. The trees were dripping along the road, but we were happy in our adventure, free, going to unknown parts. We walked along the solid green of the valley of the Isar, we climbed up hills and went down again. One of my desires, to sleep in haylofts, was fulfilled. But sleeping in haylofts is uncomfortable, really. It rained so much and we were soaked. And the wind blows through haylofts and if you cover yourself with a ton of hay you still can't get warm. Lawrence has described the crucifixes we passed, the lovely chapel he found high up in the mountains. He lit the candles on the altar, for it was evening, read all the ex-votos and forgot how tired and hungry he was.

* * *

Lawrence's birthday came as we were crossing the Alps. I had no present to give him but some edelweiss. That evening we danced and drank beer with the peasants in the Gasthaus of the village we were passing through. His first birthday together. It was all very wonderful. New things happened all the time.

* * *

How I want to recapture the gaiety of that adventurous walk into Italy, romantic Italy, with all its glamour and sunshine.

We arrived at Trento, but alas for the glamour! We could only afford a very cheap hotel and the marks on the walls, the doubtful sheets, and worst of all the W.C.s were too much for me.

The people were strangers, I could not speak Italian, then.

So, one morning, much to Lawrence's dismay, he found me sitting on a bench under the statue of Dante, weeping bitterly. He had seen me walk barefoot over icy stubble, laughing at wet and hunger and cold; it had all seemed only fun to me, and here I was crying because of the city-uncleanness and the W.C.s. It had taken us about six weeks to get there.

We took the train to Riva on the Lago di Garda. It was an Austrian garrison town at that time. Elegant officers in biscuit-coloured trousers and pale-blue jackets walked about with equally elegant ladies. For the first time I looked at Lawrence and myself; two tramps with rucksacks! Lawrence's trousers were frayed, Miriam's trousers we called them, for he had bought them with 'Miriam'. I had a reddish cotton crepe dress all uneven waves at the skirt; the colour of the red velvet ribbon had run into my panama hat. I was grateful to the three ladies who took us into their pensione and, instead of fearing the worst for their silver, sent us yellow and blue figs and grapes to our room, where we cooked our meals on the spirit lamp for economy, in fear and trembling of the housemaid. Then we got our trunks.

My sister Johanna had sent me lovely clothes and hats, some 'Paquins', much too elegant for our circumstances; but we dressed up proudly and set forth in triumph.

At Gargnano we found Villa Igea to spend the winter.

Lawrence for the first time had a place of his own. The first floor of a large villa, our windows looking over the lake, the road running underneath, opposite us the Monte Baldo in rosy sunsets. 'Green star Sirius dribbling over the lake', as Lawrence says in one of his poems.

Here began my first attempt at housekeeping. It was uphill work, in that big bare kitchen with the 'fornelli' and the big copper pans. Often the stews and 'fritti' had to be rescued, and he would come nobly from his work, never grumbling, when I called: 'Lorenzo, the pigeons are burning, what shall I do?'

The first time I washed sheets was a disaster. They were so large and wet, their wetness was overwhelming. The kitchen floor was flooded, the table drenched, I dripped from hair to feet.

When Lawrence found me all misery he called: 'The One and Only' (which name stood for the one and only phoenix, when I was uppish) 'is drowning, oh, dear!' I was rescued and dried, the kitchen wiped and soon the sheets were hanging to dry in the garden where the 'cachi' were hanging red from the trees. One morning he brought me breakfast in bed and in the Italian bedroom there was a spittoon and to my horror a scorpion was on it. To Lawrence's surprise I said, when he killed it: 'Birds of a feather flock together.'

'Ungrateful woman . . . here I am the faithful knight killing the dragons and that's all I get.'

One of the favourite walks was to Bogliacco, the next village on the Garda, where we drank wine and ate chestnuts with the Bersaglieri who seemed quiet and sad and didn't say much. My window high up over the road was a joy to me. Bersaglieri came past in their running march with a gay spark of a tenente at their head, singing: 'Tripoli sara' Italiana'. Secretly people did their bargaining under my windows, at night the youths played their guitars; when I peeped Lawrence was cross.

He was then rewriting his *Sons and Lovers*, the first book he wrote with me, and I lived and suffered that book, and wrote bits of it when he would ask me: 'What do you think my mother felt like then?' I had to go deeply into the character of Miriam and all the others; when he wrote his mother's death he was ill and his grief made me ill too, and he said: 'If my mother had lived I could never have loved you, she wouldn't have let me go.' But I think he got over it; only, this fierce and overpowerful love had harmed the boy who was not strong enough to bear it. In after years he said: 'I would write a different *Sons and Lovers* now; my mother was wrong, and I thought she was absolutely right.'

I think a man is born twice; first his mother bears him, then he has to be reborn from the woman he loves. Once, sitting on the little steamer on the lake he said: 'Look, that little woman is like my mother.' His mother, though dead, seemed so alive and *there* still to him.

Towards the end of *Sons and Lovers* I got fed up and turned against all this 'house of Atreus' feeling, and I wrote a skit called: 'Paul Morel, or His Mother's Darling'. He read it and said, coldly: 'This kind of thing isn't called a skit.'

While we were at Villa Igea Lawrence wrote also *Twilight in Italy* and most of the poems from *Look! We Have Come Through!*

His courage in facing the dark recesses of his own soul impressed me always, scared me sometimes.

In his heart of hearts I think he always dreaded women, felt that they were in the end more powerful than men. Woman is so absolute and undeniable. Man moves, his spirit flies here and there, but you can't go beyond a woman. From her man is born and to her he returns for his ultimate need of body and soul. She is like earth and death to which all return.

* * *

And always again the mail and tragedy. I was so sure I would be able to be with my children but finally my husband wrote: 'If you don't come home the children have no longer any mother, you shall not see them again.' I was almost beside myself with grief. But Lawrence held me, I could not leave him any more, he needed me more than they did.

But I was like a cat without her kittens, and always in my mind was the care, 'Now if they came where would I put them to sleep?' I felt the separation physically as if something tore at my navel-string. And

Lawrence could not bear it, it was too much for him. And then again I would turn to him and be healed and forget for a while.

Everybody seemed to condemn us and be against us and I couldn't for the life of me understand how the whole world couldn't see how right and wonderful it was to live as we did; I just couldn't. I said: 'Lorenzo, why can't people live as happily and get as much out of life as we do? Everybody could, with the little money we spend.' And he answered: 'You forget that I'm a genius,' half in fun and half seriously.

I wasn't impressed by the genius at that time, making a long nose at him, taking everything like the wind and the rain, but now I know that the glamour of it all was his genius.

He was always absolutely sure of himself, sure that the Lord was with him. Once we had a big storm on our way to Australia and I said, afraid: 'Now, if this ship goes down. . . .' He answered: 'The ship that I am on won't go down.'

Here follow some letters he wrote to my sister Else.

VILLA IGEA
VILLA DI GARGNANO
LAGO DI GARDA
14 DEC. 1912

Dear Else:

* * *

I was not cross with your letter. I think you want to do the best for Frieda. I do also. But I think you ask us to throw away a real apple for a gilt one. Nowadays it costs more courage to assert one's desire and need, than it does to renounce. If Frieda and the children could live happily together, I should say 'Go' because the happiness of two out of three is sufficient. But if she would only be sacrificing her life, I would not let her go if I could keep her. Because if she brings to the children a sacrifice, that is a curse to them. If I had a prayer, I think it would be 'Lord, let no one ever sacrifice living stuff to me – because I am burdened enough'.

Whatever the children may miss now, they will preserve their inner liberty, and their independent pride will be strong when they come of age. But if Frieda gave all up to go and live with them, that would sap their strength because they would have to support her life when they grew up.

They would not be free to live of themselves – they would first have to live for her, to pay back. It is like somebody giving a present that was never asked for, and putting the recipient under the obligation of making restitution, often more than he could afford.

So we must go on, and never let go the children, but will, will and will to have them and have what we think good. That's all one can do. You say 'Lawrence kommt mir vor wie ein Held' – I hope he may 'gehen dir aus' similarly. He doesn't feel at all heroic, but only in the devil of a mess.

Don't mind how I write, will you?

Yours sincerely,

D. H. LAWRENCE

VILLA IGEA
VILLA DI GARGNANO
LAGO DI GARDA (BRESCIA)
10 FEB. 1913

Dear Else:

* * *

Mrs K . . . has written, forwarding a lawyer's letter which was sent to . . . and which says: 'We should advise . . . to refer . . . to the Court, pending the divorce proceedings. Any request she had to make concerning the children, should be made to the Court'. That of course necessitates the engaging of a solicitor.

Frieda says, it is too long to let the children wait another six months without seeing her – they would become too much estranged. Perhaps that is true. Heaven knows how we are going to untangle these knots. At any rate, the divorce is going forward; in England, after the first hearing, the judge pronounces a decree nisi – that is, the divorce is granted unless something turns up; then at the end of the six months the divorce is made absolute, if nothing has turned up. Then Frieda is free again. Till the divorce is absolute, E . . . must have nothing to do with Frieda. So arrangements should be made through lawyers. But the children have holidays only at Easter, and can anything be settled before then? We shall have to see. This is to put you au courant. Send that wonderful book do. The sixty francs have come.

Frieda is sending a picture that I want to have framed for Prof Weber at Icking, but she says it is for you. And a thousand thanks.

D. H. LAWRENCE

1913–1914

In the spring I went from the Villa Igea to Baden-Baden and saw my father for the last time; he was ill and broken. 'I don't understand the world any more,' he said.

Lawrence walked over the big St Bernard with a friend. We met in London after a fortnight to see my children and to arrange about the divorce. We stayed with the Garnetts. One morning I met my children on their way to their school. They danced around me in complete delight. 'Mama, you are back, when are you coming home?'

'I can't come back, you must come to me. We shall have to wait.'

How I suffered not to be able to take them with me! So much of my spontaneous living had gone to them and now this was cut off. When I tried to meet them another morning they had evidently been told that they must not speak to me and only little white faces looked at me as if I were an evil ghost. It was hard to bear, and Lawrence, in his helplessness, was in a rage.

We met Katherine Mansfield and Middleton Murry at that time. I think theirs was the only spontaneous and jolly friendship that we had. We had tea with Katherine in her flat in London. If I remember rightly her room had only cushions and pouffes and a large aquarium with goldfish and shells and plants.

I thought her so exquisite and complete, with her fine brown hair, delicate skin, and brown eyes which we later called her 'gu-gu' eyes. She was a perfect friend and tried her best to help me with the children. She went to see them, talked to them and took letters from me. I loved her like a younger sister.

I fell for Katherine and Murry when I saw them quite unexpectedly on the top of a bus, making faces at each other and putting their tongues out.

We also met Cynthia and Herbert Asquith, at Margate. Cynthia seemed to me lovely as Botticelli's Venus. We also saw Eddie Marsh and

Sir Walter Raleigh and Cynthia's relations at her house, which was an unusual one, made all of ship's timber. Cynthia was always a loyal friend, even through the war, when friends were rare.

But Lawrence wanted to go away from England, also because the divorce was not finished. Later we returned to Bavaria. There Lawrence wrote *The Prussian Officer*. The strange struggle of those two opposite natures, the officer and his servant, seems to me particularly significant for Lawrence. He wrote it before the war but as if he had sensed it. The unhappy, conscious man, the superior in authority envying the other man his simple, satisfied nature. I felt as if he himself was both these people.

They seemed to represent the split in his soul, the split between the conscious and the unconscious man.

To grow into a complete whole out of the different elements that we are composed of is one of our most elemental tasks. It is a queer story and it frightened me at the time of the dark corners of Lawrence's soul, the human soul altogether. But his courage in facing the problems and horrors of life always impressed me. Often he was ill when his consciousness tried to penetrate into deeper strata, it was an interplay of body and soul and I in real agony would try to understand what was happening. He demanded so much of me and I *had* to be there for him so completely. Sometimes it was I who forced him to go deeper and roused his inner conflict. When I went away it was always terrible. He hated me for going away. 'You use me as a scientist his "dissecting rabbit", I am your "Versuchs Kaninchen",' I told him.

We wanted to go to Italy again.

The next winter we found a little cottage, 'Fiascherino', near Lerici – finding a new more southern Italy and settling down for a while like gypsies in their camp; always more adventure.

We had a large piece of land with olive trees and vegetables running down to the little bay where we bathed and kept a flat-bottomed boat, on which Lawrence went out to sea through the surf. I was on the shore watching him like a hen who has hatched a duckling and yelled in a rage: 'If you can't be a real poet, you'll drown like one, anyhow.'

Shelley was drowned not so far away. I spent lazy days lying in a hammock watching the fishermen with their beautiful red-sailed boats underneath my high rock. I watched the submarines from Spezia bobbing up and down. We had a maid, Elide, who looked after us and loved us, and her mother Felice was mostly there too. 'Bocca di mosca!' she would shout at her daughter. They loved us quite ferociously; fought to buy things cheaply for us in the market and felt absolutely responsible for us. One of Elide's griefs was that Lawrence would go out in his old clothes; she would rush after him with another coat: 'Signor Lorenzo, Signor Lorenzo', and force him to put it on, which is more than I could have done . . . When I took her along to Spezia for Christmas shopping she behaved as if she were attending the Queen of Italy at least, much to my chagrin. Nothing was too good for 'la mia Signora . . .'

We went once to visit the Waterfields at their lovely old castle, 'Aula', near Sarzana. We slept there in such a terrifically large room that it overwhelmed us, the beds looked so tiny in the vast room that we brought them close together, to make a larger spot in the vastness . . . it was a beautiful place, high up above the Magra, wide river arms underneath . . . there were flowers growing on the wide fortress walls, a Dantesque sunrise; we were impressed.

The cottage at Fiascherino had only three small rooms and a kitchen and I tried to make it look as cheerful as possible; it did not matter what I did with them, for we were out of doors most of the day; had our meals outdoors and took long walks, returning only when it grew dark, and built a fire in the downstairs room. I believe the chief tie between Lawrence and me was always the wonder of living . . . every little or big thing that happened carried its glamour with it.

But we also had sordid blows. A New York publisher had bought copies of one of Lawrence's books and sent a cheque for £25. As I had no money of my own, Lawrence said: 'You can spend that for yourself'. I took the cheque to the bank at La Spezia where they told me the date was altered, the cheque must go back to New York. It never returned. For that book Lawrence never got any money from America for about twelve years. Meanness made Lawrence always silently angry – it was something not to be thought of, but dismissed, nothing to be done, why waste your energy, then. But I, like a fool, talked furiously when I'd been disappointed. We had many such disappointments later on. With the dangerous quality of his work he accepted his more than doubtful financial position and I think one of my merits in his eyes was my never being eager to be rich or to play a role in the social world. It was hardly merit on my part. I enjoyed being poor and I didn't want to play a role in the world.

We had met many people who had villas round the bay of La Spezia, English and American. They were friendly, but I said to Lawrence: 'I don't want to be a fraud, let's tell them that we aren't married; perhaps they won't like us any more if they know how it is.'

One charming Miss Huntingdon, who had become a Catholic, was much distressed. 'I am fond of you both,' she wrote, 'and far be it from me to judge you, but I must tell you that I believe you are wrong, your life together is a mistake, a sin.' Her deep distress made me feel sorry for her, as if she had had to face the same problem and had chosen otherwise. But I was aware of the joyful acceptance and hope in me, that for my part I had chosen what was right. I don't understand, to this day, what social values really are and what meaning has the whole social game: social standards were never real to me, and the game didn't ever seem worth the candle. That winter in Fiascherino was a very happy one. He wrote *The Rainbow* there, *The Sisters* it was called at first. When Edward Garnett read it he didn't like it. This upset Lawrence, that Garnett did not follow his trend. But I said: 'You are fighting the old standards, and breaking new ground.' They said I ruined Lawrence's genius, but I know it is not so.

Lawrence was always busy, he taught me many songs, we sang by the hour in the evenings; he liked my strong voice. He sang with very little voice but, like a real artist that he was, he conveyed the music and the spirit of the song in a marvellous fashion.

We painted together, too. I can see him so absorbed and intent, licking the brush, putting it down on the paper with quick gestures, giving himself completely to everything he was doing and not understanding that I did it all so carelessly and for fun.

I remember the day the piano arrived from Spezia by sea in a little boat and we watched it bobbing around the corner of the foreland, with three Italians, very frightened, fearing to go to the bottom of the sea with it. We felt for them, for it really looked very dangerous. Then at last they pulled up on the shingly beach and it was brought up to our little cottage with terrific shouts of 'Avanti, Italiani!'

Christmas came and we had Elide's relations, about a dozen peasants, in the evening and they sang to us, very much at home with us. Elide's old mother, Felice, sang: 'Da quella parte dove si lev il sol', and 'Di' a la Marcella che lui so far l'amor', with old Pasquale, a duet. The beautiful Luigi was there, who looked so handsome picking olives from the trees; also the Maestro from Telaro, who was in love with Luigi; but she was of higher station and he, alas, wasn't in love with her. I don't know if they ever were married or not. But always the tragedy came up . . . it got me from time to time like an illness. We had trespassed the laws of men, if not of God, and you have to pay. Lawrence and I paid in full, and the others, on the contrary, had to pay for *want* of love and tenderness, and nobody likes to pay. Yet it's an eternal human law: too much happiness isn't allowed us mere mortals. And I and Lawrence seemed at times to surpass the measure of human bliss. He could be so deeply and richly happy, that young Lawrence that I have known, before the war crushed so much of his belief in human civilization . . . His deep natural love for his fellow-men . . . The deadness of them, the mechanicalness that triumphed in their souls.

I asked ' What is civilization? What is it, this man-made world that I don't understand?'

And he said: 'It's like a tree that comes forth out of a race of men, and it grows and flowers, and then it must die.' And sometimes I think that Lawrence was the last green shoot on the tree of English civilization. Anyhow, whether English civilization is dead or not, and I hope it isn't, Lawrence is the last shoot of it that has grown ahead and pierced the air.

He was always so absolutely, undeniably, *something*. 'They can't ignore me in the long run,' he would say, with clenched teeth, 'they can't get past me, much as they'd like to.' And I think they can't.

Life rattles on so mechanically, there is less and less meaning in its motor-hoots and in all the noise, all meaning is drowned. Nobody has delicate courage enough to listen to the things that give us genuine vibrating life. Our feelers for life, just quick life, are atrophied.

When I think that nobody wanted Lawrence's amazing genius, how he was jeered at, suppressed, turned into nothing, patronized at best, the stupidity of our civilization comes home to me. How necessary he was! How badly needed! Now that he is dead and his great love for his fellow men is no longer there in the flesh, people sentimentalize over him . . . Critics indeed! Had they been able to *take* instead of criticizing, how much richer their own lives might have been!

Those wonderful mornings in our little podere, getting up joyfully to that Mediterranean sun by the sea! And I'd walk through the olive trees to Telaro, for the post. It took me, the northerner, some time to see the beauty of these olive trees, so different at different times; the wind running up them turns them into quicksilver and sometimes they seem quite tired and still dark. During those early morning walks the sun threw delicate quivering shadows on the stony, mossy path. To my right was the sea. I wouldn't have been surprised meeting Christ and his disciples – it may be just as well that I didn't.

Lawrence could well teach people how to live, how to be grateful simply for life itself. He who was always so frail and so much nearer to death at every moment than most people, how religiously he appreciated every good moment! Every big and little thing! I hadn't lived before I lived with Lawrence. It was drudgery, grey tired days with endless efforts, before. With him, being in love and ecstasy was only a small part of the whole, always the whole and we two balanced in it, the universe around us for us to take as much as we could, and we took a lot of it in those eighteen years together.

Of his short life didn't Lawrence make the most! It was his deep sense of the reality of living. He knew what feeds the life-flame in a creature; it isn't Rolls-Royces or first-class hotels and cinemas. He wasn't a high-brow and he wasn't a low-brow, but with a real genius he got out of the quick of living the abiding values and said so in his writing. It is always amazing to me how little people understand him. Misunderstand him, is more like it.

I suppose when you are inside the pale you see only the palings and think they are quite splendid, but once outside, you realize how big the world is and the palings are just palings to you. You look at them in surprise: all these insurmountable obstacles, it was only rather low palings to climb over after all. But for those who feel safe inside, let them, the palings don't care, neither does the bigger world.

He was quite aware of the hostility to him, but in those days, I don't think we either of us measured the depth of it. Also as he grew more and more, the antagonism grew. We were too busy living to take much notice. Our own world, so small and poor to others on the outside, what a strong unconquerable fortress it really was!

Another thing I understood: there was no 'God-Almightiness' about him, like the universal 'I-am-everlasting' feeling of Goethe, for instance. He knew 'I am D. H. Lawrence from my head to my toes, and there I begin and there I end and my soul lives inside me. All else is not me, but I can have a relationship with all that is not me in the world, and the more I realize the otherness of other things around me the richer I am.'

It makes me laugh when I think of that American doctor who 'looked at literature' who wrote about Lawrence and saw only a diseased prurient mind in him. I think all he wanted to see was disease. Because Ursula, and Birkin, in *Women in Love*, have a good meal with beetroot and ham and venison pastry, he reads some horror into beetroot and ham and pastry. I think the horror was in the good doctor's mind for what horror is there in beetroot or ham or venison pastry? Good to eat they are, that's all. Lawrence was so direct, such a real puritan! He hated any 'haut-gout' or lewdness. Fine underclothing and all the apparatus of the seducing sort were just stupid to him. All tricks; why tricks? Passionate people don't need tricks.

In the spring of 1914 Lawrence and I went from Fiascherino to London. We stayed with a friend, Gordon Campbell, whose wife was in Ireland. The house was in Kensington. We saw a good deal of the Murrys and there were long discussions between us all. Katherine was young and yet old, like a precocious child. I never suspected so much sadness in her, then; her relation with Murry seemed so fresh and young.

We had a housekeeper, Mrs Conybear, who sang 'Angels ever bright and fair' from the basement.

Campbell was very much in love with Ireland, 'Areland' he called it. At breakfast always sad and cross, about 'Areland'.

I remember a ghastly Sunday afternoon when we wanted to amuse ourselves. We went on one of the Thames boats to Richmond – Campbell, Murry, Katherine, Lawrence and I – there were a few seedy people on the boat – a sad object of a man was playing 'Lead, Kindly Light' on a harmonium – we got more and more silent with the dreariness of that enjoyment. And then, further along, people threw sixpences from the boat into that centuries-old, awful-looking Thames mud and small boys dived for them – the Thames mud seemed to soak into our very souls and soon we could stand it no more and left the boat and got a bus to go home. Campbell, a dignified person, trod on the conductor's toe going on top and the conductor said: 'Hallo clumsy,' to Katherine's and my joy.

Finally I and Lawrence got married at a registrar's office in Kensington. Campbell and Murry went with us. On the way there Lawrence dashed out of the cab into a goldsmith's to buy a new wedding ring. I gave my old one to Katherine and with it she now lies buried in Fontainebleau.

It was quite a simple and not undignified ceremony. I didn't care whether I was married or not, it didn't seem to make any difference, but I think Lawrence was glad that we were respectable married people.

On that first visit to London Lawrence's writings were already a little known and I thought: 'What fun it is going to be to know some amusing people.' But then, oh dear, we were asked to lunch by a few lion huntresses and the human being in me felt only insulted. You were fed more or less well, you sat next to somebody whose name had also been printed in the papers, the hostess didn't know who or what you were, thought you were somebody else, and wanted to shoo you away after you were fed like chickens that had become a nuisance, and that was all. So Lawrence and I hardly went anywhere. What fun people might have had with us they never realized; perhaps they had no fun in themselves. So Lawrence and I were mostly alone.

A friend asked me once: 'But wasn't it very difficult, Lawrence and you coming from a different class, wasn't the actual contact very difficult, wasn't your sensitiveness offended?'

I don't know whether it was the genius in Lawrence or the man from the people in him, but I certainly found him more delicately and sensitively aware of me than I ever imagined anybody would be.

Once I bumped my head against a shutter and was a little stunned and Lawrence was in such an agony of sympathy and tenderness over it. It astonished me; when I had bumped my head before or hurt myself nobody seemed to bother and I didn't see why they should have done so. To be so enveloped in tenderness was a miracle in itself to me.

The War

And then the war came, quite out of the blue for us both. Lawrence was on a walking tour in the Lakes with two friends and I was in London. After Lawrence came back, I remember our having lunch with Rupert Brooke and Eddie Marsh. I see Rupert Brooke's strange fair skin, he blushed so easily, the beauty of him was strangely sad. He was coming to stay with us. Even then I thought: 'He has had enough of life, it wearies him'. He wasn't a bit happy or fulfilled. I remember Eddie Marsh saying: 'There will be war, we fear, but it may be that the Foreign Office and Earl Grey have averted it today.'

But we couldn't believe it . . . War . . .

But a politician had only said: 'Bloody peace again.'

And then it was declared. At first it seemed only exciting.

. . . Exciting indeed! Nobody realized at first what hell, what lowest demons, had been let loose.

We were at Charing Cross station and saw trains of soldiers depart. Their women were there so pale and strained looking, saying good-bye trying to be brave and not cry. It made me weep for those unknown women and their sorrow. What did I care whether these boys, boys so many of them, were English or Russian or French. Nationality was just an accident and here was grief. Lawrence was ashamed of my tears.

He himself was bewildered and lost, became abstract and mental, and couldn't feel any more. I, who had been brought up with all the 'big-drumming' of German militarism, I was scared.

Lawrence was not a pacifist, he fought all his life. But that 'World War' he condemned with all his might. The inhuman, mechanical, sheer destruction of it! Destruction for what end!

Then when Lloyd George came to power Lawrence lost all hope in the spirit of his native country. Lloyd George, who was so un-English, to stand for English prestige! It seemed incredible.

War, more war! 'Dies irae, dies illa', a monstrous disaster, the collapse of all human decency. Lawrence felt it so. I could feel only fear – all base instincts let loose, all security gone.

We were in a big crowd on Hampstead Heath one evening going home from a friend's house. In the sky, uncertain and terrible amidst the clouds, hung a Zeppelin. 'In that Zeppelin,' I thought, 'are perhaps men I have danced with when I was a girl, boys I have played with, and here they come to bring destruction and death. And if this dark crowd knew I was a German they would tear me to pieces in their fear.'

Sadly we went home. So helpless we were, at the power of all horrors. We took a small cottage out in Berkshire. Suspicion was ever present. Even when we were gathering blackberries in the nearby hedges a policeman popped up behind a bush and wanted to know who we were. Lawrence, who comes out in the open so courageously in his writings, why, why, do so many people see a sinister figure in him? The darkness wasn't in him but in those others. There is a woman even now who boasts that she turned us out of Cornwall as spies.

Our cottage was near the mill of Gilbert and Mary Cannan. And the Murrys were an hour's walk away in another cottage. We would go over to them in the dark winter nights, through bare woods and fields of dead cabbage stalks, with their smell of rottenness.

Campbell came to spend a week-end with us. He, who in London had been so elegant, with spats and top-hat, now wore an old cap and carried a very heavy stick under his arm. He looked to me like an Irish tramp. He was still weeping over his 'Areland'.

Christmas came. We made the cottage splendid with holly and mistletoe, we cooked and boiled, roasted and baked. Campbell and Koteliansky and the Murrys came, and Gertler and the Cannans. We had a gay feast.

We danced on the shaky floor. Gilbert with uplifted head sang: 'I feel, I feel like an eagle in the sky.' Koteliansky sang soulfully his Hebrew song: 'Ranani Sadekim Badanor'. Katherine, with a long, ridiculous face, sang this mournful song:

I am an unlucky man,
I fell into a coalhole
I broke my leg,
And got three months for stealing coal.

I am an unlucky man,
If it rained soup all day,
I wouldn't have a spoon,
I'd only have a fork.

She also sang:

Ton sirop est doux, Madeleine,
Ton sirop est doux.
Ne crie pas si fort, Madeleine,
La maison n'est pas a nous.

I liked this tune, but when I sang it Lawrence stopped me; it was too 'fast' for him. This occasion was the last time for years to come that we were really gay.

In the spring we went to stay with the Meynells in Sussex. We were fond of all the sons and daughters. Monica was our neighbour. We lived in the cottage that Violet had lent us. I only remember Alice Meynell as a vision in the distance, being led by Wilfred Meynell across the lawn like Beatrice being led by Dante.

I heard while there of my father's death. I did not tell anybody, I kept it to myself. When I told Lawrence he only said: 'You didn't expect to keep your father all your life?' Bertrand Russell invited Lawrence to Cambridge at that time. Lawrence had expected much of this visit. 'What did you do there? What did they say?' I asked him, when he came back.

He answered: 'Well, in the evening they drank port and they walked up and down the room and talked about the Balkan situation and things like that, and they know nothing about it.'

We had met Lady Ottoline Morrell. She was a great influence in Lawrence's life. Her profound culture, her beautiful home, 'Garsington', her social power, all meant much to Lawrence.

I felt in those days: 'Perhaps I ought to leave Lawrence to her influence; what might they not do together for England? I am powerless, and a Hun, and a nobody.' Garsington was a refuge during the war for many people and stood as a stronghold for freedom in those unfree days.

Later we took a small flat in the Vale of Heath. *The Rainbow* appeared and was suppressed. When it happened I felt as though a murder had been done, murder of a new, free utterance on the face of the earth. I thought the book would be hailed as a joyous relief from the ordinary dull stuff, as a way out into new and unknown regions. With his whole struggling soul Lawrence had written it. Then to have it condemned, nobody standing for it – the bitterness of it! He was sex-mad, they said. Little even now do people realize what men like Lawrence do for the body of life, what he did to rescue the fallen angel of sex. Sex had fallen in the gutter, it had to be pulled out. What agony it was to know the flame in him and see it quenched by his fellow men! 'I'll never write another word I mean', he said in his bitterness; 'they aren't fit for it', and for a time the flame in him was quenched.

It could not be for long; I remember with joy Frere's words: 'Lawrence is like a man so far ahead on the road, that for them he seems small.' When I think of his critics the words of Heraclitus come into my mind: 'The Ephesians would do well to hang themselves, every grown man of them, and leave the city to beardless lads, for they have cast out Hermodorus, the best man among them, saying: "We will have none who is best among us; if there be any such, let him be so elsewhere and among others".'

The best were treated so during the war. And in those dark days I had a bad time. Naturally, I came in for all Lawrence's tortured, irritable moods. His sweetness had disappeared and he turned against me as well as the rest for the time being. It all made him ill. There was not even a little hope or gaiety anywhere. We had a little flat in the Vale of Heath in Hampstead. He didn't like the Vale of Heath and he didn't like the little flat and he didn't like me or anybody else . . . And the war was everywhere . . . We were saturated with war.

CORNWALL

At Cornwall, near Zennor, we found Tregerthen cottage. As usual we made it out of a granite hole into a livable place. It cost five pounds a year rent. We had made it very charming. We washed the walls very pale pink and the cupboards were painted a bright blue. This was the entrance room; all very small but well proportioned.

There was a charming fireplace on which lived two Staffordshire figures riding to market, 'Jasper and Bridget'. On the wall a beautiful embroidery Lady Ottoline Morrell had embroidered after a drawing by Duncan Grant, a tree with big bright flowers and birds and beasts. Behind the sitting room was a darkish rough scullery, and upstairs was one big room overlooking the sea, like the big cabin on the upper deck of a ship. And how the winds from that untamed Cornish sea rocked the solid little cottage, and howled at it, and how the rain lashed it, sometimes forcing the door open and pouring into the room.

I see Katherine Mansfield and Murry arriving sitting on a cart, high up on all the goods and chattels, coming down the lane to Tregerthen. Like an emigrant Katherine looked. I loved her little jackets, chiefly the one that was black and gold like bees.

It was great fun buying very nicely made furniture for a few shillings in St Ives, with the Murrys. The fishermen were selling their nice old belongings to buy modern stuff. Our purchases would arrive tied on a shaky cart with bits of rope, the cart trundling down the uneven road. I think our best buy was a well-proportioned bedstead we got for a shilling. Then in both the Murrys' neighbouring cottage and our own such a frenzy broke out of painting chairs and polishing brass and mending old clocks, putting plates on the dressers, arranging all the treasures we had bought. After they had settled in their cottage I loved walking with Katherine to Zennor. A high wind she hated and stamped her foot at it. Later we'd sit in the sun under the foxgloves and talk, like two Indian braves, as she said. We enjoyed doing things together. I can see her round eyes when Murry painted all the chairs black with Ripolin and she said: 'Look at the funeral procession of chairs.' She told me many things from her life, but she told me them in confidence and trust.

Katherine and Lawrence and Murry had invented a place, a wonderful place where we were all going to live in complete bliss; Rananim it was called.

Lawrence thought of the new spirit of the life we would try to live there. Murry thought of the ship, and its equipment, that would take us to our island of Rananim. Katherine saw all the coloured bundles that we would have to take. By the hour we could talk Rananim.

There in Cornwall I can remember days of complete harmony between the Murrys and us, Katherine coming to our cottage so thrilled at my foxgloves, tall in the small window seat. Since then whenever I see foxgloves I must think of Katherine.

One day we went out on the sea in bright sunshine in a boat, and sang the canon:

Row, row, row your boat
Gently down the stream,
Merrily, merrily, merrily, merrily,
Life is but a dream.

I don't know why even then this canon moved me so. They were so strangely significant, those words. And I was so bad at keeping my part of the song going, to Lawrence's rage.

So much, so much was still ahead for us all. And all so wonderful. At that time we were so poor, and such nobodies, and yet so rich in dreams and gaiety! But then Lawrence would have his reactions against all this, feel that his dreams were like petty vapourings, that the only real facts were war, and a war of all the lower elements come uppermost, carrying all before them. Grimly his soul would try to understand, but in the end it could only hang on to its faith, to its own, own, unknown God.

He had to go through with it, that I knew; also I knew – however miserable I was, and he made me so – that there was a man who suffered because of his vision.

He wanted people to be as they came out of the hands of the Lord, not to violate them but gently adjust them to life in their own capacity. He didn't expect me to type. I hated it. Poor as we were he never expected me to do it. 'People should do what they enjoy, then they'll do it well,' he said.

In the first year of the war Cornwall was still not quite engulfed by it; but slowly, like an octopus, with slow but deadsure tentacles, the war spirit crept up and all around us. Suspicion and fear surrounded us. It was like breathing bad air and walking on a bog.

I remember once sitting on the rocks with Lawrence, by the sea, near our cottage at Tregerthen. I was intoxicated by the air and sun. I had to jump and run, and my white scarf blew in the wind. 'Stop it, stop it, you fool, you fool!' Lawrence cried. 'Can't you see they'll think that you're signalling to the enemy!'

I had forgotten the war for a moment.

There was an unfortunate policeman from St Ives. He had to trot up so many times to our cottage to look over and over again Lawrence's papers, to see if he were really an Englishman and his father without a doubt an Englishman, and if his mother was English. This policeman once said to me: 'Oh ma'am, if I dare only speak my thoughts, but I mustn't.' But he took the peas and beans I offered him from our field that Lawrence had ploughed with the help of William Henry from the farm, and sown with vegetables. They came up splendidly and lots of people had vegetables from this field during the war.

Our standby and friend was Katie Berryman. Her saffron cake and baked stuffed rabbit were our modest luxuries.

We had so little money, Lawrence not being wanted, nor his work, in those days when profiteers and such men were flourishing and triumphant. I remember his writing to Arnold Bennett and saying: 'I hear you think highly of me and my genius, give me some work.'

Arnold Bennett wrote back: 'Yes, I do think highly of your genius, but that is no reason why I should give you work.'

The war seemed to drive Lawrence to utter despair. He was called up for inspection and told me about it afterwards. 'You have no idea what a pathetic sight all the men were in nothing but their shirts.' How glad he was to come back to his cottage and me!

Lawrence was fond of the people at Tregerthen Farm nearby. Their Celtic natures fascinated him. He could talk by the hour with William Henry, the farmer's eldest son, ruddy and handsome.

In those days Lawrence seemed to turn against me, perhaps on account of the bit of German in me. I felt utterly alone there, on that wild Cornish moor, in the little granite cottage. Often Lawrence would leave me in the evenings, and go over to the farm, where he'd spend his time talking to William Henry and giving French lessons to Stanley, the younger son.

Sometimes at night, in the dark, the door would fly open, and it seemed as if the ancient spirits and ghosts of the place blew into my cottage. In the loneliness I seemed to hear the voices of young men crying out to me from the battlefields: 'Help us, help us, we are dying, we are dying.' Despair had blown in on the night. I thought how in the past women like Catherine of Siena had influenced events. But now what could any woman do to stem or divert this avalanche?

And then Lawrence would come home and want to quarrel with me, as if he were angry with me because I too felt sad and hopeless and helpless.

It was only at the very last, and out of one's final despair, that there arose a hope and a belief. But the outer world was viler every day.

I remember coming home from Zennor with a loaf of Katie Berryman's bread in Lawrence's rucksack. Coastguards suddenly pounced on us from behind a hedge and said: 'Let us look at your rucksack, you have a camera in there.'

I could feel Lawrence swooning with rage. I opened the rucksack and held the loaf of bread under their noses. I had to show my contempt, if they hanged me for it the next moment. I believe they would have liked to.

It was no wonder Lawrence went almost mad at times at the creeping foulness around us, he who came out so completely in the open. And I knew that he felt so helpless, as if all that he believed in was utterly lost, he who by his genius felt responsible for the spirit of his England, he whose destiny it was to give England a new direction.

If only the war could end! But it went on, was present wherever you went, there was no escaping it. One evening at Cecil Grey's place, Bosigran Castle, we were sitting after dinner, when there came a knock at the door and four coast-watchers stood there ominously.

'You are showing a light.'

To Grey's dismay it was true. He had a new housekeeper from London and the light from her bedroom could be seen at sea.

As we stood there I shivered with alarm. I had before this been under suspicion of giving supplies to the German submarine crews. As for the suspicion, we were so poor at the time – a biscuit a day we might have spared for the submarines, but no more.

I took a secret pleasure in the fact that our coast-watchers were all covered with mud. They had fallen into a ditch listening under the windows.

Fortunately Grey had an uncle who was an admiral. That saved him, and us. As for Lawrence, he just looked at those men. What a manly job theirs was, listening under other people's windows!

A few days later I came home from Bosigran Castle to the cottage.

Lawrence was away, had driven to Penzance. In the dusk I entered the cottage alone. Immediately I was inside I knew by instinct something had happened, I felt overwhelming fear. With shaking knees I went to the farm. Yes, I was told, two men had asked for us.

I was full of foreboding, even though Lawrence, coming home later, didn't share my fear.

But then early next morning there appeared a captain, two detectives, and my friend the policeman. The captain read us a paper that we must leave the county of Cornwall in three days. Lawrence, who lost his temper so easily, was quite calm.

'And what is the reason?' he asked.

'You know better than I do,' answered the captain.

'I don't know,' said Lawrence.

Then the two awful detectives went through all our cupboards, clothes, beds, etc., while I, like a fool, burst into a rage:

'This is your English liberty, here we live and don't do anybody any harm, and these creatures have the right to come here and touch our private things.'

'Be quiet,' said Lawrence.

He was so terribly quiet, but the iron of his England had stabbed his soul once more, and I knew he suffered more than I.

In the background stood my friend the policeman, full of sympathy. How sad I was, and desperate. But nothing could be done, so we left Cornwall, like two criminals. When we were turned out of Cornwall something changed in Lawrence for ever.

We went to London where H. D. lent us her flat in Mecklenburg Square. It had a very large room. Richard Aldington was home on leave at the time and in the evening we met and were very gay.

Where did we get the courage to be gay? I don't know.

Lawrence invented wonderful charades. Once we played the Garden of Eden. Lawrence was the Lord, H. D. was the tree, Richard Aldington waving a large chrysanthemum was Adam, and I was the serpent, and a little scared at my part.

A few days later Cynthia Asquith invited us to the royal box that Lady Cunard had lent her at Covent Garden.

Lawrence trimmed his beard, we made ourselves very fine, and went to listen to *Aïda*.

Very few people wanted to be friendly to us in those days. I was a Hun and Lawrence not wanted.

That was the time of air raids over London, the time there was such a strain on people's nerves. During the air raids we were supposed to go into the cellar, but Lawrence always refused to go; he stayed in bed. And it was certainly very depressing being in the cellar with all the other gloomy people. So I spent my time during air raids running up and down stairs imploring Lawrence to come to the cellar. But he'd never do it.

We met Gertler in those days and he used to tell us funny stories about his experiences during air raids, especially one sudden one when he lost his head and kept running up and down the stairs of a strange house. Campbell also told about air-raid experiences, how once in Hampstead Heath he'd found himself buried under a heap of terrified housemaids coming home from a dinner party.

Yet underneath all this gaiety, we were so dulled and bitter. 'Dancing while Rome burns'. But if Nero enjoyed his burning Rome, we did not. And Lawrence's helplessness to stem this lavaflood of death to all that is best in man made him savage underneath and again I had a bad time . . . It was torture to live, and to live with him.

I felt helpless and an outcast, and only a burden and a difficulty for Lawrence.

I, the Hunwife in a foreign country!

Then we went to Hermitage in Berkshire. The country there is so quiet and English with its woods. Our simple life in the cottage healed him a lot.

I saw my son, who was in the O.T.C., and it seemed terrible that he would have to fight against his own relations, perhaps, and I said: 'Let me hide you somewhere in a cave or in a wood, I don't want you to go and fight, I don't want you to be killed in this stupid war.' But he was shocked.

All this time we were followed by detectives. Detectives had even gone to my first husband and asked him if he knew anything against me.

While we were there in Hermitage the armistice came. I nearly said peace came. But it was not peace, it is not peace yet. The war has bred not peace but awful gargoyle children of hate and resentment, and has only left death as the desirable, clean thing, almost.

Lawrence and My Mother

Lawrence and my mother were fond of one another; she was a wonderful mother to us, her three daughters. We were all three different and yet she helped and understood us, and was there for us in our hours of need – alas, there were plenty of them for the three of us. But she was equal to all the awful situations we found ourselves in. My eldest sister Else wanted to study, when studying for women in Germany was still *infra dig.*; I remember walking through the crowds of men students into a lecture hall at Heidelberg with my sister at sixteen and feeling like a real martyr. My sister Johanna had lovely names for my mother, like 'Goldfasanchen', my little golden pheasant – it was so quaint to hear her, worldly and elegant, being so tender with my mother, and she half loving it and saying: 'What do you want now?' She had taught me the love for poetry from early childhood. Especially after the war she and Lawrence became great friends. She lived in her 'Stift', at Baden-Baden, a kind of home for women, mostly widows of distinguished men, Excellencies and so on. It was a very dignified life. We three sisters loved to meet there and stay with my mother. We had to be on our best behaviour, except in my mother's beautiful rooms, where all the wildness of our childhood came back, especially for my sister Johanna and me. Lawrence sat on the sofa, happily, while my mother tried to give him all the things for tea that he liked – 'Pumpernickel' and 'Truffelleberwurst' – and we played wild games of bridge.

Sometimes, when Lawrence wanted to complain about me, she would say: 'I know her longer than you, I know her.'

He wrote his *Fantasia of the Unconscious* in the woods behind the Altes Schloss. We stayed in a rough little inn at Ebersteinburg. I remember that we had some friends to dinner and a chicken flew into the soup tureen.

Then Lawrence, in the meagre after-the-war days, would scour the country for some cream for her.

She was very happy in Lawrence's life and mine, it meant so much to her, but she always trembled that the women in the Stift might read his books.

He was so polite to them and they liked him, again he was the Herr Doktor.

At Ebersteinburg he would go out in the morning and take his book and fountain pen. I would find him later on, leaning against a big pine tree; it was as if the tree itself helped him to write his book, and poured its sap into it.

Then we would go down to Baden to my mother in the afternoon and take her our wildflowers or some honey or fruit or nuts; or we would go for long walks and make the place our own as usual. Looking over the Rheintal or listening to the music in the Kurpark. Baden was no longer the Baden of Turgeniev and archdukes and grand dukes and the Prince of Wales; no, it was after the war, would-be elegant.

Lawrence and my mother in her wisdom and ripeness understood each other so well. She said to me: 'It's strange that an old woman can still be as fond of a man as I am of that Lorenzo.'

Happy was their relationship. Only the last time, when my mother was so frail and old herself, being with Lawrence who was so very ill, they got on each other's nerves, and when she saw him often so irritable with me, she said: 'He isn't grateful to you for all you do for him.' But I did not feel like that myself; I was glad to do everything for him I possibly could. It seemed little enough.

Then when she and I were going to meet for the first time after his death, we were afraid to meet. She knew what his death meant to me and I what it meant to her. So we avoided our common grief; there was no need of words.

I remember after she had been indoors for weeks, coming to Baden and taking her out on one of those first tender spring days we get in the north, just the first whisper of spring. To feel her respond to this coming renewal of the earth in an almost sacred happiness was very moving to me.

I think after Lawrence's death her desire to live left her. Less than a year after he died telling me: 'You have many friends, you have much to live for yet,' I got a telegram: 'Come.'

I went but it was too late. In the train I listened as it were to the sound of the wheels: 'Is she still alive? Is she dead?' At the door of the Stift I was told: 'The Frau Baronin died two hours ago.'

She lay for the last time in her bedroom, the rocks of the Altes Schloss looking in through the window. 'Lawrence is there for me,' she had said. We, her three daughters, stood by her bedside, she for the first time not welcoming me with open arms as always. She lay with her silver hair like thistledown, in gentle and peaceful death – she who had sustained our lives for half a century with the strength and harmony of her nature.

I remember my mother saying to me once: 'But it's always you in Lorenzo's books, all his women are you.' There was an expression on her face I could not get. Is she pleased at this or is she not? My sister Nusch was the only person that ever could take a liberty with him. She could lightly jump on his knee and say in her broken English: 'O Lorenzo, you are so nice, I like your red beard.' He felt happy in the atmosphere of my mother and of us three sisters, so free and open and gay. Only when my sister Nusch and I had our long female talks, he did not like it, he had to be in it.

We spent some weeks at Zell-am-See with Nusch, her husband and children at her villa. We bathed and boated and Lawrence wrote his *Captain's Doll* there.

One day the peasants from my sister's shooting-lodge high up in the mountains brought us some honey and left. The honey was found to be full of worms. 'Hadu,' said Lawrence, full of rage, to my nephew, 'you and I will take this honey back to them.' So up they marched to the lodge, in the heat of the afternoon, Lawrence and Hadu, and arrived at the peasant's hut to find them in the midst of a meal; in the very middle of the table Lawrence planted the jar of honey and left without a word. The peasants remained petrified. 'If honesty, common-and-garden honesty goes,' Lawrence told me once, 'then all is lost, life becomes impossible.'

After the War

The first snow has fallen, it's a still, black and white world. All the gold of the autumn has gone. On the mountains it was green-gold where the aspens turned, and the oakbrush was red-gold and there was yellow-gold in the tall sunflowers all along the road to Taos. The sage brush bloomed pale yellow and the fields and openings of the woods were yellow with small sunflowers. The mountains looked like tigers with their stripes of gold and dark pine trees. And the golden autumn sun lit it all. Now it has gone, this golden world: the frost and the snow have taken it away. I am writing in the sun on the snowy hill behind the cabins, where the Indians had their camp; where Lawrence and I slept in the summer, years ago, and again a grey squirrel scolded me for intruding; I wonder if it is the same grey squirrel. The snow drips from the cedar trees that are alive with birds; it is melting fast; in the desert below it has gone. The pinto ponies look bright like painted wooden toys against the snow. The black and white pigs follow me grunting and the black cats look shiny and black on the whiteness, delicately trotting after me. I have seen tracks of wild turkeys, of deer and bears, in the Gallina. I am now leaving that English autumn there in Berkshire, with its blackberry hedges and mushroom fields and pale sunsets behind a filigree of trees.

I am leaving Lawrence behind, who doesn't want to come to Germany so soon after the war. I go on my journey, a nightmare of muddle, my trunks stolen. I arrive in Baden, so glad to see my sisters and my mother, but, oh, so many, many dead that had been our life and our youth. A sad, different Germany.

We had suffered so much, all of us, lost so much. And money was scarce.

Meanwhile Lawrence had gone to Florence and I went to join him. I arrived at four o'clock in the morning. 'You must come for a drive with me,' he said, 'I must show you this town.' We went in an open carriage, I saw the pale crouching Duomo and in the thick moonmist the Giotto tower disappeared at the top into the sky. The Palazzo Vecchio with Michelangelo's David and all the statues of men, we passed. 'This is a men's town,' I said, 'not like Paris, where all statues are women.' We went along the Lungarno, we passed the Ponte Vecchio, in that moonlight night, and ever since Florence is the most beautiful town to me, the lily town, delicate and flowery.

Lawrence was staying at a pensione on the Lungarno with Norman Douglas and Magnus.

The English there in Florence still had a sense of true hospitality, in the grand manner. And yet it struck me all as being like 'Cranford', only it was a man's 'Cranford'. And the wickedness there seemed like old maids' secret rejoicing in wickedness. Corruption is not interesting to me, nor does it frighten me: I find it dull.

Nobody knows Norman Douglas that doesn't know him in German. When he talks German you know something about him that you don't know if you only know him in English. I was thrilled at the fireworks of wit that went off between Lawrence and Douglas. They never quarrelled. I understood that Douglas had to stand up for his friend Magnus and to Lawrence's logical puritanical mind Magnus presented a problem of human relations. When we had gone to Capri and Magnus was in trouble at Montecassino, Lawrence went there and lent him some money, and yet we had so very little then.

Later Magnus appeared at our Fontana Vecchia at Taormina, having fled from Montecassino. He came almost taking for granted that we would be responsible for him, that it was our duty to keep him. This disturbed Lawrence.

'Is it my duty to look after this man?' he asked me.

To me it was no problem. Had I been fond of Magnus, had he had any meaning, or purpose – but no, he seemed only anti-social, a poor devil without any pride, and he didn't seem to matter anyhow. With the money Lawrence had lent him, he stayed at the best hotel in Taormina, to my great resentment, we who could not afford to stay even in a second-rate hotel. I felt he made a fool of Lawrence, and afterwards, when we went to Malta, crossing second class from Palermo, whom should I discover gaily swanking and talking to an English Navy officer but Magnus on the first-class deck! The cheek of the man! He had written to Lawrence: 'I am sweating blood till I am out of Italy.' I knew his sort, people always sweating blood and always going to shoot themselves. But Magnus, anyhow, did commit suicide at the end. It was a shock, but there was nothing else for him to do. It seemed to me he had had put his money on the wrong horse. He thought the splendour of life lay in drinking champagne, having brocade dressing gowns, and that kind of thing. But Lawrence felt deeply disturbed by Magnus and did feel a responsibility for him.

There is a letter from Douglas to Lawrence in which Douglas says: 'Go ahead, my boy, do as you like with Magnus's work.' Lawrence wanted to pay the Maltese young men who had helped Magnus, hence the publication of Magnus's memoirs with Lawrence's introduction.

From Florence we went to Capri. I didn't like Capri; it was so small an island, it seemed hardly capable to contain all the gossip that flourished there. So Lawrence went to Sicily and took Fontana Vecchia for us, outside Taormina.

Living in Sicily after the war was like coming to life again. Fontana Vecchia was a very simple but big-roomed villa.

* * *

Fontana Vecchia had a large podere to it. Great 'vasche' were on the rocky slope toward the sea, pools of green water to feed the lemon and orange trees. The early almond blossoms pink and white, the asphodels, the wild narcissi and anemones, all these we found during our walks. Nothing new would escape Lawrence and we never got tired finding new treasures.

We went on a jolly expedition to Syracuse with Renee and John Juta and Insole. Trains had their own sweet way in Italy then and arrived when they felt like it. I remember being much impressed by how Renee Hansard, with the experience of a true colonial, was fortified with a hamper of food and a spirit lamp so we could have tea at any time.

She pulled out her embroidery with its wools from a neat little bag. She turned the railway car into a live little temporary home. The quarries of Syracuse impressed me much. Here at Syracuse the flower of the Athenian youth had been defeated; in these quarries the Greek men had been put to starve while the ladies of Syracuse took their walks along the top of the quarries to see them slowly die. A sinister dread impression it left in me. I doubt whether centuries can clean a place of such inhumanity, the place will retain and remember such horrors.

Syracuse and its splendour have gone. Man is more cruel than nature but whenever he has been so he pays for it.

Of our winter excursion to Sardinia Lawrence has described every minute, it seems to me, with extraordinary accuracy.

Garibaldi, the picturesque, had begun his campaign here in Sicily with his thousand, with his Anita and his South American experience.

Along our rocky road the peasants rode past into the hills on their donkeys, singing loudly, the shepherds drove their goats along, playing their reed pipes as in the days of the Greeks. We had an old Greek temple in the garden; there was the beautiful Greek theatre at Taormina, facing the Etna; what a marvellous stage for a play, not a modern play, alas, but how I longed to see one of the old giants like Sophocles there. How I longed for the old splendour of life to come back to us in those shabby after-the-war days.

'Give me a little splendour, O Lord,' would be my prayer.

There in Taormina, in the whole of Sicily, one could feel the touch of the hands of many civilizations: Greek and Moorish and Norman and beyond into the dim past.

Old Grazia did our shopping and I loved watching Lawrence doing the accounts with her, her sly old Sicilian face spying his, how much she could rook him.

'She can rook me a little, but not too much,' he would say, and he kept a firm hand on her.

The sun rose straight on our beds in the morning, we had roses all winter and we lived the rhythm of a simple life, getting up early, he writing or helping in the house or getting the tangerines from the round little trees in the garden or looking at the goat's new kids. Eating, washing up, cleaning the floor and getting water from the trough near the wall, where the large yellow snake came to drink and drew itself into its hole in the wall again.

Wherever Lawrence was, the surroundings came alive so intensely. At the Fontana Vecchia we mostly cooked on charcoal fires, but on Sundays he lit the big kitchen stove for me, and I, who had become quite a good cook by now, made cakes and tarts, big and little, sweet pies and meat pies and put them on the sideboard in the dining room and called them Mrs Beeton's show.

Once we had lunch with three friends at their villa. It was a jolly lunch.

We had some white wine that seemed innocent, but it was not. When we left, going home, I felt its effects but soon got over it.

'We must hurry, because those two English ladies are coming to tea.'

So we hurried home and unfortunately the white Sicilian wine affected Lawrence later. The very English ladies came and Lawrence was terribly jovial and friendly with them. I tried to pull his sleeve and whispered: 'Go away,' but it was no use.

'What are you telling me to go away for?' he said.

I could see the two visitors being very uneasy and wanting to leave.

'No, no, you must have some mimosa, I'll get you some,' Lawrence insisted. So he went with them through the garden, tried to climb a small mimosa tree and fell.

The ladies hurried away.

Next day Lawrence was chagrined and he met one of the ladies and tried to apologize to her, but she was very stiff with him, so he said: 'Let her go to blazes.'

I think from this incident arose the story that Lawrence was a drunkard. Poor Lawrence, he who could not afford wine and didn't want it, who was so naturally abstemious. I have seen him drunk only twice in all my life with him.

We stayed at Taormina in the heat and I remember when the mulberries were ripe and delicious and he climbed a big mulberry tree in his bathing suit. The mulberries were so juicy and red and they ran down his body so that he looked like one of those very realistic Christs we had seen on our walk across the Alps years ago.

He wrote *Birds, Beasts and Flowers* and *Sea and Sardinia* at Fontana Vecchia, and also *The Lost Girl. Sea and Sardinia* he wrote straight away when we came back from Sardinia in about six weeks. And I don't think he altered a word of it. His other works, especially the novels, he wrote many times, parts of them anyhow. Sometimes I liked the first draft best, but he had his own idea and knew the form he wanted it to take.

One day I found the manuscript of *Sea and Sardinia* in the W.C. at Fontana Vecchia. So I told him: 'But why did you put it there, it's such a pity, it's so nicely written and tidy.' I had then no idea it might have any value, only regretted the evenly written pages having this ignominious end. But no, he had a passion for destroying his own writing. He hated the personal touch.

'I would like to burn all my writing. Print is different. They can have it in print, my stuff.'

Just as he wanted Lawrence, the private person, separate from Lawrence the writer, the public man. He guarded his privacy ferociously. He liked best to meet people who knew nothing about it. He really disliked talking about his writing. 'They don't like it, anyhow,' he would say. But I read every day what he had written; his writing was the outcome of our daily life.

I had to take in what he had written and had to like it. Then he was satisfied and did not care for the approval of the rest of the world. What he wrote he had lived and was sure of. Travelling with him was living new experiences vividly every minute.

Then from Fontana Vecchia, we were really leaving Europe for the first time.

We did so much with the little money we had, making homes and unmaking them.

We unmade our beloved Fontana Vecchia and went to Palermo where the 'facchini' were so wild and threw themselves on our luggage; I can see Lawrence struggling amongst a great crowd of them, waving his umbrella about, equally wild. It was midnight and I was terrified.

An American friend gave me the side of a Sicilian cart I had always longed for. It had a joust painted on one panel, on the other St Genevieve. It was very gay and hard in colour. I loved it. Lawrence said: 'You don't mean to travel to Ceylon with this object?'

'Let me, let me,' I implored. So he let me. And off we set for Naples. There we were bounced in the harbour into our P. & O. boat. We arrived nearly too late, the gang-plank was pulled up immediately the minute we got on board. How we enjoyed that trip! Everybody feeling so free and detached, no responsibility for the moment, people going to meet husbands or wives, people going to Australia full of the wonders that were coming to them, and Lawrence being so interested and feeling so well. How tenderly one loves people on boats! They seem to become bosom friends for life. And then we went through the Suez Canal into the Red Sea, Arabia Deserta on one side, so very deserta, so terrifying. Then one morning I woke up and I was sure I could smell cinnamon; the ship stopped and we were in Colombo. It struck me: 'I know it all, I know it all.' It was just as I expected it. The tropics, so marvellous these black people, this violent quick growth and yet a little terrifying, a little repulsive, as Lawrence would say. We stayed with the Brewsters in a huge bungalow with all those black servants in the background. In the morning the sun rose and we got up and I always felt terrified at the day and its heat. The sun rose higher and the heat would rise. We went for a walk and I saw a large thing coming towards us, large like a house, an elephant holding a large tree with its trunk! Its guide made him salaam to us, the great animal – young natives would come and pay visits to us and the Brewsters, who were interested in Buddhism. Lawrence became so terribly English and snubbed them mostly. Some young Cingalese said I had the face of a saint! Didn't I make the most of it and didn't Lawrence get this saint rubbed into him! Then we had the fantastic experience of a Pera-Hera given in honour of the Prince of Wales. Such a contrast was the elegant figure of the Prince sitting on the balcony of the Temple of the Tooth amongst the black seething tropical mass of men. The smell of the torches and the oily scent of dark men. Great elephants at midnight, and the heat in the dark. The noise of the tom-toms that goes right through some dark corner in one's soul. The night falls so quickly and the tom-toms begin and we could see the native fires on the hills all around. Noises from the jungle; those primeval cries and howls and the brainfever bird and the sliding noises on the roof and the jumps in the darkness outside. How could one rest under such a darkness that was so terribly alive!

The climate didn't suit Lawrence and we had to leave. Lawrence was not well and happy in Ceylon. The tropics didn't suit him.

I was so enthralled with the life around us, it was like living in a fairy-tale. We would go to Casa Lebbes, a little jewelshop at Number 1 Trincomalee Street in Kandy, and look at his jewels. He would pull out a soft leather bundle, undo it, and put before our eyes coloured wonders of sapphires, blue and lovely yellow ones, and rubies and emeralds. Lawrence bought me six blue sapphires and a yellow one: they were round in order to make a brooch in the form of a flower. The yellow one was the centre and the blue petal-shaped ones formed a flower around it. Also he bought me a cinnamon stone and a little box of moonstones. The blue sapphire flower I have lost, as I have lost so many things in my life, and the moonstones have disappeared, only the cinnamon stone remains. I wanted to go to Australia; it attracted me. Off we set again, trunks, Sicilian cart, and all, and went to Perth. Only Englishmen and Australians on the boat and it really felt as if one was going to the end of the earth.

We stayed only a little while near Perth and went a long way into that strange vague bush, everything so vague and dim, as before the days of creation. It wasn't born yet. Vague, remote, and unborn it made one feel oneself. There we stayed with Miss Skinner, whose manuscript Lawrence was looking over: *The Boy in the Bush.* Later on, as I look back, it's all vague to me. Then, after a few weeks, we went on to Sydney.

We arrived in Sydney Harbour – nice it was not knowing a soul.

A young officer on the boat had told me: 'The rain on the tin roofs over the trenches always made me think of home.' Sydney.

And there they were, the tin roofs of Sydney and the beautiful harbour and the lovely Pacific Coast, the air so new and clean. We stayed a day or two in Sydney, two lonely birds resting a little. And then we took a train with all our trunks and said: 'We'll look out of the window and where it looks nice we'll get out.' It looked very attractive along the coast but also depressing. We were passing deserted homesteads: both in America and Australia, these human abandoned efforts make one very sad. Then we came to Thirroul; we got out at four and by six o'clock we were settled in a beautiful bungalow right on the sea. Lined with jarra the rooms were, and there were great tanks for rainwater and a stretch of grass going right down to the Pacific, melting away into a pale blue and lucid, delicately tinted sky.

But what a state the bungalow was in! A family of twelve children had stayed there before us: beds and dusty rugs all over the place, torn sailing canvases on the porches, paper all over the garden, the beautiful jarra floors grey with dust and sand, the carpet with no colour at all, just a mess, a sordid mess the whole thing. So we set to and cleaned, cleaned and cleaned as we had done so many times before in our many temporary homes! Floors polished, the carpet taken in the garden and scrubbed, the torn canvases removed. But the paper in the garden was the worst; for days and days we kept gathering paper.

But I was happy: only Lawrence and I in this world. He always made a great big world for me, he gave it to me whenever it was possible; whenever there was wonder left, we took it, and revelled in it.

The mornings, those sunrises over the Pacific had all the wonder of newness, of an uncreated world. Lawrence began to write *Kangaroo* and the days slipped by like dreams, but real as dreams are when they come true. The everyday life was so easy, the food brought to the house, especially the fish cart was a thrill: it let down a flap at the back and like pearls and jewels inside the cart lay the shiny fishes, all colours, all shapes, and we had to try them all.

We took long walks along the coast, lonely and remote and unborn. The weather was mild and full of life, we never got tired of the shore, finding shells for hours that the Pacific had rolled gently on to the sand.

Lawrence religiously read the *Sydney Bulletin*. He loved it for all its stories of wild animals and people's living experiences. The only papers Lawrence ever read were the *Corriere della Sera*, in the past, and the *Sydney Bulletin*. I wonder whether this latter has retained the same character it had then; I haven't seen it since that time. It was our only mental food during that time.

I remember being amazed at the generosity of the people at the farms where we got butter, milk, and eggs; you asked for a pound of butter and you were given a big chunk that was nearly two pounds; you asked for two pints of milk and they gave you three; everything was lavish, like the sky and the sea and the land. We had no human contacts all these months: a strange experience: nobody bothered about us, I think.

At the library, strangely enough, in that little library of Thirroul we found several editions of Lawrence's condemned *Rainbow*. We bought a copy – the librarian never knew that it was Lawrence's own book. Australia is like the 'Hinterland der Seele'.

Like a fantasy seemed the Pacific, pellucid and radiant, melting into the sky, so fresh and new always; then this primal radiance was gone one day and another primeval sea appeared. A storm was throwing the waves high into the air, they rose on the abrupt shore, high as in an enormous window. I could see strange sea-creatures thrown up from the deep: swordfish and fantastic phenomena of undreamt deep-sea beasts I saw in those waves, frightening and never to be forgotten.

And then driving out of the tidy little town into the bush with the little pony cart. Into golden woods of mimosa we drove, or wattle, as the Australians call it. Mostly red flowers and yellow mimosa, many varieties, red and gold, met the eye, strange fern trees, delicately leaved. We came to a wide river and followed it. It became a wide waterfall and then it disappeared into the earth. Disappeared and left us gaping. Why should it have disappeared, where had it gone?

Lawrence went on with *Kangaroo* and wove his deep underneath impressions of Australia into this novel. Thirroul itself was a new little bungalow town and the most elegant thing in it was a German gun that glistened steely and out of place there near the Pacific.

I would have liked to stay in Australia and lose myself, as it were, in this unborn country but Lawrence wanted to go to America. Mabel Dodge had written us that Lawrence must come to Taos in New Mexico, that he must know the Pueblo Indians, that the Indians say that the heart of the world beats there in New Mexico.

This gave us a definite aim, and we began to get ready for America, in a few weeks.

* * *

We sailed from Sydney for San Francisco. It was a smallish boat with a stout jolly captain. We passed Raratonga and went on to Tahiti, always in perfect weather in the Pacific. Nothing but flying fish, porpoises, sky, the great sea, and our boat. Then Tahiti. It must have been so marvellous in the past, those gentle, too gentle handsome natives, with their huts, the perfection of the island in itself. But the joy of it was gone. The charming native women, who offered me old beads and flowers, made me sad in their clumsy Mother Hubbard garments. I know how European diseases were wiping the natives out, the contact with Europe fatal to them. In the evening we saw a cinema in a huge kind of barn; there was a native king, enormous; he was in a box near the stage with several handsome wives. We had travelled with a cinema crowd from Tahiti. Near our cabin two of the young stars had their cabin. They seemed to sleep all day and looked white and tired in the evening. Cases of empty champagne bottles stood outside their cabin in the morning. One of them I had seen flirt quite openly with a passenger but when we arrived in San Francisco I saw her trip so innocently into the arms of a young man who was waiting for her. I remember in San Francisco how the moon at night made such a poor show above all the lights of the town.

We went into a cafeteria and did not know how to behave; how to take our plates and food.

America

We travelled from San Francisco to Taos in great expectation. It was September and the journey through the inner American desert very hot. We got out at Lamy to be met by Mabel Dodge who had brought us here. And as we looked out we saw Mabel standing there in a turquoise blue dress with much of the silver-and-turquoise Indian jewellery and by her side a handsome Indian in a blanket with a large silver belt going across his chest. I looked at Mabel. 'She has eyes one can trust,' I said to myself. And afterwards I always kept to this: people are what they are, whatever they may occasionally do.

When we came to Santa Fe all the hotels were full, so Mabel asked Witter Bynner to take us in. He did: us, the trunks, Sicilian cart and all.

The next morning we drove up through the vast wonderful desert country, with its clear pure air, driving through the Rio Grande canyon deep down by the river and then coming up on to the Taos plateau. Coming out of the canyon to the mesa is an unforgettable experience, with all the deep mountains sitting mysteriously around in a ring, and so much sky.

Mabel had prepared us a house all to ourselves in her 'Mabel-town'. The house stood on Indian land and belonged to Tony. It was a charming adobe house, with Mexican blankets and Indian paintings of Indian dances and animals, clean and full of sun.

A new life for us – and we began it straight away. Out from the pueblo to the east of us, a few miles away, came the feel of the Indians, so different from anything we had ever known. We neither of us wanted to stunt about it, but we were very happy. Tony went for two days with Lawrence to the Navajo country. I spent the days with Mabel and her friend Alice Corbin.

They asked me many questions, which I answered truthfully, giving the show away completely as usual. Then Mabel, with her great energy, took us all over the country: we saw the pueblo, we bathed in a hot radium spring by the Rio Grande. Mabel and Lawrence wanted to write a book together: about Mabel, it was going to be. I did not want this. I had always regarded Lawrence's genius as given to me. I felt deeply responsible for what he wrote. And there was a fight between us, Mabel and myself: I think it was a fair fight. One day Mabel came over and told me she didn't think I was the right woman for Lawrence and other things equally upsetting, and I was thoroughly roused and said: 'Try it then yourself, living with a genius, see what it is like and how easy it is, take him if you can.'

And I was miserable thinking that Lawrence had given her a right to talk like this to me. When Lawrence came in, he saw that I was unhappy, and somebody had told him that Mabel's son John Evans had said: 'My mother is tired of those Lawrences who sponge on her.' This may have been pure malice, but Lawrence was in a fury too; not for nothing was his beard red, and he said: 'I will pay the rent of the house and I'll leave as soon as I can.'

And then he would draw me in a flood of tenderness and love and we would be washed clean of all our apartness and be together again. And Lawrence would rave against Mabel as only he could rave. When I wanted to stick up for her I would get it: 'All women are alike, bossy, without any decency; it's your business to see that other women don't come too close to me.'

That's what he said. It was all very well, but I didn't know how to do it.

We had learned to ride: a long thin Don Quixote of a Mexican had taught us how in a few rides across the open desert. I was terribly happy, feeling the live horse under me. Later on, Azul, my horse, would go like the wind with me and he seemed always aware of me when I was a bit scared.

So we left Mabel's ambient and went to live at the Del Monte Ranch, under the mountains. We had a log house, and the Hawks lived at the big house and in the lower log cabin lived two Danish painters who had come to stay with us; they had come from New York in the most trying old Lizzie that ever went along the road.

She coughed and trembled at the tiniest hill, she stuck and had to be shoved: she was a trial.

It was a real mountain winter. So sharp, knifey cold at night; snow and ice, and the Danes and Lawrence had to chop lots of wood.

We rode into the Lobo Canyon over the logs under the trees and one had to look out for one's head and knees when the horses tore along under the trees. Lawrence would say later on: 'If you were only as nice with me as you are with Azul.'

The friendship and fight with Mabel went on, off and on. She was so admirable in her terrific energy, in her resources and intelligence, but we couldn't get on, somehow.

I remember riding along in the car, when Lawrence said to her: 'Frieda is the freest human being I know.' And I said to him, afterwards: 'You needn't say nice things about me, just to make other people mad.'

Tony would sing his Indian songs when driving. I had told him: 'In our country, Tony, one crow means bad luck and two good luck.' So he would watch for crows and say: 'Two crows, Frieda.'

In the spring we went to Mexico with Witter Bynner and Spud Johnson. After the hard winter, I clamoured for a first-rate hotel in Mexico City. But it wasn't a success, the first-rate hotel, after all; it seemed dull and a bit unclean; the ladies were so very painted and the men not attractive.

The journey across the lonely desert had been strange. The stations were only a few miserable houses and a big water tank and fine dust blew in at the windows of the car, filling one's eyes and ears and nose, all one's pores with very fine sand.

Mexico City seemed like a would-be smart and grand lady to me, but she hadn't quite brought it off. The shabby parts were the most interesting. The Volador Market and all the fascinating baskets and ropes and saddles and belts, pots and dishes and leather jackets.

One day we were in the cathedral plaza of Mexico City, Bynner and Spud and I, when on the top of the church we saw a red flag being hoisted. A crowd collected, soldiers appeared. Bynner and Spud had dashed into the dark hole of the door of the church tower. It was crowding with people. I stayed in the plaza, watching the tower on which were Bynner and Spud, fearing for their fate. My relief when they appeared after an hour was great.

In the Museum we saw among the Aztec relics coiled snakes and other terrifying stone carvings, Maximilian's state carriage. That took me back to my childhood. One of the impressive figures of my childhood had been a Graf Geldern, long, lean, sad, and loosely built like a Mexican, in the uniform of a colonel of the 'Totenkopfhusaren'. He had been to Mexico with Maximilian. How he afterwards took Prussian service I don't know. When they shot Maximilian, they played 'La Paloma'. He had asked for it.

Lawrence went to Guadalajara and found a house with a patio on the Lake of Chapala. There Lawrence began to write his *The Plumed Serpent*. He sat by the lake under a pepper tree writing it. The lake was curious with its white water. My enthusiasm for bathing in it faded considerably when one morning a huge snake rose yards high, it seemed to me, only a few feet away. At the end of the patio we had the family that Lawrence describes in *The Plumed Serpent*, and all the life of Chapala. I tried my one attempt at civilizing those Mexican children, but when they asked me one day: 'Do you have lice too, Nina?' I had enough and gave up in a rage. At night I was frightened of bandits and we had one of the sons of the cook sleeping outside our bedroom door with a loaded revolver, but he snored so fiercely that I wasn't sure whether the fear of bandits wasn't preferable. We quite sank into the patio life. Bynner and Spud came every afternoon, and I remember Bynner saying to me one day, while he was mixing a cocktail: 'If you and Lawrence quarrel, why don't you hit first?' I took the advice and the next time Lawrence was cross, I rose to the occasion and got out of my Mexican indifference and flew at him.

All that time in Mexico seems to me, now, as if I had dreamt it, dreamt it intensely.

We went across the pale Lake of Chapala to a native village where they made serapes; they dyed the wool and wove them on simple looms. Lawrence made some designs and had them woven, as in *The Plumed Serpent*.

Lawrence could only write in places where one's imagination could have space and free play, where the door was not closed to the future, where one's vision could people it with new souls to be born, who would live a new life.

I remember the Pyramids at Teotihuacan, that we saw with Spud and Bynner, I hanging around behind. It was getting dusky and suddenly I came on a huge stone snake, coiling green with great turquoise eyes, round the foot of a temple. I ran after the others for all I was worth.

I got a glimpse of old Mexico then, the old sacrifices, hearts still quivering held up to the sun, for the sun to drink the blood: there it had all happened, on the pyramid of the Sun.

And that awful goddess, who, instead of a Raphael bambino, brings forth an obsidian knife. Fear of these people who don't mind killing and don't mind dying. And I had seen a huge black Christ, in a church, with a black beard and long woman's hair and he wore little white, frilly knickers. Death and sacrifice and cruel gods seemed to reign in Mexico under its sunshine and splendour of flowers and lots of birds and fruit and white volcano peaks.

We went into a huge old Noah's Ark of a boat, called 'Esmeralda', on the Lake of Chapala, with two other friends and Spud. Three Mexicans looked after the boat. They had guitars and sang their melancholy or fierce songs at the end of the boat. In the evening, we slowly drifted along the large lake, that was more like a white sea, and, one day, we had no more to eat. So we landed on the island of the scorpions, still crowned by a Mexican empty prison, and only fit for scorpions. There Lawrence bought a live goat, but when we had seen our Mexican boatmen practically tearing the poor beast to pieces, our appetites vanished and we did not want to eat any more.

Lawrence's visions which he wrote in *The Plumed Serpent* seem so interwoven with everyday life. The everyday and the vision running on together day by day. That autumn we returned to America and spent some time in New Jersey. Lawrence remained in America and went again to Mexico. I went to Europe.

So I went to England alone and had a little flat in Hampstead to see something of my children. It was winter and I wasn't a bit happy alone there and Lawrence was always cross when I had this longing for the children upon me, but there it was, though now I know he was right: they didn't want me any more, they were living their own lives. I felt lost without him. Finally he came and wrote this cross and unjust letter to my mother:

HOTEL GARCIA
GUADALAJARA
JALISCO, MEXICO
10 NOVEMBER, 1923

My dear Mother-in-Law,
I had the two letters from Frieda at Baden, with the billet-doux from you.
Yes, mother-in-law, I believe one has to be seventy before one is full of
courage. The young are always half-hearted. Frieda also makes a long,
sad nose and says she is writing to the moon – Guadalajara is no moon-
town, and I am completely on the earth, with solid feet.

But I am coming back, am only waiting for a ship. I shall be in
England in December. And in the spring, when the primroses are out, I
shall be in Baden. Time goes by faster and faster. Frieda sent me
Hartmann von Richthofen's letter. It was nice. But the women have more
courage these days than the men – also a letter from Nusch, a little sad but
lively. I hope to see her also in the spring. One must spit on one's hands
and take firm hold. Don't you think so?

I was at the Barranca, a big, big ravine, and bathed in the hot springs
– came home and found the whole of Germany in my room.

I like it here. I don't know how, but it gives me strength, this black
country. It is full of man's strength, perhaps not woman's strength, but it
is good, like the old German beer-for-the-heroes, for me. Oh, mother-in-
law, you are nice and old, and understand, as the first maiden
understood, that a man must be more than nice and good, and that heroes
are worth more than saints. Frieda doesn't understand that a man must
be a hero these days and not only a husband; husband also but more. I
must go up and down through the world, I must balance Germany against
Mexico and Mexico against Germany. I do not come for peace. The devil,
the holy devil, has peace round his neck. I know it well, the courageous old
one understands me better than the young one, or at least something in me
she understands better. Frieda must always think and write and say and
ponder how she loves me. It is stupid. I am no Jesus that lies on his
mother's lap. I go my way through the world, and if Frieda finds it such
hard work to love me, then, dear God, let her love rest, give it holidays.
Oh, mother-in-law, you understand, as my mother finally understood,
that a man doesn't want, doesn't ask for love from his wife, but for

strength, strength, strength. To fight, to fight, to fight, and to fight again. And one needs courage and strength and weapons. And the stupid woman keeps on saying love, love, love, and writes of love. To the devil with love! Give me strength, battle-strength, weapon-strength, fighting-strength, give me this, you woman!

England is so quiet: writes Frieda. Shame on you that you ask for peace today. I don't want peace. I go around the world fighting. Pfui! Pfui! In the grave I find my peace. First let me fight and win through. Yes, yes, mother-in-law, make me an oak-wreath and bring the town music under the window, when the half-hero returns.

D. H. L.

(TRANSLATED FROM THE GERMAN)

But I think he was right; I should have gone to meet him in Mexico, he should not have come to Europe; these are the mistakes we make, sometimes irreparable.

Finally he came and I was glad. Just before Christmas he came and we had some parties and saw some friends, but we wanted to go back to America in the spring and live at the ranch that Mabel Luhan had given me. She had taken me to the little ranch near Taos and I said: 'This is the loveliest place I have ever seen.' And she told me: 'I give it you.' But Lawrence said: 'We can't accept such a present from anybody.' I had a letter from my sister that very morning telling me she had sent the manuscript of *Sons and Lovers*, so I told Lawrence: 'I will give Mabel the MS. for the ranch.' So I did.

Murry was coming to America too. First we went to Paris, where we stayed as in our own home at the Hotel de Versailles.

Lawrence wanted me to have some new clothes. Mabel Harrison, who had a large studio opposite the hotel, told us of a good tailor nearby. Lawrence went with me. The stout little tailor draped himself with the cape we bought to show me how to wear it. 'Voyez-vous, la ligne, Madame.' He made me some other clothes and Lawrence remarked with wonder: 'How is it possible that a man can throw all his enthusiasm into clothes for women?'

We went to Strassburg and Baden-Baden, a strange journey for me, going through French territory that had been German just a few years ago.

In the spring we went to America again and Dorothy Brett came with us. We only stayed a few days in New York and went onto Taos. We stayed with Mabel Luhan but, somehow, we didn't get on. I was longing to go to the ranch and live there. Lawrence was a bit afraid to tackle the forlorn little ranch. We had some ten or a dozen Indians to build up the tumble-down houses and corrals and everything. Then he loved it. We had to mend the irrigation ditch and we were impressed by the way Mr Murry dragged huge pipes through the woods, just over no road, to the mouth of the Gallina Canyon of which we had the water rights. And I cooked huge meals for everybody. We all worked so hard. Brett, as everybody called her, straight from her studio life, was amazing for the hard work she would do. One day we cleaned our spring and carried huge stones until we nearly dropped. The spring is in a hollow, and I loved watching the horses play when they came to drink there, shoving each other's noses away from the water level and then tearing up the bank. We did it all ourselves for very little money for we didn't have much. We got a cow and had four horses: Azul, Aaron, and two others; and then we got chickens, all white ones, Leghorns. The beautiful cockerel was called Moses and Susan was the cow's name.

Lawrence got up at five o'clock each morning. With the opera glasses my mother had given him, he looked for Susan, who was an independent creature and loved to hide in the woods. There he would stand, when at last he had found her, and shake his forefinger at her – to my delight – and scold her, the black cow.

I made our own butter in a little glass churn and the chickens flourished on the buttermilk, and so did we in this healthy life. We made our own bread in the Indian oven outside, black bread and white and cakes, and Lawrence was terribly fussy about the bread, which had to be perfect. He made cupboards and chairs and painted doors and windows. He wrote and irrigated and it seems amazing that one single man got so much done. We rode and people stayed with us, and he was always there for everybody as if he did nothing at all. He helped Brett with her pictures and me with my poor attempts.

It was a wonderful summer; there were wild strawberries that year, and back in the canyon raspberries as big as garden ones, but I was afraid to get them because I had heard that bears love raspberries. Bears won't do you any harm except when they have young. There were bears in the

| 171 |

canyon – that seemed indeed the end of the world! The Brett had a tiny shanty in which she lived. She adored Lawrence and slaved for him.

In the autumn we went again to Mexico City. It was fun and we saw several people. In Mexico you could still feel a little lordly and an individual; Mexico has not yet been made 'safe for democracy'.

An amusing thing happened: Lawrence had become a member of the PEN club and they gave an evening in his honour. It was a men's affair and he put on his black clothes and set off in the evening, and I, knowing how unused he was to public functions and how he really shrank from being a public figure, wondered in the hotel room how the evening would go off. Soon after ten o'clock he appeared.

'How was it?'

'Well, they read to me bits of *The Plumed Serpent* in Spanish and I had to sit and listen and then they made a speech and I had to answer.'

'What did you say?'

'I said: here we are together, some of us English, some Mexicans and Americans, writers and painters and business men and so on, but before all and above all we are *men* together tonight. That was about what I said. But a young Mexican jumped up: "It's all very well for an Englishman to say I am a man first and foremost, but a Mexican cannot say so, he must be a Mexican above everything."'

So we laughed, the only speech that Lawrence ever made falling so completely flat. They had missed the whole point, as so often.

Just as it was said of him that he wasn't patriotic; he who seemed to me England itself, a flower sprung out of its most delicate, courageous tradition, not the little bourgeois England but the old England of Palmerston, whom he admired, when men were still men and not mere social beings.

One day William Somerset Maugham was expected in Mexico City; so Lawrence wrote to him if they could meet. But Maugham's secretary answered for him, saying: 'I hear we are going out to a friend's to lunch together who lives rather far out; let's share a taxi.'

Lawrence was angry that Maugham had answered through his secretary and wrote back: 'No, I won't share a car.'

Brett came with us and she had a story from her sister, the Ranee of Sarawak, where Maugham had stayed and he and his secretary had nearly got drowned, shooting some rapids, I think. So there had been feeling there. And our hostess had a grudge against the secretary. Maugham sat next to me and I asked how he liked it here. He answered crossly: 'Do you want me to admire men in big hats?'

I said: 'I don't care what you admire.' And then the lunch was drowned in acidity all round. But after lunch I felt sorry for Maugham: he seemed to me an unhappy and acid man, who got no fun out of living. He seemed to me to have fallen between two stools as so many writers do. He wanted to have his cake and eat it. He could not accept the narrow social world and yet he didn't believe in a wider human one. Commentators and critics of life and nothing more.

When I met other writers, then I knew without knowing how different altogether Lawrence was. They may have been good writers, but Lawrence was a genius.

The inevitability of what he elementally was and had to say at any price, his knowledge and vision, came to him from deeper secret sources than it is given to others to draw from. When I read Aeschylus and Sophocles, then I know Lawrence is great, he is like these – greatest in his work, where human passions heave and sink and mingle and clash. The background of death is always there and the span of life is felt as fierce action. Life is life only when death is part of it. Not like the Christian conception that shuts death away from life and says death comes after: death is always there. I think the great gain of the war is a new reincorporation of death into our lives.

Then we went down to Oaxaca. We had again a house with a patio. There Lawrence wrote *Mornings in Mexico*, with the parrots and Corasmin, the white dog, and the mozo. He rewrote and finished *The Plumed Serpent* there. There was malaria in Oaxaca, it had come with the soldiers, and the climate didn't suit him.

I went to the market with the mozo and one day he showed me in the square, in one of the bookshops, an undeniable caricature of Lawrence, and he watched my face to see how I would take it. I was thrilled! To find in this wild place, with its Zapotec and undiluted Mexican tribes, anything so civilized as a caricature of Lawrence was fun. I loved the market and it was only distressing to see the boy with his basket so utterly miserable at my paying without bargaining: it was real pain to him. But the lovely flowers and everything seemed so cheap.

Meanwhile Lawrence wrote at home and got run down. The Brett

173

came every day and I thought she was becoming too much part of our lives and I resented it. So I told Lawrence: 'I want the Brett to go away,' and he raved at me, said I was a jealous fool. But I insisted and so Brett went up to Mexico City. Then Lawrence finished *The Plumed Serpent*, already very ill, and later on he told me he wished he had finished it differently. Then he was very ill. I had a local native doctor who was scared at having anything to do with a foreigner and he didn't come. Lawrence was very ill, much more ill than I knew, fortunately. I can never say enough of the handful of English and Americans there: how good they were to us. Helping in every way. I thought these mine-owners and engineers led plucky and terrible lives. Always fever, typhoid, malaria, danger from bandits, never feeling a bit safe with their lives. And so I was amazed at the 'Selbstverständlichkeit' with which they helped us. It was so much more than Christian, just natural: a fellow-Englishman in distress: let's help him. Lawrence himself thought he would die.

'You'll bury me in this cemetery here,' he would say, grimly.

'No, no,' I laughed, 'it's such an ugly cemetery, don't you think of it.'

And that night he said to me: 'But if I die, nothing has mattered but you, nothing at all.' I was almost scared to hear him say it, that, with all his genius, I should have mattered so much. It seemed incredible.

I got him better by putting hot sandbags on him, that seemed to comfort his tortured inside.

One day we had met a missionary and his wife, who lived right in the hills with the most uncivilized tribe of Indians. He didn't look like a missionary but like a soldier. He told me he had been an airman, and there far away in Oaxaca he told me how he was there when Manfred Richthofen was brought down behind the trenches and in the evening at mess one of the officers rose and said: 'Let's drink to our noble and generous enemy.'

For me to be told of this noble gesture made in that awful war was a great thing.

Then I remember the wife appeared with a very good bowl of soup when Lawrence was at his worst, and then prayed for him by his bedside in that big bare room. I was half afraid and wondered how Lawrence would feel. But he took it gently and I was half laughing, half crying over the soup and the prayer.

While he was so ill an earthquake happened into the bargain, a thunderstorm first, and the air made you gasp. I felt ill and feverish and Lawrence so ill in the next room – dogs howled and asses and horses and cats were scared in the night – and to my horror I saw the beams of my roof move in and out of their sheaves.

'Let's get under the bed if the roof falls!' I cried.

At last, slowly, slowly, he got a little better. I packed up to go to Mexico City. This was a crucifixion of a journey for me. We travelled through the tropics. Lawrence in the heat so weak and ill and then the night we stayed half-way to Mexico City in a hotel. There, after the great strain of his illness, something broke in me. 'He will never be quite well again, he is ill, he is doomed. All my love, all my strength, will never make him whole again.' I cried like a maniac the whole night. And he disliked me for it. But we arrived in Mexico City. I had Dr Uhlfelder come and see him. One morning I had gone out and when I came back the analyst doctor was there and said, rather brutally, when I came into Lawrence's room: 'Mr Lawrence has tuberculosis.' And Lawrence looked at me with such unforgettable eyes.

'What will she say and feel?' And I said: 'Now we know, we can tackle it. That's nothing. Lots of people have that.' And he got slowly better and could go to lunch with friends. But they, the doctors, told me:

'Take him to the ranch; it's his only chance. He has T.B. in the third degree. A year or two at the most.'

With this bitter knowledge in my heart I had to be cheerful and strong. Then we travelled back to the ranch and were tortured by immigration officials, who made all the difficulties in the ugliest fashion to prevent us from entering the States. If the American Embassy in Mexico hadn't helped we would not have been able to go to the ranch that was going to do Lawrence so much good.

Slowly at the ranch he got better. The high clear air, short sunbaths, our watching and care, and the spring brought life back into him. As he got better he began writing his play *David*, lying outside his little room on the porch in the sun.

I think in that play he worked off his struggle for life. Old Saul and the young David – old Samuel's prayer is peculiarly moving in its hopeless love for Saul – so many different motifs, giant motifs, in that play.

Mabel took us to a cave along the road near Arroyo Seco and he used it for his story *The Woman Who Rode Away*. Brett was always with us. I liked her in many ways; she was so much her own self.

I said to her: 'Brett, I'll give you half a crown if you contradict Lawrence,' but she never did. Her blind adoration for him, her hero-worship for him was touching, but naturally it was balanced by a preconceived critical attitude towards me. He was perfect and I always wrong, in her eyes.

When the Brett came with us Lawrence said to me: 'You know, it will be good for us to have the Brett with us, she will stand between us and people and the world.' I did not really want her with us, and had a suspicion that she might not want to stand between us and the world, but between him and me. But no, I thought, I won't be so narrow-gutted, one of Lawrence's words, I will try.

So I looked after Brett and was grateful for her actual help. She did her share of the work. I yelled down her ear-trumpet, her Toby, when people were there, that she should not feel out of it. But as time went on she seemed always to be there; my privacy that I cherished so much was gone. Like the eye of the Lord, she was; when I washed, when I lay under a bush with a book, her eyes seemed to be there, only I hope the eye of the Lord looks on me more kindly. Then I detested her, poor Brett, when she seemed deaf and dumb and blind to everything quick and alive. Her adoration for Lawrence seemed a silly old habit. 'Brett,' I said, 'I detest your adoration for Lawrence, only one thing I would detest more, and that is if you adored me.'

When I finally told Lawrence in Oaxaca: 'I don't want Brett such a part of our life, I just don't want her,' he was cross at first, but then greatly relieved.

How thrilling it was to feel the inrush of new vitality in him; it was like a living miracle. A wonder before one's eyes. How grateful he was inside him! 'I can do things again. I can live and do as I like, no longer held down by the devouring illness.' How he loved every minute of life at the ranch. The morning, the squirrels, every flower that came in its turn, the big trees, chopping the wood, the chickens, making bread, all our hard work, and the people and all assumed the radiance of new life.

He worked hard as a relaxation and wrote for hard work.

* * *

Going Back to Europe

At the end of the summer he became restless again and wanted to go to Europe. To the Mediterranean he wished to go. So on the coast, not far from Genoa, we found Spotorno, that Martin Secker had told us was not overrun with foreigners. Under the ruined castle I saw a pink villa that had a friendly look and I wondered if we could have it. We found the peasant Giovanni who looked after it. Yes, he thought we could. It belonged to a Tenente dei Bersaglieri in Savona. We were staying at the little inn by the sea, when the Bersaglieri asked for us. Lawrence went and returned. 'You must come and look at him, he is so smart.' So I went and found a figure in uniform with gay plumes and blue sash, as it was the Queen's birthday. We took the Bernarda and the Tenente became a friend of ours. Lawrence taught him English on Sundays, but they never got very far.

My daughter, Barbara, now grown up, was coming to stay with me. She was coming for the first time. I was beside myself with joy to have her. I had not waited in vain for so many years and longed for these children. But Lawrence did not share my joy. One day at our evening meal came the outburst: 'Don't you imagine your mother loves you,' he said to Barby; 'she doesn't love anybody, look at her false face.' And he flung half a glass of red wine in my face. Barby, who besides my mother and myself was the only one not to be scared of him, sprang up. 'My mother is too good for you,' she blazed at him, 'much too good; it's like pearls thrown to the swine.' Then we both began to cry. I went to my room offended.

'What happened after I went?' I asked Barby later on.

'I said to him: "Do you care for her?" "It's indecent to ask," he answered; "haven't I just helped her with her rotten painting?"' Which again puzzled me because he would gladly help anybody. It did not seem a sign of love to me. Then my daughter Elsa came too. But evidently to counterbalance my show Lawrence had asked his sister Ada and a friend to come and stay, so there were hostile camps. Ada arrived and above me, in Lawrence's room with the balcony, I could hear him complaining to her about me. I could not hear the words but by the tone of their voices I knew.

His sister Ada felt he belonged to her and the past, the past with all its sad memories. Of course it had been necessary for him to get out of his past as I had, of equal necessity, to fight that past, though I liked Ada for herself.

Lawrence was ill with all this hostility. I was grieved for him. So one evening I went up to his room and he was so glad I came. I thought all was well between us. In the morning Ada and I had bitter words. 'I hate you from the bottom of my heart,' she told me. So another night I went up to Lawrence's room and found it locked and Ada had the key. It was the only time he had really hurt me; so I was quite still. 'Now I don't care,' I said to myself.

He went away with Ada and her friend, hoping at the last I would say some kind word, but I could not. Lawrence went to Capri to stay with the Brewsters.

But I was happy with the two children. The spring came with its almond blossoms and sprouting fig-trees. Barby rushed up the hills with her paintbox, her long legs carrying her like a deer. We lay in the sun and I rejoiced in her youthful bloom. Then a picture arrived from Lawrence. There was Jonah on it, just going to be swallowed by the whale. Lawrence had written underneath: 'Who is going to swallow whom?'

But I was still angry.

Finally Lawrence came from Capri, wanting to be back. The children tried like wise elders to talk me round. 'Now Mrs L.' (so they called me) 'be reasonable, you have married him, so now you must stick to him.'

So Lawrence came back. 'Make yourself look nice to meet him,' the children said. We met him at the station all dressed up. Then we all four had peace. He was charming with Elsa and Barby, trying to help them live their difficult young lives. 'Elsa is not one of those to put the bed on fire, because there is a flea in it,' Lawrence said of her.

But for his sister Ada he never felt the same again.

* * *

Lawrence wanted to go further into the heart of Italy. The Etruscan tombs and remains interested him. But the ranch too called him.

However the idea of having to struggle with immigration officials, thinking of his tuberculosis, scared him. So he went to Florence, with Elsa and Barby. After a short time they went back to England.

Friends told us of a villa to let in the country about Florence. So we took a car and went out by the Porta Federicana through dreary suburban parts till we came to the end of the tramline.

It was April, the young beans were green and the wheat and the peas up, and we drove into the old Tuscan landscape, that perfect harmony of what nature did and man made. It is quite unspoiled there still. Beyond Scandicci we passed two cypresses and went to the left on a small, little used road. On the top of one of those Tuscan little hills stood a villa. My heart went out to it. I wanted that villa. It was rather large, but so perfectly placed, with a panorama of the Valdarno in front, Florence on the left, and the umbrella-pine woods behind.

'I do hope it is this one that's to let,' I said to Lawrence, and my wish was fulfilled; we could have the villa, we could live in the Mirenda. We were thrilled by the peasants who belonged to the podere . . . the Orsini, Bandelli, and Pini. The Orsini had a wild feud with the Bandelli. The Bandelli fascinated me; a loosely built, untamed father and easy-going mother, and two beautiful wild girls, Tosca and Lila, and three beautiful boys . . . My special favourite was Dino, who was so gently grey-eyed and angelic, but you knew perfectly well how he would laugh at you behind your back. So polite he was, carrying parcels for me, such exquisite manners at ten years old! Then I discovered that he looked very pale and ill at times and they told me that he had a rupture, and, with the brutality of boys, he told me the boys at school jeered at him for it. So I went with him to Doctor Giglioli in Florence and poor Dino was to have an operation. His sisters and I took him to the hospital, first decking him out with new shirts and vests. He was miserable, but chiefly miserable because they had put him among the women, him, a maschio. He was put to bed and, when we left him there, he crept under the sheets and shook with misery. Alas, next day, who appeared at home? Dino! He had crept about the place, seen a man under an anaesthetic, and fled. It was like putting a wild creature into a hospital. Then we persuaded him to go back, chiefly by telling him that, once operated, no one could laugh at him any more. So back he went, this time he had made up his mind. He was a plucky boy, and afterwards they told me at the hospital how they had never had a better, braver patient. It was a jolly hospital, this Florence one, so human and friendly, not at all prisonlike or too much white starch of nurses, white tiles, whitewash, white paint about, that one's very blood turns white. No, there your friends came to see you, everybody took a friendly interest in everybody else; well, such is life, here we are ever so ill, one day, then we get ever so well again, and then we die; 'Ah, signora, cosí è la vita.' And after the operation Dino was a prouder and more important person than he had ever been in his life, with his chicken-broth and good foods, and his new vests and shirts and socks, and two hankies and actually some eau de Cologne. And proudly he told his sisters, in superior knowledge, when they asked for the WC: 'There is a thing, and you pull, you must pull, see?' They not having seen such an arrangement before!

Then Dino came home and he brought me flowers and fruit and we were very fond of each other, although he never felt quite at ease with me.

Our servant was Giulia, from the Pini family. There was the Pini father, a zio, and a poor old zia, who had been buried in an earthquake and occasionally had fits, and Pietro who also helped Giulia about the house, arriving each morning to feed the chickens and goats, and Stellina, the horse. Giulia had to cut the grass every day with a sickle to feed all the animals. In the morning she was barefoot and shabby, but in the afternoon, when she heard a motorcar with visitors, she would appear at the Mirenda in high-heeled shoes and a huge bow in her hair. We loved Giulia . . . never was anything too much for her, gay and amusing and wise, she was.

For the first time, there near Florence, I got the Italian, especially the Tuscan, feel of things. In Florence, the ancient unbroken flower of a culture made its deep mark on me. The Misericordia, how deep it impressed me, the voluntary, immediate effort to help one's neighbour in distress. And when people pass it to the youngest and the oldest take off their hats to it . . . To me this seems real culture . . . The Misericordia dates from the twelfth century and was founded by a facchino, an interesting story in itself.

Oh, the strange, almost ferocious intelligence of the Florentines!

What a pleasure it was to walk from the Villa Mirenda, and take the tram in Scandicci to Florence! The handsome Tuscan girls with their glossy, neatly-done hair in the tram . . . a chicken, sitting, tenderly held by its owner in a red hankie, its destiny either a sick friend or the mercato. Bottles of wine are hidden from the Dazio men, men friends embrace each other, somebody sees a relation and yells something about the 'pasta' for midday, and so on, while we sail gaily on for Florence. There we would rush to Orioli's shop, hear his news and all the news of our friends. We would each dash out and do our exciting shopping. Shopping in Florence was still fun, not the dreary large-store drudgery . . . There are the paper shops, leather shops, scent shops, stuffs; one glorious shop sells nothing but ribbons, velvet and silk, all colours and sizes, spotted and gold and silver. Another shop, all embroidery silks. Then to have your shoes made is so comfortable . . . the shoemaker feels your foot more important than the measuring. And then the '48' . . . what didn't we buy at the '48'!

Marionettes and pots and pans, china and glasses and hammers and paints. We would collect our things at Orioli's and drive home with Pietro and Giulia, furnishing the great kitchen at the Mirenda so conveniently with a few pounds, Lawrence designing a large kitchen table and brackets from which the pots hung. We painted the shutters of the Mirenda, and the chairs, green; we put 'stuoie', thick pale grass matting, on the red-tiled floor in the big sitting-room. We had a few Vallombrosa chairs, a round table, a piano, hired, a couch and an old seat. The walls were syringed white with the syringe one uses to put verderane on the vines . . . that was done fast, and the sun poured into the big room so still and hot. The only noises came from the peasants, calling or singing at their work, or the water being drawn at the well. Or best, and almost too fierce, were the nightingales singing away from early dawn, almost the clock round . . . an hour or two's rest at midday in the heat. The spring that first year was a revelation in flowers, from the first violets in the woods . . . carpets of them we found, and as usual in our walks we took joyful possession of the unspoiled, almost mediaeval country around us. By the stream in the valley were tufts of enormous primroses, where the willow trees had been blood red through the winter. On the edge of the umbrella-pine woods, in the fields, were red and purple big anemones, strange, narrow-pointed, red and yellow wild tulips, bee orchids and purple orchids, tufts of tight-scented lavender . . . flowers thick like velvety carpets, like the ground in a Fra Angelico picture.

Our carriage and the Stellina were so small, I felt like sitting in a doll's perambulator. One day I went shopping with Pietro in Scandicci, when he had tooth-ache; he wore a red hankie round his poor swollen cheek, and on top of the hankie perched a hat, a bit sideways, with the Italian chic in it. He was very sorry for himself, and so was I, but none of the people we passed seemed to think us a funny sight, and we must have been, in that tiny barroccino, Pietro with his tooth-ache and his hankie by my side.

The Italians are so natural, one has tooth-ache and why hide it? Pietro would tell me: 'Si, signora, questa sera vado a fare all'amore con la mia fidanzata.' The fidanzata had only one eye, she was pretty, but in a self-conscious way she always kept the side *with* the eye toward one.

Christmas came and I wanted to make a Christmas tree for all the peasants. I told Pietro: 'Buy me a tree in Florence, when you go to market.'

'What,' he said, 'buy a tree, signora? Ah, no, one doesn't buy a tree, I'll get the signora one from the prete's wood.'

On Christmas Day, or rather Christmas Eve, at four in the morning I heard a whisper: 'Signora! Signora!' under my window. I looked out and there was Pietro with a large beautiful tree. He brought it in and how Lawrence and I and Giulia and Pietro enjoyed trimming that tree. There were pine cones on it and we put gold and silver paper around these cones and Pietro would yell: 'Guarda, guarda, signora, che bellezza!' while Lawrence and I went on trimming the tree with a lot of shiny things bought at the '48'; silver threads that we called 'Christ Child hair' when I was small, and also lots and lots of candies. The Christmas tree looked so beautiful in that big white empty room, not a bit Christian, and how the peasant children loved their cheap wooden toys and how carefully they handled them, so precious were they. They had never had toys before. The grown-ups loved it too. We had difficulty in making them all go home again.

Such a sweetness and perfection of successive flowering Florence meant to us. We walked in the afternoons, almost awed through so much unknown, unobtrusive loveliness . . . the white oxen so carefully ploughing, between the cypresses, and flowers in the wheat, and beans and peas and clover! At twilight we would come home and light our stove in the big sitting-room, the stove that had been there for centuries, used as it had been to keep the silkworms warm in the winter . . . now it warmed us. We had no pictures on the walls, but Maria Huxley had left some canvases behind and I said: 'Let's have some pictures.'

Then, mixing his paints himself, boldly and joyfully, Lawrence began to paint. I watched him for a few hours, absorbed, especially when he began a new one, when he would mix his paints on a piece of glass, paint with a rag and his fingers, and his palm and his brushes. 'Try your toes next,' I would say. Occasionally, when I was cooking pigeons that tasted of wine because they had fed on the dregs of grapes from the wine-press, or washing, he would call me, and I would have to hold out an arm or a leg for him to draw, or tell him what I thought of his painting.

He enjoyed his painting . . . with what intensity he went for it! Then he wrote *Lady Chatterley*. After breakfast – we had it at seven or so – he would take his book and pen and cushion, followed by John the dog, and go into the woods behind the Mirenda and come back to lunch with what he had written. I read it day by day and wondered how his chapters were built up and how it all came to him. I wondered at his courage and daring to face and write these hidden things that people dare not write or say.

For two years *Lady Chatterley* lay in an old chest that Lawrence had painted a greeny yellow with roses on it, and often when I passed that chest, I thought: 'Will that book ever come out of there?'

Lawrence asked me. 'Shall I publish it, or will it only bring me abuse and hatred again?' I said: 'You have written it, you believe in it, all right, then publish it.' So one day we talked it all over with Orioli; we went to a little old-fashioned printer, with a little old printing shop where they had only enough type to do half the book – and *Lady Chatterley* was printed. When it was done, stacks and stacks of *Lady C* . . ., or Our Lady, as we called it – were sitting on the floor of Orioli's shop. There seemed such a terrific lot of them that I said in terror: 'We shall never sell all these.' A great many were sold before there was a row; first some did not arrive at their destination in America, then there came abuse from England . . . but it was done . . . his last great effort.

He had done it . . . and future generations will benefit, his own race that he loved and his own class, that is less inhibited, for he spoke out of

183

them and for them, there in Tuscany, where the different culture of another race gave the impetus to his work.

One winter we went to Diablerets and stayed in a little chalet. Aldous Huxley and Maria, Julian Huxley and Juliette, and their children shared a big villa nearby. Maria read *Lady C.* there and Juliette was shocked at first. But then it was meant to be a shock. I can see Aldous and Lawrence talking together by the fire. I remember Aldous patiently trying to teach me to ski, but my legs tied themselves into knots with the skis and I seemed to be most of the time sitting in the snow collecting my legs.

We went for picnics in the snow, the Huxleys ski-ing, Lawrence and I in a sledge. I saw Diablerets again later on in the summer – I didn't recognize it, so completely different it looked in the snow.

I think the greatest pleasure and satisfaction for a woman is to live with a creative man, when he goes ahead and fights – I found it so. Always when he was in the middle of a novel or writing I felt happy as if something were happening, there was a new thing coming into the world. Often before he conceived a new idea he was irritable and disagreeable, but when it had come, the new vision, he could go ahead, and was eager and absorbed.

We had a very hot summer that year and we wanted to go to the mountains. One hot afternoon Lawrence had gathered peaches in the garden and came in with a basket full of wonderful fruit – he showed them to me – a very little while after he called from his room in a strange, gurgling voice; I ran and found him lying on his bed; he looked at me with shocked eyes while a slow stream of blood came from his mouth. 'Be quiet, be still,' I said. I held his head, but slowly and terribly the blood flowed from his mouth. I could do nothing but hold him and try to make him still and calm and send for Doctor Giglioli. He came, and anxious days and nights followed. In this great heat of July nursing was difficult – Giulia, all the peasants – helped in every possible way. The signor was so ill – Giulia got down to Scandicci at four in the morning and brought ice in sawdust in a big handkerchief, and milk, but this, even boiled straightaway, would be sour by midday. The Huxleys came to see him, Maria with a great bunch of fantastically beautiful lotus, and Giglioli every day, and Orioli came and helped. But I nursed him alone night and day for six weeks, till he was strong enough to take the night train to the Tyrol.

This was another inroad his illness made. We both fought hard and won.

People came to see us at the Mirenda. Capitano Ravagli had to come to Florence for a military case – he came to see us and showed Lawrence his military travel-pass. When Lawrence saw on it: *Capitano Ravagli* deve *partire* (must *leave*) *at such and such a time* . . . he shook his head and said resentfully: 'Why "must"? why "must"? there shouldn't be any *must*. . . .'

One Sunday afternoon Osbert and Edith Sitwell came. They moved us strangely. They seemed so oversensitive, as if something had hurt them too much, as if they had to keep up a brave front to the world, to pretend they didn't care and yet they only cared much too much. When they left, we went for a long walk, disturbed by them.

That autumn we gave up the Mirenda. Lawrence had been so ill there and wanted the sea. I went to pack up at the Mirenda, it was a grief to me. I had been so very happy there except for Lawrence's illness. How great the strain was at times, always the strain of his health. The last ounce of my strength seemed to be drained at times but I had my reward. He got better and I always knew however tired I might be he felt worse than ever I could. Making another effort my own strength grew. I never had time to think of my own health, so it looked after itself and it never let me down. The peasants at the Mirenda, the very place itself, the woods with their umbrella-pines, the group of buildings, seemed sad at being left.

The peasants took all the belongings we had collected and carried them away on their backs, like gnomes they crept under their loads down the path. When I gave a last look from the two cypress trees along the road there stood the Mirenda upon its hill in the evening sun, with its shutters closed, old and solid, it seemed as if its eyes had closed for sleep, to dream of the life that had been and gone.

Lawrence had gone to Port Cros with Richard Aldington, Brigit Patmore, and Dorothy Yorke – Arabella we called her.

I joined them there. Port Cros seemed an island of mushrooms – I had never seen so many as there on the moist warm ground of the undergrowth. We had a donkey and a man who worked for us and brought up the food from the little harbour below. Lawrence was not well and I remember how we all did our best on the top of that island to help him in every way.

We drank coffee in the inner space of the small fortress we lived in. The donkey looked on and Richard jumped up to play the brave toreador, waving his blue scarf at the donkey. Jasper was its name. Jasper fled into the bushes but its long ears stuck out and he had to peep at Richard – he hadn't got the bullfight idea, but was intrigued.

Richard was an education in itself to me: he knew so much about Napoleon, for instance, and made me see Napoleon from a different angle, the emotional power he had over his men. Richard told me of his war experiences, death experience and beyond death; it seemed to melt one's brain away; Richard began writing his *Death of a Hero* there in Port Cros. One day we went bathing in the bluest little bay, when an octopus persecuted Brigit and Richard had to beat it away.

We wanted to go to the mainland, not to be so far away with Lawrence so frail. So we left for Toulon, gay Toulon with its ships and sailors and shops, real sailors' shops, with boxes adorned with shells, ships made of shells, long knives from Corsica, on which was written: 'Che la mia ferita sia mortale'.

Near Toulon, at Bandol, in the hotel Beau Rivage we stayed all winter. A sunny hotel by the sea, friendly and easy as only Provence can be. We seemed to live completely the life of a 'petit rentier', as Rousseau le Douanier has painted it. Lawrence wrote *Pansies* in his room in the morning, then we went to have our aperitif before lunch in a cafe on the sea-front. There was a small war memorial, a gay young damsel that would please any poilu. We knew all the dogs of the small place, we saw the boats come in, their silvery loads of sardines glittering on the sand of the shores. Lawrence was better that winter in health. He watched the men playing 'boccia' on the shore, after lunch. We seemed to share the life of the little town, running along so easily. We went with the bus to Toulon. We saw the coloured soldiers. We went to a beautiful circus. Yes, easy and sunny was this winter in Bandol.

The Huxleys came and later on they found a house across the bay at Sanary. I see us sitting in the sunny dining-room of the Beau Rivage, and Lawrence saying to Maria: 'No, Maria, you would not be a bit nice if you were really very rich.'

In the spring we went to Spain from Marseilles – to Barcelona, from there to Mallorca. Mallorca still has a depth to it, a slight flavour of Africa, a distance in its horizon over the sea.

Our hotel was by a small bay. Deliciously hot, the days went by. We went all over the island, always wary not to tire Lawrence. I bathed in the heat of midday and climbed the rocks with the little bay entirely to myself. But one day I looked around and saw a Spanish officer on a splendid horse, looking out towards the sea; I was disturbed in my loneliness and wanted to dash to my bathing cloak and go away. I sprang on to a heap of seaweeds that had a hole underneath it and rocks. Like a gunshot my ankle snapped, I collapsed sick with pain. The officer rode up and offered me his horse that danced about. I thought: what a waste of a romantic situation; the ankle hurts so much, I can't get on to a prancing horse – if I could only be alone with this pain.

Lawrence appeared, got two young men to take me to the hotel in their car. The ankle did not hurt any more, but it was broken.

Lawrence wanted me to go to London to be there for the exhibition of his paintings. A gay flag with his name was flying outside the Warren Gallery when I went there. His pictures looked a little wild and overwhelming in the elegant, delicate rooms of the galleries. Never could I have dreamed that a few pictures could raise such a storm. I had not realized their potency in the big, bare rooms of the Mirenda, where they had been born so naturally, as if Tuscany had given its life to them. I was astonished. Then the police came and put them in the cellar of Marlborough Street Police Station to be destroyed. I was worried lest the cellar be damp and so destroy them that way. But no, they were saved; it was a fight, though.

Meanwhile Lawrence was ill in Florence. What with the abuse of *Lady Chatterley* and the disapproval of the pictures, he had become ill. Orioli telegraphed in distress. So off I set on my journey to Florence, my ankle still wobbly and aching and with constant worry in my mind of how I would find Lawrence. Orioli told me that after receiving my telegram saying I was coming, he had said: 'What will Frieda say when she arrives?' And Lawrence had answered: 'Do you see those peaches in the bowl? She will say, "What lovely peaches", and she will devour them.' So it was. After my first look at Lawrence, when his eyes had signalled to me their relief, 'She is here with me,' I felt my thirst from the long journey and ate the peaches.

He always got better when I was there. But Orioli told me how scared he had been when he had seen Lawrence, his head and arms hanging over the side of the bed, like one dead.

We left the heat of Florence for the Tegernsee to be near Max Mohr. We had a rough peasant house, it was autumn. Lawrence rested a great deal. My sister Elsa came to see him, and Alfred Weber. When he was alone with Alfred Weber, he said to him: 'Do you see those leaves falling from the apple tree? When the leaves want to fall you must let them fall'. Max Mohr had brought some doctors from Munich, but medicine did not help Lawrence. His organism was too frail and sensitive. I remember some autumn nights when the end seemed to have come. I listened for his breath through the open door, all night long, an owl hooting ominously from the walnut tree outside. In the dim dawn an enormous bunch of gentians I had put on the floor by his bed seemed the only living thing in the room. But he recovered and slowly Max Mohr and I travelled with him south again to Bandol.

After the Mirenda we seemed to live chiefly for his health. Switzerland and the sea one after the other seemed to do him most good. He did not want any doctors or cures. 'I know so much better about myself than any doctor,' he would say. His life became a struggle for health. And yet he would rise above it so amazingly and his spirit brought forth immortal flowers right up to the very end. One of his desires was to write a novel about each continent. Africa and Asia still he wanted to do. It was not given to him to do so. As one of my Indian friends here said: 'Why didn't Mr Lawrence write about the whole world? He knew all about it.' When he had read *The Lost Girl* he said: 'What happened to those people afterwards? I want to know their story till they die.'

Here these Indians seem to understand him so immediately – better, I believe, than his white fellowmen.

* * *

Nearing the End

Now I am nearing the end . . . I think of Bandol and our little villa 'Beau Soleil' on the sea, the big balcony windows looking toward the sea, another window at the side over-looking a field of yellow narcissus called 'soleil' and pine-trees beyond and again the sea. I remember sunny days when the waves came flying along with white manes, they looked as if they might come flying right up the terrace into his room. There were plants in his room and they flowered so well and I said to him: 'Why, oh why, can't you flourish like those?' I remember what a beautiful and strange time it was. One day a cat, a big handsome yellow-and-white cat came in; Lawrence chased it away. 'We don't want it. If we go away it'll be miserable. We don't want to take the responsibility for it'; but the cat stayed, it insisted on it. Its name was 'Micky' and it grew more and more beautiful and never a cat played more intelligently than Micky . . . he played hide-and-go-seek with me, and Lawrence played mouse with him . . . Lawrence was such a convincing mouse . . . and then he insisted: 'You must put this cat out at night or it will become a bourgeois, unbeautiful cat.' So very sadly, at nightfall, in spite of Micky's remonstrances I put him out into the garden. To Mme Martens, the cook, Lawrence said: 'Vous lui donnez à manger, il dort avec moi, et Madam l'amuse.'

But in the morning at dawn Micky and I appeared in Lawrence's room . . . Micky took a lying leap on to Lawrence's bed and began playing with his toes, and I looked at Lawrence to see how he was . . . his worst time was before dawn when he coughed so much, and I knew what he had been through . . . But then at dawn I believe he felt grateful that another day had been given him. 'Come when the sun rises,' he said, and when I came he was glad, so very glad, as if he would say: 'See, another day is given me.'

The sun rose magnificently opposite his bed in red and gold across the bay and the fishermen standing up in their boats looked like eternal mythological figures dark and alive against the lit-up splendour of the sea and sky, and when I asked him: 'What kind of a night did you have?' to comfort me, he would answer: 'Not so bad . . .' but it was bad enough to break one's heart . . . And his courage and unflinching spirit, doing their level best to live as long as he possibly could in this world he loved so much, gave me courage too. Never, in all illness and suffering, did he let the days sink to a dreary or dull or sordid level . . . those last months had the glamour of a rosy sunset . . . I can only think with awe of those last days of his, as of the rays of the setting sun . . . and the setting sun obliterates all the sordid details of a landscape. So the dreary passages in our lives were wiped out and he said to me: 'Why, oh why did we quarrel so much?' and I could see how it grieved him . . . our terrible quarrels . . . but I answered: 'Such as we were, violent creatures, how could we help it?'

One day the charming old mother of Mme Douillet who was at the Hotel Beau Rivage brought us two goldfish in a bowl; 'Pour amuser Monsieur', but, alas, Micky thought it was 'pour amuser Monsieur le chat'. With that fixed, incomprehensible cat-stare he watched those red lines moving in the bowl . . . then my life became an anxious one . . . the goldfish had to go in the bathroom on a little table in the sun. Every morning their water was renewed and I had to let it run for half an hour into the bowl. That was all they got, the goldfish, no food. And they flourished . . . 'Everything flourishes,' I said to Lawrence imploringly, 'plants and cats and goldfish, why can't you?' And he said: 'I want to, I want to, I wish I could.'

His friend Earl Brewster came and massaged him every day with coconut oil . . . and it grieved me to see Lawrence's strong, straight, quick legs gone so thin, so thin. . . and one day he said to me: 'I could always trust your instinct to know the right thing for me, but now you don't seem to know any more . . .' I didn't . . . I didn't know any more . . .

And one night he asked me: 'Sleep with me,' and I did . . . all night I was aware of his aching inflexible chest, and all night he must have been so sadly aware of my healthy body beside him . . . always before, when I slept by the side of him, I could comfort and ease him . . . now no more . . . He was falling away from life and me, and with all my strength I was helpless . . .

Micky had his eye on the goldfish. One sad evening at tea-time the bathroom door was left open . . . I came and found both goldfish on the floor. Mickey had fished them out of the bowl. I put them in quickly, one revived, a little sadder and less golden for his experience, but the other was dead. Lawrence was furious with Micky. 'He knew we wanted him to leave those goldfish alone, he knew it. We feed him, we take care of him, he had no right to do it.'

When I argued that it was the nature of cats and they must follow their instincts he turned on me and said: 'It's your fault, you spoil him, if he wanted to eat me you would let him.' And he wouldn't let Micky come near him for several days.

I felt: 'Now I can do no more for Lawrence, only the sun and the sea and the stars and the moon at night, that's his portion now . . .' He never would have the shutters shut or the curtains drawn, so that at night he could see the sky. In those days he wrote his *Apocalypse*; he read it to me, and how strong his voice still was, and I said: 'But this is splendid.'

I was reading the New Testament and told Lawrence: 'I get such a kick out of it, just the same as when Azul gallops like the wind across the desert with me.'

As he read it to me he got angry with all those mixed-up symbols and impossible pictures.

He said: 'In this book I want to go back to old days, pre-Bible days, and pick up for us there what men felt like and lived by then.'

The pure artist in him revolted! His sense of the fitness of things never left him in the lurch! He stuck to his sense of measure and I am often amused at the criticism people bring against him . . . criticisms only reveal the criticizers and their limitations . . . If the criticizer is an interesting person his criticism will be interesting, if he isn't then it's a waste of time to listen to him. If he voices a general opinion he is uninteresting too, because we all know the general opinion *ad nauseum*. 'My flesh grows weary on my bones' was one of Lawrence's expressions when somebody held forth to him, as if one didn't know beforehand what most people will say!

One day Lawrence said to himself: 'I shan't die . . . a rich man now . . . perhaps it's just as well, it might have done something to me.' But I doubt whether even a million or two would have changed him!

One day he said: 'I can't die, I can't die, I hate them too much! I have given too much and what did I get in return?'

It sounded so comical the way he said it, and I ignored the depth of sadness and bitterness of the words and said: 'No, Lawrence, you don't hate them as much as all that.' It seemed to comfort him.

And now I wonder and am grateful for the superhuman strength that was given us both in those days. Deep down I knew 'something is going to happen, we are steering towards some end', but every nerve was strained and every thought and every feeling . . . Life had to be kept going gaily at any price.

Since Doctor Max Mohr had gone, we had no doctor, only Mme Martens, the cook. She was very good at all kinds of tisanes and inhalations and mustard plasters, and she was a very good cook.

My only grief was that we had no open fireplaces, only central heating and, thank goodness, the sun all day. Lawrence made such wonderful efforts of will to go for walks and the strain of it made him irritable. If I went with him it was pure agony walking to the corner of the little road by the sea, only a few yards! How gallantly he tried to get better and live! He was so very clever with his frail failing body. Again one could learn from him how to handle this complicated body of ours, he knew so well what was good for him, what he needed, by an unfailing instinct, or he would have died many years ago. . . and I wanted to keep him alive at any cost. I had to see him day by day getting nearer to the end, his spirit so alive and powerful that the end and death seemed unthinkable and always will be, for me.

And then Gertler sent a doctor friend to us, and when he saw Lawrence he said the only salvation was a sanatorium higher up . . .

For the last years I had found that for a time mountain air, and then a change by the sea, seemed to suit Lawrence best. Lawrence had always thought with horror of a sanatorium, we both thought with loathing of it. Freedom that he cherished so much! He never felt like an invalid, I saw to that! Never should he feel a poor sick thing as long as I was there and his spirit! Now we had to give in . . . we were beaten. With a set face Lawrence made me bring all his papers on to his bed and he tore most of them up and made everything tidy and neat and helped to pack his own trunks, and I never cried . . . His self-discipline kept me up, and my admiration for his unfailing courage. And the day came that the motor stood at the door of our little house, Beau Soleil . . . Micky the cat had been taken by Achsah Brewster. She came before we started with armfuls of almond blossoms, and Earl Brewster travelled with us . . . And patiently, with a desperate silence, Lawrence set out on his last journey. At Toulon station he had to walk down and up stairs, wasting strength he could ill afford to waste, and the shaking train and then the long drive from Antibes to the 'Ad Astra' at Vence . . . And again he had to climb stairs. There he lay in a blue room with yellow curtains and great open windows and a balcony looking over the sea. When the doctors examined him and asked him questions about himself he told them: 'I have had bronchitis since I was a fortnight old.'

In spite of his thinness and his illness he never lost his dignity, he fought on and he never lost hope. Friends brought flowers, pink and red cyclamen and hyacinths and fruit . . . but he suffered much and when I bade him 'good night' he said: 'Now I shall have to fight several battles of Waterloo before morning.' I dared not understand to the full the meaning of his words. One day he said to my daughter:

'Your mother does not care for me any more, the death in me is repellent to her.'

But it was the sadness of his suffering . . . and he would not eat and he had much pain . . . and we tried so hard to think of different foods for him. His friends tried to help him, the Di Chiaras and the Brewsters and Aldous and Maria Huxley and Ida Rauh.

Wells came to see him, and the Aga Khan with his charming wife. Jo Davidson did a bust of him.

One night I saw how he did not want me to go away, so I came again after dinner and I said: 'I'll sleep in your room tonight.' His eyes were so grateful and bright, but he turned to my daughter and said: 'It isn't often I want your mother, but I do want her tonight to stay.' I slept on the long chair in his room, and I looked out at the dark night and I wanted one single star to shine and comfort me, but there wasn't one; it was a dark big sky, and no moon and no stars. I knew how Lawrence suffered and yet I could not help him. So the days went by in agony and the nights too; my legs would hardly carry me, I could not stay away from him, and always the dread, 'How shall I find him?' One night I thought of the occasion long ago when I knew I loved him, when a tenderness for him rose in me that I had not known before. He had taken my two little girls and me for a walk in Sherwood Forest, through some fields we walked, and the children ran all over the place, and we came to a brook . . . it ran rather fast under a small stone bridge. The children were thrilled, the brook ran so fast. Lawrence quite forgot me but picked daisies and put them face upwards on one side of the bridge in the water and then said: 'Now look, look if they come out on the other side.'

He also made them paper boats and put burning matches into them; 'this is the Spanish Armada, and you don't know what that was.' 'Yes we do,' the older girl said promptly. I can see him now, crouching down, so intent on the game, so young and quick, and the small girls in their pink and white striped Viyella frocks, long-legged like colts, in wild excitement over such a play-fellow. But that was long ago . . . and I thought: 'This is the man whom they call sex-obsessed.'

I slept on his cane chair several nights. I heard coughing from many rooms, old coughing and young coughing. Next to his room was a young girl with her mother, and I heard her call out: 'Mama, Mama, je souffre tant!' I was glad Lawrence was a little deaf and could not hear it all. One day he tried to console me and said: 'You must not feel so sympathetic for people. When people are ill or have lost their eyesight there is always a compensation. The state they are in is different. You needn't think it's the same as when you are well.'

After one night when he had suffered so much, I told myself: 'It is enough, it is enough; nobody should have to stand this.'

He was very irritable and said: 'Your sleeping here does me no good.' I ran away and wept. When I came back he said so tenderly: 'Don't mind, you know I want nothing but you, but sometimes something is stronger in me.'

We prepared to take him out of the nursing home and rented a villa where we took him . . . It was the only time he allowed me to put on his shoes, everything else he always did for himself. He went in the shaking taxi and he was taken into the house and lay down on the bed on which he was to die, exhausted. I slept on the couch where he could see me. He still ate. The next day was a Sunday. 'Don't leave me,' he said, 'don't go away.' So I sat by his bed and read. He was reading the life of Columbus. After lunch he began to suffer very much and about tea-time he said: 'I must have a temperature, I am delirious. Give me the thermometer.' This is the only time, seeing his tortured face, that I cried, and he said: 'Don't cry,' in a quick, compelling voice. So I ceased to cry any more. He called Aldous and Maria Huxley who were there, and for the first time he cried out to them in his agony. 'I ought to have some morphine now,' he told me and my daughter, so Aldous went off to find a doctor to give him some . . . Then he said: 'Hold me, hold me, I don't know where I am, I don't know where my hands are . . . where am I?'

Then the doctor came and gave him a morphine injection. After a while he said: 'I am better now, if I could only sweat I would be better . . .' and then again: 'I am better now.' The minutes went by, Maria Huxley was in the room with me. I held his left ankle from time to time, it felt so full of life, all my days I shall hold his ankle in my hand.

He was breathing more peacefully, and then suddenly there were gaps in the breathing. The moment came when the thread of life tore in his heaving chest, his face changed, his cheeks and jaw sank, and death had taken hold of him . . . Death was there, Lawrence was dead. So simple, so small a change, yet so final, so staggering. Death!

I walked up and down beside his room, by the balcony, and everything looked different, there was a new thing, death, where there had been life, such intense life. The olive trees outside looked so black and close, and the sky so near: I looked into the room, there were his slippers with the shape of his feet standing neatly under the bed, and under the sheet he lay, cold and remote, he whose ankle I had held alive only an hour or so ago . . . I looked at his face. So proud, manly and splendid he looked, a new face there was. All suffering had been wiped from it, it was as if I had never seen him or known him in all the completeness of his being. I wanted to touch him but dared not, he was no longer in life with me. There had been the change, he belonged somewhere else now, to all the elements; he was the earth and sky, but no longer a living man. Lawrence, my Lorenzo who had loved me and I him . . . he was dead . . .

Then we buried him, very simply, like a bird we put him away, a few of us who loved him. We put flowers into his grave and all I said was: 'Good-bye, Lorenzo,' as his friends and I put lots and lots of mimosa on his coffin. Then he was covered over with earth while the sun came out on to his small grave in the little cemetery of Vence which looks over the Mediterranean that he cared for so much.

Conclusion

Now that I have told my story in such a condensed way, letting blow through my mind anything that wanted to blow, I know how little I have said – how much I could say that perhaps would be more interesting.

But I wrote what rose up, and here it is.

FRIEDA LAWRENCE
KIOWA RANCH
SAN CRISTOBAL
NEW MEXICO

PART III

Extracts from Frieda's Fictionalized Memoirs

English Marriage

Throughout her fiction, as here, Frieda casts herself as Paula. In this chapter, which is unabridged, Ernest Weekley is thinly disguised as Charles Widmer, and we hear of Frieda's first trip to England, her wedding night and her profound disappointment in conventional married life. Manya is Frieda's elder sister, Else.

Charles Widmer had gone for a holiday that he had well earned . . . They had offered him the headmastership of a small public school in the north of England. So the world felt good to him and he went to the Black Forest and fell in love with its running brooks and the mountain walks and the peasants and the good wine. He met the young Paula and he fell in love with her too. He was no longer in his first youth, but of the age when a man falls head over heels or not at all. He asked her to marry him and she said yes.

It did not seem very real to her. She was engaged, going to another country, life seemed to draw its curtains apart for her to step into it. How he seemed to love her! He trembled when he came near and kissed her! Something big had suddenly entered her world, she knew, though she didn't understand it. He had told her of his people. 'They are very simple,' he said, 'but they will love you, because I love you and I have not been a bad son.' The quiet man who was greying at the temples became a youth again under her laugh. He told her of the struggle of poverty in his home, of his parents' unselfish devotion to each other and their ten children. She could feel his sense of responsibility, that had been there and grown strong, when at seventeen he earned his living as a schoolmaster and a hard earning it seemed to Paula as she listened. Later on he had gone on schoolmastering and taken the nights to prepare for a Cambridge scholarship. Then he told her with a smile for which she loved him, 'I went home one day and surprised them by telling them casually after dinner: "By the way you had dinner with a scholar of Trinity".'

Paula felt firm ground under her feet for the first time in her life. Here was something different from her own home life. There in his English home she felt the solidity of family life, an intimate circle, an ideal to strive after. Her own home had been such a scattered thing. There was no grit. Only the moment's satisfaction, good times, counted. Paula wanted more. She had always battled with her parents and their shallow, cynical outlook on life. In spite of their vitality they had failed intrinsically and obstinately, perversely made the best of things. There was this simple, strong man who loved her. Paula thanked God for him. She would be a good wife to him, she would love him; he was poor, but what did she care, she was not afraid of poverty. His life had been solitary, hard grinding; she would bring him the bright side of life. Her own power she did not doubt. Only sometimes he frightened her. When in a fit of reverence he kissed her feet, which seemed to her rather large, ordinary feet in not too elegant boots, then she felt uncomfortable. It flattered her vanity on one hand, on the other she accepted it placidly as the behaviour of men in love. But dimly, this ideal Paula that she knew did not exist made her uneasy. But she would live up to it; she would try and be that sampler of all the virtues he thought [her]. Paula was thinking over these things as she walked towards the fountain in the wood where she would meet him. She climbed up through the pinewood, where young beech leaves were waving loosely like butterflies in the morning wind, shining golden in the sun. Two red squirrels with black, beady eyes chased each other in front of the [path] brown with last year's leaves, with sunlit golden patches here and there. She came slowly nearer, watching the squirrels, who, seeing her, ran up a pine tree chattering angrily. Paula got more excited as she neared the fountain. She was conscious of her pink and white frock with the pink and white sunbonnet that [he] loved so much. She thought more of her effect on him than of himself. At last she saw him standing in the entrance of a sombre pine wood, the trees forming a deep archway behind him. He was like a man lifted out of ordinary life. He did not know anything, he was nothing by himself, his sole being was in that approaching pink and white girl. His emotion almost paralysed him. Paula felt slightly uncomfortable, she went up to him. He took her in his arms, gently, tenderly, repressing his passion, so as not to frighten her. 'My snowflower,' he said . . .

. . . When she went with her mother and future husband to England to pay a visit to her future relations and met them at Dover, her heart sank. She wanted to cry. 'Don't be a goose,' her mother whispered. The parents, the old stately father and the lively stout mother, talked away to the son, or rather only the mother talked and she could not understand their English. They were all so foreign, such strangers, what had she to do with them, what could she ever have to do with them? She looked out of the train at the soft green countryside, everything seemed so near, a little village humped in the hedged-in fields with a church steeple showing. 'What a wonderful cow one would make here,' she said to herself, 'or a frog'; everything was low-lying and near horizon where the sun was setting behind heavy clumps of trees. How different the country was from the towns! The towns were not soft and peaceful but grim with an iron determination and power.

Charles' parents lived in a suburb of London, and Paula was fond of them. She had never met people of their stamp. When Grandpa read a chapter from the Bible to the household in the morning, with an arm round a grandchild, he was impressive like Moses with his square white beard and handsome, rather unchanging, face. The lively Granny really ruled the roost; it only seemed as if Grandpa were the head, and Paula admired her female tactics. Granny adored her clever sons, the girls took second place. There was a warm and cosy atmosphere about the house with big joints of meat and juicy pies on the dinner table. The great event of the week was Sunday-morning church. There was such a bustle and running up and downstairs till everybody was ready. Then Grandpa, all brushed up in his top-hat and tail-coat with a little select bunch of flowers in his buttonhole, set forth down the road, and Granny in her silk cape and bonnet trimmed with violets trotted beside him to keep up with his long straight strides. Then there was church, so different from the services Paula had known at home; here men knelt to pray, which they had not done at home, and she missed the strong soldiers' voices that had filled the church with a great sound. The congregation looked so eminently lady and gentlemanlike in their Sunday clothes; 'They don't have to pray, the old Adam is dead in them for sure' thought Paula.

She went to visit three old maiden aunts with Charles. They lived in a small town pretty as a coloured postcard. They kept a little select tobacco shop. The middle aunt wrote poetry for the local paper, but the eldest was lovely, like old ivory, in black satin with a lace-fringed black silk apron. Their old house was curtained and double-curtained not to let any air in at all.

Their most joyful possession was a doll's house, a perfect doll's house with little lamps and cradles and plates and knives and forks. It seemed a symbol of their own lives. And yet they told Paula the grim story of how their father spent many nights with a loaded gun on the new grave of a dead daughter, afraid of body-snatchers. Queen Victoria was a near and dear potentiality in their lives.

Then Paula's wedding day came. For the last time she shared her bedroom with Manya, the bedroom where they had romped so wildly in the evenings, acting Lady Macbeth and the old Moor of Schiller's Rauber. Their clothes lying about like on a battlefield. It was a gay wedding down at the big old peasant inn and they drove into Freilburg where they were married in the little English church. But William the manservant, who had been part of the family and knew all their likes and dislikes, and Emma the cook, whose love letters Manya had written for her in the kitchen, wept aloud when Paula went away and everybody was sad at her going . . .

And now they were married, the train was sliding along through sunny apple orchards, vines, the earth looked bright and fruitful. Paula felt very happy . . . Also she expected something to happen, she did not know quite what it was, but it would make her very happy, happier than she had ever been. They travelled first class and were alone. He sat in a corner, ill at ease, miserable, tired. He was married, this happy creature was his wife. Yet she felt so far away in her virginity, he was almost in despair. The question of sex relations was terrifying to him, he was almost virgin himself. In spite of his age and strong passions he had never let himself go. Sex was suppressed in him with ferocity. He had suppressed it so much, put it away so entirely, that now, married, it overwhelmed him. His love had been of the ideal, pure adoration kind, sex he had not let enter consciously. How he suffered now! Paula saw it in his face. She got frightened suddenly. Perhaps, after all, the lovely thing that she expected would not happen. He hardly said a word. From time to time he gripped her hand with his long, beautiful hand tightly, while his body was held stiff and unbending. Paula began to feel sad, she put her head against the red plush and went to sleep till the end of the journey. She woke with a start. They were at Lucerne. The lights were reflected in the lake, a beautiful warm night, E [*sic*] was strung to an unbearable pitch. Their two rooms looked out on the lake, carts and people and a happy life went still on under their windows. Paula sat down on the window-seat and looked out, uneasy herself.

'Will you have something to eat?' he asked.

'No, thank you,' she answered. 'What nice big rooms they are.'

'Yes,' he said. 'Paula,' he braced himself to it, 'I must tell you we aren't really married yet. Come to me.'

She came and sat on his knee. She could feel his legs tremble underneath her, she could smell his homespun.

'My little love, you are not yet my wife.'

'Oh yes,' she said, 'I knew.'

The cheerfulness, the frankness of the answer confused him. 'Go to bed, my child. I'll go and drink something, then I will come and say good night to you.'

He got up and went, almost relieved, Paula thought. She was sad, she had imagined it all so differently. 'He used to kiss my feet in stupid boots,' she thought, 'why doesn't he kiss my real toes? He treats me like an old dowager Empress.' A big old oak cupboard, beautifully carved with a stiff Eve and an Adam that looked like the 'missing link', held her attention. She had taken some of her clothes off. Suddenly she climbed up the old cupboard, the frills of her knickers flapping from her climbing legs. Triumphantly she reached the top and sat there, wondering what he would do if he couldn't find her; she laughed, but as she thought of his serious, immobile face, she climbed down again sadly and quickly got into the great big bed that was let into a recess, it seemed like sinking into the earth.

Two hours afterwards she stood on the balcony in her light blue dressing-gown for only comfort. She was in an unspeakable torment of soul. It had been so horrible, more than horrible. 'Oh God,' she thought. How she would love to fling herself from the window! 'Only housemaids jump from windows,' she said disdainfully. Couldn't she get away? 'No, I am married, I am married,' rang in her ears. She had expected unspeakable bliss and now she felt a degraded wretch. Her pride was gone, she was nothing. Why did men marry women they loved, she asked herself, why didn't they leave them and never touch them, that would be real love instead of this horror. And he slept. He slept. She stamped her foot in impotent rage. He was sleeping while she was in utter despair. Oh God, how she hated him for it, hated him helplessly, miserably. She was bound to him nevertheless, that was the horror, she was bound to that man whom she could hear breathing. Her whole inner self was on fire. She could not bear it. 'My wedding night,' she said in cynical misery. 'I wonder if many women have felt my joy!' The lights were still slipping like a scale on the waves of the lake, the water lapped under her window, the night got slightly greyer, dawn was coming. With a shiver it went through her body, she was exhausted by her emotions. She went indoors and slept a heavy, miserable sleep . . .

Paula and her husband arrived in grim November in the north of England. It was awful. Grey and damp, and her little house was always dark. Widmer was busy and Paula was helpless in her housekeeping. She tried to learn the routine of the English middle-class woman's life. You did the shopping in the morning, after lunch you paid some calls or somebody called on you, there was the ceremony of tea and then there was dinner . . .

This horrid gnawing at her heart, how irritating, how maddening it was! She believed he was good, better than she was herself, he felt so firm and going his way so sure of himself. Yes, he was better, he knew what was right and wrong, she didn't. She could understand how a person could steal, lie, murder, love another man when one was married. To him there was an absoluteness, she knew he simply could not have done any of these lawless things. It impressed her very much and yet somehow she felt so different herself; she knew for certain that never could she have his rigid code of morals, she even did not really want it.

But it was nice to feel him at the back of her days, solid and firm, her rock of ages. He bored her a bit occasionally, she felt again today that curious sensation that she must run, run away. And in the evening she put on an old hat, ran out of the house, tore up the Mapperley hill. The lanterns gave a cheerful light; in rhythmic distances the burring noise of the trams as they boiled up the hill came near and passed again, and she had a glorious feeling of escape, of freedom as she ran on and on the dark road where the wind was catching the trees on the top of the plain. Then she would go back to her house quietly, sane again.

She entered the front door. In the hall the gas was turned down and the curious undescribable smell of the sunless hall damped her spirits. She went into the study where a bright fire burnt; the walls were books, the whole room seemed books, books on the writing-table, books on the floor. And then the smell of his pipe, it was so evidently a man's room, his room, she liked it. She threw herself down on the hearthrug with a novel, one side of her baking comfortably at the fire. These evenings when the children were asleep and he was lecturing were a treat to her.

She had got utterly absorbed in her novel when he came in, tired to death after his two evening lectures. He ran up the stairs, his step so much like his father's. His face was white with exhaustion, his eyes brilliant with his effort. A wave of tenderness rose in her at sight of him, so tired, working so hard, so uncomplainingly for the children and her. The maid brought a plate of soup for him on a tray. He gave her a look and sat down eating it, the spoon so neatly held in his beautiful hand.

'I am a damn good lecturer,' he said, wiping his drooping moustache with his napkin, shaking his head proudly.

She admired him then, when he exulted in his work. She could see him rousing his hearers, trying to get some understanding into them, grateful for the slightest sign of progress, slaving for years and years. She could never have that patience, that faithfulness in small things, duties and so on. Then he ate some bread and cheese, he made neat little 'breads' as Paula called them, a little piece of bread, butter and cheese. Paula snatched one for herself, they looked so appetizing. He laughed happily. Then he emptied a glass of beer at one go, she seemed to hear it sizz down his parched, tired throat. Then he drew up to the fire, she slipping out of his chair's way.

'You condescend to speak to me tonight,' he said. 'Yesterday you were so absorbed in your book that you did not answer my questions except with an occasional grunt.'

'Sorry,' she said, 'is it as bad as that? Lord, but this is exciting. I love Stendhal.'

'He is supposed to be something wonderful,' he answered.

'I don't care a twopenny damn what he is supposed to be,' she burst out, 'but I have not read anything that's got hold of me like this, *Le Rouge et le Noir.*'

'I daresay, it's the kind of modern stuff you like,' he said, 'with your Nietzsches and Platos.'

'Do you remember,' she laughed, 'when I had my Plato fit on and I began at breakfast, "Socrates says". You banged the table as if it were Socrates and said "Curse Socrates."'

'Yes,' he said, 'you get your measles late, most people have done with Platos at your age, but your fits!' And he sighed wearily, comically . . .

At last the spring came, the lovely English spring with its primroses, the sea of bluebells under the ancient oaks in Sherwood Forest, and the violets in the hedges and the ferns uncurled. She was waiting for a baby to be born. She knew nothing about babies. She was frightened for the baby. But otherwise she was immensely glad. Her son was born in June. Like most mothers she was convinced it was the first and only child born in the world. When he drank so eagerly, grasping her breasts, she felt she was feeding the universe. She adored him with a secret passion and would have liked to take him away to a hidden place and have him all to herself. She played games with him, popping up behind his curtains and saying: '*Bonjour Monsieur,*' and he laughed with his whole little body, gurgling at her. Two little girls were born, and she was amazed how good the children seemed, how considerate and how they amused her! She loved embroidering small clothes for them, and their neat clothes hung on the fender in the nursery at night ready for the morning. On Sunday morning they all had breakfast together in her big bed and they would listen to her German fairy-stories, that were often sad; then they would hide their faces in the sheets with distress for the fate of the little princess, and Paula felt mean at having made them sad. Their existence seemed a joy in itself, when they ran on such light feet after a ball or jumped dripping wet out of the bath to the nursery fire. They spoke English and German, but when she spoke German to her boy in a tram or train, he would pull her skirt and whisper: 'Don't speak German, people are looking at us.'

In the outer world a Boer War was going, people were singing: 'The soldiers of the Queen, my lads', and Boers were being confined in concentration-camps and there were a few pro-Boers in England. England loomed large and powerful, much more grim than its gentle landscape. Paula admired the English tremendously. Their restraint, their discipline, above all their awareness of the other person, seemed so truly civilized to her. She pondered over their ideal of fair play. Fair play seemed to her that you helped the little fellow against the big fellow, but that was not English fair play. You only stood by and saw that neither side had an advantage or played a mean trick. She also realized how ironclad was the form of the very minds of the people. Their laws were more set than Moses' Ten Commandments, especially the un-written ones. One's life was moulded and set and one could not get out. That was terrifying. Paula knew she would never become a good middle-class Englishwoman. It seemed mediaeval, you were born into a class and a million to one chances you would die in it. Why a class at all? Not like America where the poorest devil dreams that he might be president one day, where every workman felt he had a right to a house, a car, a radio, an icebox, a bathroom and a cottage in the country. No European workman would have the cheek to claim in his wildest dreams so much, and yet why not? There was political freedom in England, but it was not social freedom. Only America had known so far what actual personal liberty meant, a possibility to become anything you wanted to be. When Paula went into the kitchen Laura the cook resented it, the kitchen was her domain. When Paula asked politely after her family, Laura snubbed her, that was her business. And the routine! On Monday the cold Sunday joint for lunch, and Tuesday washday, and Wednesday ironing, and Thursday and Friday cleaning, and Saturday the kitchen premises. Thursday was Paula's 'at home day' and on Friday afternoon she sang at a women's choir, the St Cecilia. Women's suffrage was in the air. Paula never understood about politics or races or armies . . .

Octavio

This chapter is a barely fictionalized account of Frieda's first love affairs. Paula's 'great friend' with the automobile is Will Dowson; Manya, again, is her elder sister, Else; Octavio is a full portrait of Otto Gross. A few of Octavio's letters – more of the same kind as those reproduced here – have been omitted.

How well she knew later on the form of English life! One landed at Southampton, and one could know what day of the week it was. This was a Saturday afternoon because the men in white flannels were playing cricket, or were mowing the strip of lawn of their semi-detached houses. There was the Dorothy Perkins blooming over a little arbour, and the beds of marguerites and geraniums were flourishing more or less, according to the house. There were the same curtains in the houses, of art linen, the good daddies were wheeling perambulators in the street, there were the fields so unbelievably green in the moist climate that you longed to be a cow or a frog. Young people would be climbing over the stiles. Had it been a Tuesday, washing day, the semi-detacheds would have the washing out. How long, often, the washing took to dry in the damp air! Everything was on so small a scale and so known.

She had seen train after train pour into London in the early morning. There were bank-clerks and small officials and shop assistants. 'Hallo, George. Fine day today'. And then the whole compartment would be buried behind newspapers. 'And in the evening,' Paula thought, 'George will go home to his little semi-detached in the suburb, to his little wife and a little George, and mow his lawn and, for excitement, collect stamps perhaps. One day George will fall ill and have pneumonia and die, and the other men in the train next morning will say, "Have you heard about poor old George?"' And that would be the end, and poor old George had not had much of a show.

Paula had tried hard to be a good English *bourgeoise* and do as the other women did. She went shopping in the morning, because to shop in the afternoon would have been unthinkable. She called in the afternoon on other women, and in the evening there would be a dinner somewhere. But she was not happy. The winter came so dark and grey. In her small house, the beautiful wedding presents she had had of Bohemian glass and old silver and beautiful rugs looked out of place . . .

She had so far lived in the spirit of her people. Never had she been in contact with the issues of life. Neither death nor illness nor poverty, none of the things that hurt mankind deep into living, had come her way. She had spent her days an unbroken, sleeping force. People had loved her, she had loved them. But she had longed, longed madly for things she did not know, could not express. At the bottom of her being lay an uncertainty, everything was so puzzling. She did not know what was right. She argued fiercely with the men, she gripped with keen hands anything that came her way. The strength of her emotions often made people misunderstand her. She threw her whole self at them with the force of a battering ram; she was too much for them as a rule, they did not want such fierce contact, so they did not understand her as she thought and she used to feel humble and a fool. People seemed to her mostly concerned with the accessories of their lives not with the life itself, that they seemed to leave severely alone. This Paula did not understand.

Today she was in one of those cross, longing, nothing-is-right moods. She had seen her sister Manya and it made her sad. Manya had married an officer in one of the crack regiments, and the Manya of whom as a kid she had been so fond, whose blood was her blood, how could she have grown like that? Paula had met Manya at the station of the little village. Never had such an elegant person stepped out of the little, slow trains of this side line. Manya in travelling costume. Shepherd's plaid perfectly fitting her figure, the ideal of all tailors. A little travelling hat, well shoed and gloved as the French say, she stepped forth from the train. Her swaggering movements calmed down at sight of Paula.

'How are you dear?' she said. Her hard voice took on a softer tone for the sister she was fonder of than anybody. Manya talked. Paula in her simple, white garments walked round her, watching every detail of her dress; it pleased her, this perfection. Only the face, where was the face of the little sister, the dreamy eyes and the freshness and the something that had made her so dear? She was a beautiful woman, the scale of exquisite colouring that rejoiced painters was there, but the cheeks seemed too broad over the tight, high collar, and the eyes that had animated the face had lost their importance.

'And now,' asked Manya, 'tell me, are you really satisfied in your life, have you got all you want?'

'All I want; good God, but don't you see I try to, to . . .', Paula stopped.

'Ah,' said Manya. 'No, your life gives me the creeps, you poor dear. I must have change and the fittings round me and the men. Paula, you have no idea how they spoil me. The flowers I get, and the women, how jealous they are of me. Their faces are a study; oh the frumps, the frumps, I don't wonder men are bored to death with the tame cats!' Before Paula's eyes rose scores of humble, thin, unattractive women. Paula felt sorry for them, yet laughed. 'Yes,' Manya went on, 'the girls, the stacks and stacks of unmarried girls.' She pulled down her full mouth in disdain. 'Anyway, it's something to be married! How the men hate them, the poor virgins. We married women have a better time! I don't think! I laughed [*sic*]. 'And you, how are you, tell me about you?'

But Paula heard the pity in Manya's voice . . . And Paula almost felt a pitiful figure. She wanted to explain to Manya that she did not mind so much about garments and motors and grandeur, but she knew it wasn't true; she did like clothes and nice things, but they were only a part of life, not a small one either. Paula thought of Manya's little girl, Henrietta, who would be another Manya some day. Little Henrietta was already the image of her mother, and suddenly Paula saw a procession of Manya-Henriettas down the ages. She wondered at the futility of it. The why of these temporary beings distressed her fearfully. She would have liked to say something to make Manya understand what she felt and thought. But to her horror she was convinced that never as long as the world stands could she have explained to this dear creature, whom she still loved. Down in her heart Paula held the picture of an adorable little girl; to this picture Paula clung, she could still see it through Manya's elegance, the hard voice. Manya seemed to have drawn a horsehair net of fashion over her very soul. Yes, she had a horsehair quality about her. But instead of saying anything Paula talked *chiffons*. None of her garments deserved that elegant term, but Manya, good-natured as she was, often gave Paula some of her own garments that she had tired of.

These made Paula perfectly happy. A real 'Paquin', a wonderful creation of shrimp colour and a steely blue mixed with chiffon, was Paula's special joy. It had to be freshened up and to Paula's distress let out in places, but in spite of all it was perfect joy. Manya had only paid a flying visit; she made a grand stage entrance and the exit had been quick . . .

Paula had one great friend who had one of the first automobiles in England. He would drive into the forests with her, where the great hoary oaks stood apart from each other. There were pools of bluebells between them, and the primroses were big as pennies! Then she felt alive again; there weren't only dull teas and servants and grimy towns. But she always longed to go home.

As often as she could she took her children with her to Germany, to the security of her old home. On one of her visits she went to stay with a friend at Munich, the Munich before the war. Laura, the friend, seemed like a woman of another age. She was like an archaic Roman figure. She had the most astonishing, fine, honey-coloured hair. When it was not piled on her head, it covered her in a great mantle to her feet, like a Lady Godiva. Her face was still, with simple lines; her nose a little long, like an Etruscan's.

The first morning of her stay, Laura said, 'Come and let's have breakfast'. Paula looked around. There was no sign of breakfast to be seen.

'No. Put your coat on. We have breakfast at the *Kaffeehaus*.'

At the *Kaffeehaus* Laura had breakfast and wrote her letters and telephoned to her friends. Paula was introduced to an anarchist friend with the most ferocious ideas; but he looked as though he would not hurt a fly. An emancipated young countess joined them; she wrote for the *Jugend*. More and more people appeared: socialists and painters and poets, and they were all full of talk, and they seemed to come to the *Kaffeehaus* to let off steam. Paula was thrilled. As they were mostly more anxious to talk than to listen, they liked Paula because she was a grateful audience. She did not swallow all they said, but their keenness in itself was exciting.

She met a young psychologist who had been a pupil of Freud's. Octavio talked to her about Freud; she had never heard of him before. 'Yes,' thought Paula, 'these clever Jews.' They know where the crux of humanity lay, in love and work. Right from Adam and Eve they had known it.

'You see, my story of Adam and Eve is quite different,' she told Octavio. 'The Lord can't have been such a bad psychologist as not to have known that Eve would want the apple the minute it was forbidden. He really wanted Adam and Eve to eat it. And when they had eaten it, they weren't ashamed of their nakedness at all. "Look, Adam. There is a pool down by those willows and we will have a swim, and then we'll dry ourselves in the sun. Hurrah! I shall have a small Adam, and you will make him a cradle out of the willows, and then you'll work to get us something to eat while I sing to the baby." As for Freud's complexes and Karl Marx's labour, that is all the wrong side of the medal. Call it love and work and it all looks quite different.'

Octavio was amused. She told him Mark Twain's saying: 'What a pity Adam hadn't swallowed the snake instead of the apple.'

Octavio, with the help of his research in psychology, had built up in his imagination a new form of living for human beings. Octavio came from the Austrian Alps and had the light strong frame of a mountaineer; he was the first vegetarian she had ever met. 'I won't eat your nasty carcasses,' he would say, and he drank no alcohol.

Paula's old world was tumbling about her ears. She had accepted, more or less without thinking it out for herself, the human society she had been born into. It had never occurred to her that it could possibly change. But now she believed it could, and it must. She was all for it. People were choked in their lives; it was all set, the whole show, from beginning to end, from birth to death, and there was no fun and no adventure and no mystery.

Paula fell in love with Octavio and his vision of a new society. She began to question the old order. She read the great writers with a new understanding. The world had suddenly become a large growing place with endless possibilities.

Paula went back to England and her children. With the uncanny second-sight of children, one of her little girls said to her, 'You are not our old mother. You have got our old mother's skin on, but you are not our mother that went away.' The child was right.

Octavio's letters came.

'*My dearest:*
'*I am grateful that you exist and that I have been privileged to know you.*

Thank you for all the strength and courage and hope that has come to me through you. Only now that you have gone I slowly begin to understand what a renewal of all my forces you have given me: you who have shown me living and coloured what has so far been only a bodiless dream to me, a vague longing for fulfilment. I have actually seen and loved what previously seemed only a possibility, a vision I hardly hoped to see in the flesh.

'In the past all the paralysing doubts had attacked my vision of a future, of all mankind's future. But now these doubts have no longer any point of attack. Now I know. The woman that I have dreamed of for coming generations I have known and loved. Is it really possible, can it exist? Am I dreaming or is it really true? It is like a miracle, like a greeting from the future that you have come to me. Now I know what men will be like who will no longer be tainted by all the things I hate and combat. I know it through you, the only living human being today that has remained free from all the false shame and sham Christianity and false democracy, free from all the accumulated bunk, remained free through your own strength.

'How did you accomplish this, you golden child, with your laughter and your love, banishing from your soul all the curse and dirt of two thousand sombre years? Have you then no idea, dearest, of the great thing you have given me, no idea of the incomparable strength that came to me in these days? It was given me to see actually my dream of a future; and when it proved more beautiful than I had ever thought it possible, do you know how glad and strong it made me? You have taught me to laugh. Now I am sure of myself, sure as I never was before. Thank you, dearest.

O.'

Another letter:

'Dearest:
'First of all a thousand thanks for your last letter, that you always let me see afresh the lavishness of your soul. Have you then no idea of what you yourself are, of your own genius, and how elementally power and warmth well out of everything that you have filled with your life? It is as if out of your letter streamed the warmth of your body, so sweet and powerful, like a wave of happy, liberating bliss, as you live and give, you whom I love with such joy!

'*I felt the richness of your soul in every moment of bliss; particularly then your soul unfolds itself, don't you know it? You are so free, so open, and yet is your soul shy, dearest; only the most intense, most intimate feeling reveals it. It is so wonderful that in those moments of utter bliss one senses your great capacity for friendship, one feels the light of your spirit fill one's soul. When consciousness is lost in deadening bliss, above all then one feels the nearness of your soul. You are wonderful, my dearest, wonderful.*

O.'

Paula did not for a moment think that she was as wonderful as Octavio thought her, and it did not interest her; what thrilled her was his vision, his new approach to human problems. She was passionately grateful. He had given her a new faith: the human world could be happier and better than it was, and more charitable. People were tight in themselves and could not get out; they were like closed oysters.

* * *

Another letter:

'. . . *I implore you for news. I am anxious, very anxious about you. Not that I am uneasy about your love. Since that night on the ship fear is no longer permissible, but I fear for your courage in the future, that your strength may not be equal to the annihilating, strangling smallness of life in that dead, grey, cold milieu. I know that you can never adjust yourself to that world and its destructive strength. I am afraid for you, afraid for your power of resistance, your power to remain whole, just as hardly any of the free, proud animals can survive captivity. Just because of your marvellous nature, just because you are free and born for freedom, because of this I am afraid for you. What will become of you in this eternally foreign and, for you, impossible world? Remain strong and free. You must not go under. Help must come.*

O.'

Paula had met Octavio again. Together they had crossed at night from Holland to England. They had sat in the still, warm night, and it seemed to Paula they were crossing over into an unknown world. She was frightened, but it could not be helped. Her old world was gone.

'Dearest one', he wrote,
'Now I can see how the highest and the deepest is liberating itself in you, how you are growing conscious in quiet strength, how a proud harmony is completing itself in you. You have the great simplicity of expression that is a sign of the rarest beings. I am not far enough on yet to speak of it. I only know that my love is filled with immense gratitude for your being and your growth. You know that you are the affirmation in my life, the flowering fruitful yes, the future that has come to me . . .'

* * *

'Yes, I know you as far as you can be known. You are so close to me and yet always so marvellously new, and ever new . . .'

* * *

It was not true when Octavio wrote her that she was free and harmonious – far from it. Chaos raged in her soul. How could she stand all alone against all the millions of other people, their weight and power? She loved her children; they fascinated her, their difference of character, the things they said and did, and the fun she had with them. When her boy went to school, she would stand at the window making faces at him, and he would look up a little anxious that nobody else saw her. She seemed so much nearer to them than the grown-up people. 'They are so good, these children,' she thought, 'so considerate with me! They must never be aware that I am going through this hell.'

Octavio wrote:

'I fear you want to commit self-deception to be able to deceive others, not to have to tell an honest lie. This I fear, that you lack the honesty for an honest lie. You say as you did before that you have no right to destroy the existence of a good man. But don't you see that you destroy your own right of self-determination, this right that can never be lost either through pact or sense of duty? How can you overlook that, if you don't want to overlook it?'

And another torturing letter came:

'I have come to know what a fateful influence you have become in my life, what dominant powers pour from you into me, and how clearly your image fits into my world and all I strive for. You give me the wonderful

strength to make me a genuine human being, and at the same time live for an idea. One must have both to be worthy of loving you . . .'

* * *

'Paula, I need you because you make me sure and great . . .'

* * *

Paula sat by the piano when this letter came. She was trying to make a noise to drown the uproar in her heart; and the tears dropped on the keys. She wanted to go to Octavio. She wanted to live that bright life that he held out to her. How she wanted to go, now, at once. He had wakened up her soul in her, that had lain coiled up and asleep, and now it had become a frightening tiger and she had it on her hands. She could not go to him. How could she leave her children? They were so small! She could not burden him with them. He lived for his vision. The everyday life he ignored. On visions alone you can't live. He hardly knew whether it was night or day. She was no Bohemian. How were they going to live? She would let him down, he who had given her her own soul. She would not help him. He would have to go his way and she her own that looked so grim and miserable. She would be quite alone with that tiger of a soul on her hands. She knew somehow that something was wrong in him; he did not have his feet on the ground of reality.

His last letter came. 'I can never lose you because you will never lose yourself.'

Then later she heard that he had been a doctor in the World War, and had died. How he must have suffered! He, who had dreamed of a glorious coming day for all men, saw before him the torn bodies and broken spirits of the young that he had dreamed his dreams of happiness for! No wonder he died, as so many had died with their hopes denied and broken.

Andrew

The record of her meeting with D. H. Lawrence (Andrew) and their passion is, sadly, incomplete in Frieda's manuscripts. This edited version from the *Memoirs*, however, captures some of their time together. Frieda's three children appear towards the end of this section with their real names, this chapter being part of notebook fragments that were never translated into fiction.

Paula

* * *

She felt cut off and alone in a world of millions, living her inner life unrelated to the outer one. She was a fanatic. She had believed that all people had an inner life or wanted to go on and get more out of their living on this earth, but she found it was not so. Most of them hung on like grim death to their known selves and would prefer death to changing. But in her heart she listened to a little persistent voice: 'You have had much, and you will have more.'

And one sunny spring morning Andrew walked into her life, naturally and inevitably as if he had always been there, and he was going to stay. In a sovereign way he took her for himself; she was his and he would never let her go again while he lived; he would kill her rather. She liked it. He wanted her, he needed her, and that was bliss. Nothing else mattered; all the misery of loneliness, of unconnectedness, was gone. Together they took hold of the earth, the solid earth, never to lose it again entirely, neither of them. He was at home in both worlds, the material and the adventurous spiritual one. He was so much of a piece, so simple, that it took her some time to realize that he was a great man. He was trusting with her, completely generous. 'Take me, all of me, I am yours.' It almost frightened her. He forced the responsibility of himself on to her; she did not want to take it. She was not as sure of everything as all that, especially of what she thought. She had found that thoughts were shifting and contradictory things. And he would hammer away at her, trying to make her commit herself finally, and she often would not. He lived what he believed, and believed what he lived. There was no discrepancy, no compromise; and she had to be the same.

* * *

Andrew

* * *

Andrew had walked through the 'gates of the walled defences' and found himself in the wilderness and was cutting a path through it for others to follow if they wished. So together they were gloriously alone. It was adventure all the time. His writing was adventure in the wilderness of human experience; so little was really known of what happens inside us, we were only at the very beginning of consciousness. What happens inside of others remains always [a] vague mystery we get at best a glimpse [of] now and then. Andrew's genius gave him a deeper understanding. Instinctively people knew that his words were not so harmless, and neither was he. Society insists on its members being 'embedded in its matrix', and it will not let you 'walk out of its walled defences'.

Paula was so sure she knew little about others. It was as much as she could do to feel right about her own self. She did not really want a connexion, especially not an emotional one, with others. Yet in her own way she passionately wanted people to be happy. She felt responsible for humanity in a vague, helpless way. And there was Andrew who felt more responsible than she did. It would be a fight, and she never thought of possible defeat. Most people think of their own welfare first; not so Andrew. The bigger task always stood first. He needed so little for himself: enough decent food, good water, a simple but clean and healthy place to live in, not in a town but on the land. He had very few personal belongings: a few shirts and underwear, all very tidy, and a few clothes. On the few occasions that his socks had holes in them – he was so light on his feet – Paula would mend them with red and green and blue wool. 'They are more fun this way,' she told him as he looked at them in astonishment.

His movements were so sure and to the point. She never remembered him breaking anything accidentally. He had his own life under complete control. Poor as they were he always had enough money to buy a book he wanted, or a box of paints, or a present for somebody; there was always enough for both of them, but there were no luxuries in their lives.

Especially at the times when Andrew worked, Paula felt alive with the richness of her days. After lunch they would go for long walks and find flowers and berries and mushrooms; daffodils and bluebells and primroses in English woods; almond blossoms and asphodel in Sicily; big ferns and mimosa, so many different kinds, in the Australian bush; red-hot-poker and Mariposa lilies in New Mexico. The house was full of flowers. As a friend had written: 'Always when I see foxgloves, I think of the Elmers. Again I pass in front of their cottage and in the window, between the daffodil curtains with the green spots, there are the great sumptuous blooms. "And how beautiful they are against the whitewash," cry the Elmers. As is their custom when they love anything, they make a sort of fiesta. With foxgloves everywhere, and then sitting in the middle of them, like blissful prisoners, dining in an encampment of Indian braves.'

The very fact that they were poor seemed to give them a more immediate connexion with the things that don't cost a cent. The sun and moon and stars and trees and clouds and contact with people and animals. Most of the very rich people Paula had known were longing to get out of their sumptuous homes, to put on old clothes and get into the wilderness somewhere and rough it in a hut, and broil their own steaks over a self-made oven, and moaned when they had to return to their riches.

* * *

They had been together for nearly a year . . . There had sprung up no grand passion between them a year ago. They had not wanted to fall in love, but inevitably, against their will, they had to submit to something blind and strong that drew them together. They had fought, they had suffered a great deal in this year; for days they were quite swamped by the misery they had inflicted on so many people by their union, but always triumphantly rose that love between them and justified what they had done. They were sitting in the great, white room with the big windows looking over the lake, ultramarine blue in the sunlight, the bamboos at the side bowing in the slight breeze. The lake was dotted with white and pink and yellow sails like butterflies breathing quietly.

Across, Monte Baldo sloped into the lake, brown and lazy, like the back of a prehistoric monster. Some window-panes opposite were brilliant suns reflecting the setting sun rays. Andrew was absorbed in finishing a sketch. A bold bridge leaping in one bound easily, gracefully, over a deep chasm. The white, frothing water rushing underneath, cypresses pointing up out of a mist of olive trees. Andrew stepped back from his easel, put his head slightly on one side, then quickly took a step forward and gave a darker touch to the cypresses. He stood back again, yes, he was satisfied. 'Come and look,' he said, 'now aren't those cypresses wonderful?'

Paula rose lazily from the couch where she had been reading, curled up in comfortable, cat fashion. She looked at the picture critically. 'Not quite soft and misty enough for me,' she answered, 'but the bridge is a joy. I want the olives different though.'

He resented her lofty criticism, but reluctantly effaced some hard parts. '*La posta*', rang from the gate the deep voice of the Italian postman that they liked so much. Paula went to the door. '*Buona sera, signora*,' he said to her, handing her a letter.

She looked at it frightened. On the big couch she sat down and opened it. She could not believe what she read. The husband whom she had left promised her the children from time to time. 'I could never be quite hard on a woman,' he had written at first. However, she had suffered at the thought of her three children who had meant life to her, till Andrew had come. She had looked on their spending these Easter holidays with her as a certainty. But now her husband wrote, 'I have done with you, I want to forget you and you must be dead to the children. You know the law is on my side.'

'The law,' Paula cried with blazing eyes, clutching at the nearest thing to vent her rage. 'The law! Can they undo the fact that those children are mine, that I bore them, that they are flesh of my flesh? The law,' she said bitterly, contemptuously, 'it takes much count of human nature.'

Andrew was irritated at the form her deep disappointment took. 'It's no good going on like that,' he said, tapping the table with his fist. But Paula went on, let loose her anger on the universe at large, at the injustice that was done her as she thought. Andrew felt helpless, her grief was something beyond him, he could not cope with it. His oversensitive, oversympathetic nature could not bear the suffering imposed on her and on him. He shut himself off from her. But she did not notice, she was blinded by the pain of her disappointment.

All night she lay looking across the lake where in the blue night one solitary light shone; she was conscious of nothing but this light and the pain in her limbs, her arms, that had longed to hold her children. Tomorrow would be Sunday. She thought of the Sunday mornings, when the three had come to her bed, when she had pillow fights with them in spite of the disapproving nurse, when they rode on her raised knees and she made them tumble down. She saw Joy's little neck, the head thrown back laughing like nobody in the world laughed when she tumbled off her seat.

The next day Paula went about blind and dumb, incapable to think, to act, just doing household things, the tears running down her face; she did not notice them except when they touched her hands or tickled her nose. Andrew suffered to see her like this. He could not get near her, he might as well have got near an avalanche. Anaesthetized with suffering Paula went on for two or three days thinking of the children. She was one great wound where her children had been bleeding her to death.

Andrew was getting beside himself. He was a delicate man always. On the third day he developed a bad cold and had to stay in bed. Absently, mechanically Paula looked after him. At last in self-preservation, knowing that they could neither of them bear this, he said to her in a detached voice from his bed, 'Paula, we really cannot go on like this. You see for yourself that it makes me ill; if things are as they are between us, if you behave like that, I think you had better leave me, go to the children altogether and leave me.'

Paula was stung into reality for the first time for days. 'Oh,' she wailed, 'don't say it, don't. Don't leave me in the lurch now, don't send me away. You know I love you, you know I can't leave you. But can't you see what it means to me, the children?'

'No,' he said quickly, 'no man can understand it.'

'Oh, but you won't try,' she cried, 'you are jealous of them, you kill me when you don't recognize the mother in me.'

'Very well,' he said, 'I can't then, and so we had better make an end.'

'Oh,' Paula cried crouching on the floor like under a blow, holding her arms. 'Oh, but what of our love, that should not fail; you told me you would die if I left you!'

'That phrase has done a lot of harm in our lives already, you know it isn't true now,' he said.

'Yes,' she cried bitterly, 'I have made you stronger.'

'Yes,' he said, 'and if a thing is a failure, it is better to acknowledge it than to go on being miserable.'

These last words seemed to kill Paula's remaining wits. She became a wounded animal. The mother in her bleeding, and the man whom she loved so deeply giving her this blow was too much for her. She was ashamed, a hunted animal that nobody wanted; she was utterly alone and ashamed; she wanted to creep away somewhere in a dark corner where nobody should see her misery and shame. Him, whom she had loved and trusted, he told her to go. She felt ashamed to be sent away as if she had some disease, nobody wanted her.

She put on a hat mechanically and wandered out of the house, slinking along the walls like a dog afraid of a hiding. A bell started ringing, hitting her raw senses like a blow. She went along the walls through the narrow street of the dark Italian village, slowly, mechanically. At the end of the village she turned to the road leading along the lake. On her right rose the bare layers of rock. The road lay in front of her white in the sun; far away the sky melted into the lake in a haze, the lake lay blue at her left. She left the road and walked on the sand and stones to the water. Little waves were lapping, coming on the land with a wicked little sound. The sun and the clear water were weaving little moving patterns of light over the round stones. Paula's heart beat when she saw those stones. She had become an unconscious mass of life; she did not reason, she did not feel resentment; life went on in her in spite of herself. Only staring at those stones with the pattern of moving light over them did she know that she trembled all over. Something had gone down in her, something was broken that would never be whole again. She accepted it all, the suffering that had left her so raw, she accepted it, but she could stand no more. She envied those stones with their skin of limpid water that protected them from the air and wind; there was shelter down there. The waves were lapping, gently swishing at her feet. She felt so flayed herself, her misery was like a shameful disease to her. She wanted to hide, to creep away from things. The water was licking her feet rhythmically. Slowly, mechanically, she took off her things, her boots, her underclothes. She wanted to be one of those stones under the clear, protecting water. She would creep into the water. Slowly she sat down, slipping into the shallow water gradually, slipping deeper and deeper. Now the waves touched her breast; she caught her breath, then the waves went over her gently lapping. Her arms and legs relaxed, she sank back in the water . . .

I met him in the dark passage of Colet house. He looked so big in his grey long flannel trousers and blue blazer. He ran easily towards me, stopped, came nearer and stopped again.

'You,' he said, 'you,' in a voice wavering with unbelief.

'Monty,' I answered, 'can you come with me now for half an hour without anybody knowing?'

'Yes,' he said, 'but I must ask Mr Wicroff first.'

'Tell him it's your aunt,' I said.

He ran away and soon came back, his cap on his head, joyfully. 'We will go and have tea together. Where do you come from and are you alone?'

'I have come from Germany to see you. You are a big boy.'

He did not dare to look at me; at first only sideways he glanced. We ordered tea and strawberries and cream from a nice barmaid who smiled at us. Then I wept when we sat together so near, and I had to ask him for his hanky and he gave it me, a big grubby school hanky.

'There, I mustn't make an exhibition of myself,' I said, and he looked at me full of manly love and support. Then we talked. I asked him how I could see the little ones, without anybody knowing, and he thought and made a plan calmly and self-possessed. Then he looked at me full of love.

'You look pretty fit,' he said admiringly. His eyes filled with tears. He asked me what I did, what I lived on, and I said, 'I wrote a novel.' He looked with his old impish smile at the ambitious mother. Then he said, 'You know it's a bad lookout, you don't make much money by writing. Now I'll show you St Paul's, the grounds.'

'I want a photograph of it.'

'No, I'll draw you a picture,' he said. I always felt his love strong and whole.

I told him, 'You know I couldn't stand Nottingham and the life any more, you can't understand things now, but you will later on. I want to be able to see you,' I said.

'Shall I ask Papa?' he said. 'I will,' his big grey eyes again full of tears and a manly love shining in them as I have never felt before in my life. It was the most wonderful thing I have seen and I humbly thanked God in my heart for it.

'I don't know,' I said.

We walked round St Paul's, I so proudly by the side of him, with a red rose for a brooch. We passed a bitterly weeping kid, I gave it a penny and it stopped like clockwork. It pleased Monty. I gave him half a crown.

'I'll share it with the little ones.' He told me, full of pride, that Elsa was so clever at school, always first, that Barby was a little lazy but that she drew so well. Then I took him to the station, where he [slipped] away quickly. Afterwards I saw him sitting on the platform, reading a letter I had given him, his eyes full of tears . . .

Last Chapter – Friends

This chapter was put together by E. W. Tedlock from a number of diverse papers of Frieda's, and is necessarily more fragmented than the previous ones. It tells of Frieda (Paula) living alone in Mexico in the period immediately following Lawrence's death. Ravagli (Dario) is in Europe, collecting Lawrence's (Andrew's) ashes to bury them in Taos.

Never since Andrew's death had she been alone. She knew that she had not accepted the fact that Andrew was really dead.

* * *

Andrew's death had been so quiet and proud, so still, and inevitably his life had stopped. And death was there. He had given her so much of life, the glamour of all creation, he had made her feel and now he had given her the last and supreme gift: death in its dignity. She had felt death's silent splendour. Andrew's life was accomplished, his sincere efforts were ended. Nothing would disturb him any more.

She remembered singing quietly to him in the night by his bed where he lay dead, he had always listened to her, even when he was angry. But now he listened no more. She had felt a curious exultation. It was fulfilled. Her own self seemed to fall away from her. There was not only the little everyday personal world, there was the great universe, the great whole of creation to whom all belongs, plants and animals and men, alive or dead; the universe was one forever. For the first time she felt the wholeness of the world as if before it had been a flat coin, now she had a sense of its depth, of its roundness. But the live man, he had gone, she could hear him still and feel his presence in her soul. She had lived so absolutely in his world, the bright, noble world that had been his, she was still living in it. But now she was alone. Dario had gone and stood no longer between her and her loneliness, and like a dark figure she saw Andrew standing in front of her bed as if asking her: 'Come and join me.' She became ill and was taken to a nursing home. A great fear was upon her, she could not fight it. A crisis came, would she live or die? The engines of the trains were screaming their arrival, but there was nobody in the train for her; Andrew was dead, he couldn't come, and Dario was far away. A struggle went on in her between life and death. Then slowly in the centre of her a sweet, patient small impulse rose and asserted itself. No, she was not going to die yet. The number of her dead had grown larger and larger, friends and parents, people she had loved were dead. But she herself would live still and see the clouds and the rain and feel the warmth of summer and doubly would she be grateful for being just that, alive. Let people fight about Communism and Fascism, in the end the two were the same, a mere fight for control, and what then? You had to live from a deeper self than mere will. They missed the point of living, these would-be controllers. When you had control, what did it amount to? 'They have missed the bus,' Paula thought. We are not born in little black shirts, nor little red ones, but in our skins. And we live in it and then die in it. Even if everybody had ten cars and twenty radios and forty iceboxes it would not make them rich inside themselves. You had to get your own natural inheritance back, your own joy in the living universe round you. It was this that was lost, nothing else. However much you took away from other people it wouldn't do you any good. There were those who wanted to hang on like grim death to what they had and the others who wanted to take it away from them, and it wasn't the point at all. 'Forget about it,' Paula wanted to say to them, 'it won't make you happy, begin really to live from your own best human inside and see what happens. Resentment and having fixed ideas won't get you anywhere.'

Especially resentment Paula wanted to conquer. Let people be mean to her personally, she would not let it alter her nature and sour her life. That's what they wanted: to bore a hole into her wholeness; she would not let them triumph but would cut herself off from this new devil of malevolence. This was her fight, now, not to fight others, but fight to keep her own integrity . . .

Dim and drowsy the days went by; Paula was feeling very weak. Impatiently she waited for Dario to return, but he could not come at once. He was bringing her husband's ashes from Europe. How grateful Paula felt that Dario had a respect almost as her own for Andrew's memory. She had after Andrew's death wanted to take his remains to the ranch to which he had meant to return.

In the autumn Dario had built a small chapel, very simple, on the hill under the steep mountains. The hill had wild flowers growing on it, sunflowers and red and pink cactus and michaelmas daisies and little cypress trees. Andrew had loved the spot.

* * *

She was at peace now, Dario was there, he made it possible for her to live the simple life she loved on this spot of the earth that she loved; this spot that they could turn into a living centre, this meant genuine living to her.

* * *

How big the price was that Paula had to pay for Andrew's love. So many people hated her, because he had come her way and not theirs. Well, she paid, but it had been worth it through all eternity.

Bibliography

There are thousands of critical publications on Lawrence, so the following list is necessarily highly selective. It includes only works that have been quoted directly in the introduction, have profoundly influenced my own thinking or whose primary focus is Frieda Lawrence herself.

Barr, Barbara, 'Step-daughter to Lawrence', *London Magazine*, Aug/Sept 1993, 23-33 and Oct/Nov 1993, 12-23

Battersby, Christine, *Gender and Genius: Towards a Feminist Aesthetics* (London, Women's Press, 1989)

Beauvoir, Simone de, *The Second Sex* (1949; Harmondsworth, Penguin, 1972)

Bedford, Sybille, *Aldous Huxley: The Apparent Stability* (1973; London, Paladin, 1987) and *Aldous Huxley: The Turning Points* (1974; London, Paladin, 1987)

Brett, Dorothy, *Lawrence and Brett: A Friendship* (1933; Sante Fe, 1974)

Brown, Keith (ed.), *Rethinking Lawrence* (Milton Keynes, Open University Press, 1990)

Bynner, Witter, *Journey with Genius* (London, Peter Nevill, 1953)

Carswell, Catherine, *The Savage Pilgrimage* (London, Secker and Warburg, 1932)

Chadwick, Whitney and Courtivron, Isabelle de, *Significant Others: Creativity and Intimate Partnership* (London, Thames and Hudson, 1993)

Colls, R., and Dodd, P. (eds.), *Englishness: Politics and Culture 1880-1920* (London, Croom Helm, 1986)

Daly, Mary, *Pure Lust* (London, Women's Press, 1984)

Dinnerstein, Dorothy, *The Rocking of the Cradle and the Ruling of the World* (London, Women's Press, 1987)

Dunmore, Helen, *Zennor in Darkness* (1993; Harmondsworth, Penguin, 1994)

Faludi, Susan, *Backlash: The Undeclared War Against Women* (London, Chatto and Windus, 1992)

Feinstein, Elaine, *Lawrence's Women: The Intimate Life of D. H. Lawrence* (London, HarperCollins, 1993)

Fussell, Paul, *Abroad: British Literary Travelling Between the Wars* (Oxford, Oxford University Press, 1980)

Garnett, David, *The Golden Echo* (London, Chatto and Windus, 1953)

Green, Martin, *The von Richthofen Sisters: The Triumphant and the Tragic Modes of Love* (London, Weidenfeld and Nicholson, 1974)

Huxley, Aldous, *The Genius and the Goddess* (London, Chatto and Windus, 1955)

Iles, Teresa *All Sides of the Subject: Women and Biography* (New York, Teachers College Press, 1992)

Irvine, Peter and Kiley, Anne (ed.) 'D. H. Lawrence and Frieda Lawrence: Letters to Dorothy Brett', *D. H. Lawrence Review*, Spring 1976

Jackson, Rosie, *Mothers Who Leave: Behind the Myth of Women Without Their Children* (London, Pandora, 1994)

Lacy (ed.), *Letters to Thomas and Adele Seltzer*, (Santa Barbara, Black Sparrow Press, 1976)

Lawrence, D. H., *Fantasia of the Unconscious and Psychoanalysis and the Unconscious* (1923; Harmondsworth, Penguin, 1971). Lawrence's fiction, poetry and essays are all published by Penguin, as well as being available in other editions.

Lea, F. A., *The Life of John Middleton Murry* (London, Methuen, 1959)

Leavis, F. R., *D. H. Lawrence: Novelist* (1955; Harmondsworth, Penguin, 1964)

Light, Alison, *Forever England: Femininity, Literature and Conservatism Between the Wars* (London, Routledge, 1991)

Lucas, Robert, *Frieda Lawrence: The Story of Frieda von Richthofen and D. H. Lawrence* (London, Secker and Warburg, 1973)

Luhan, Mabel Dodge, *Lorenzo in Taos* (New York, Knopf, 1932)

MacLeod, Sheila, *Lawrence's Men and Women* (London, Heinemann, 1985)

Maddox, Brenda, *Nora: A Biography of Nora Joyce* (London, Hamish Hamilton, 1988)

Maddox, Brenda, *The Married Man: A life of D. H. Lawrence* (London, Sinclair Stevenson, 1994)

Mailer, Norman, *The Prisoner of Sex* (London, Weidenfeld and Nicholson, 1971)

Miller, Henry, *The World of Lawrence: A Passionate Appreciation* (London, John Calder, 1985)

Millet, Kate, *Sexual Politics* (1969; London, Rupert Hart-Davis, 1971)

Mitchell, Juliet, *Psychoanalysis and Feminism* (Harmondsworth, Penguin, 1974)

Moore, Harry T., and Montague, Dale B. (eds.), *Frieda Lawrence and Her Circle: Letters from, to and about Frieda Lawrence* (London, Macmillan, 1981)

Moore, Harry T., *The Collected Letters of D. H. Lawrence* (Harmondsworth, Heinemann, 1962)

Moore, Harry T., *The Intelligent Heart: The Story of D. H. Lawrence* (1955; London, Penguin, 1960)

Moore, Harry T. and Roberts, Warren, *D. H. Lawrence* (1966; London, Thames and Hudson, 1988)

Murry, John Middleton, *Son of Woman* (London, 1931)

Nehls, Edward (ed.), *D. H. Lawrence: A Composite Biography* (Madison, Wisconsin, 1957-59)

Russell, Bertrand, *Autobiography* (London, Allen and Unwin, 1967)

Sagar, Keith, *The Life of D. H. Lawrence* (London, Methuen, 1980)

Smith, Anne (ed.), *Lawrence and Women* (London, Vision, 1978)

Smith, Grover, *Letters of Aldous Huxley* (London, Chatto and Windus, 1969)

Spender, Stephen (ed.), *D. H. Lawrence: Novelist, Poet, Prophet* (London, Weidenfeld and Nicholson, 1973)

Squires, Michael (ed.), *D. H. Lawrence's Manuscripts: The Correspondence of Frieda Lawrence, Jake Zeitlin and Others* (London, Macmillan, 1991)

Storch, Margaret, *Sons and Adversaries: Women in William Blake and D. H. Lawrence* (Knoxville, University of Tennessee Press, 1990)

Tedlock, E. W. (ed.), *Frieda Lawrence: The Memoirs and Correspondence* (London, Heinemann, 1961)

Thornycroft, Rosalind, *Time Which Spaces us Apart* (completed by Chloë Baynes, published in a limited private edition, Batcombe, Somerset, 1991)

Tomalin, Claire, *Katherine Mansfield: A Secret Life* (1987; Harmondsworth, Penguin, 1988)

West, Anthony, *D. H. Lawrence* (London, Arthur Baker, 1950)

Notes

1. All the italicized sections running through my text are verbatim quotations from Frieda's daughter, Barbara Barr. They are transcribed from the author's personal interview with Barbara, made in Radda, Italy, 16 November 1993, and are reproduced with Barbara Barr's permission.
2. I would have preferred some other way of referring to Frieda than by her Christian name alone, as this remains an unfortunate convention when men are habitually referred to by their surnames, but there seemed no other brief way of avoiding confusion with D. H. Lawrence.
3. Daly, *Pure Lust*, has an index reference to 'Lawrence, D. H. as a wife beater', and pp. 212–3 cites a newspaper article about a four-day convention on Lawrence – a 'festival' that, to her indignation, not only honoured 'that misogynist' by claiming he venerated women, but seemed to be defending wife battering.
4. Quoted by Whitney Chadwick in 'Living Simultaneously: Sonia and Robert Delaunay', in Chadwick, ed., *Significant Others*, p. 34.
5. Lucas, *Frieda Lawrence*, p. 253.
6. Carswell, *The Savage Pilgrimage*. This quote encapsulates the way in which women are frequently constructed as elemental nature. See de Beauvoir, *The Second Sex* and Dinnerstein, *The Rocking of the Cradle and the Ruling of the World*, for further discussions of the unconscious drives behind this.
7. Luhan, *Lorenzo in Taos*, p. 36.
8. Lucas, p. 85. In 1928, Rhys Davies similarly likened Frieda to a lionness.
9. Tomalin, *Katherine Mansfield*, p. 118.
10. Leavis, *D. H. Lawrence*, pp. 49–50.
11. Frieda Lawrence, *Memoirs*, p. 374.
12. Luhan, quoted Lucas, p. 188.

13. Sagar, *The Life of D. H. Lawrence*, p. 57.

14. Miller, *The World of Lawrence*, p. 36.

15. Frieda, letter to Richard Aldington, January 1949, in *Frieda Lawrence and Her Circle*, eds. Harry T. Moore and Dale B. Montague, p. 91.

16. The cover of *Frieda Lawrence and Her Circle*.

17. Lucas, p. 3.

18. Miller, pp. 32–3.

19. Huxley's letter to Mary Kelly, 21 November 1957, in *Letters of Aldous Huxley*, ed. Grover Smith. Previously, in *The Genius and the Goddess*, Huxley had betrayed his own fantasies of Frieda by having his narrator go to bed with her counterpart and then killing her in a nasty car accident – perhaps a piece of unconscious revenge for a sense of helplessness in the face of her sexual power and emotional indifference to him.

20. Moore and Roberts, *D. H. Lawrence*, p. 27.

21. This was the subject of Marina Warner's excellent Reith lectures in 1994, particularly the first one, 'Monstrous Mothers'.

22. *Memoirs*, p. 43.

23. *Memoirs*, p. 275.

24. Letter to Monty, 1954, *Memoirs*, pp. 339–40.

25. Letter to Murry, 1954, *Memoirs*, p. 342.

26. Weekley formed no further intimate relationships, never remarried and, once the children were set up with his relatives in London, lived a lonely life in his Nottingham digs, immersed in his books. His publications were to include *An Etymological Dictionary of Modern English* (1924), *Words, Ancient and Modern* (1927) and *The English Language* (1929). He gained an honorary doctorate from Nottingham University in 1951.

27. Frieda, letter to Else Jaffe, 1954, *Memoirs*, p. 340.

28. Moore, *The Intelligent Heart*, p. 531.

29. *Memoirs*, pp. 339–40.

30. Barr, *London Magazine*, Aug/Sept 1993, p. 29.

31. Barr, *London Magazine*, Aug/Sept 1993, p. 31.

32. Gross' version of psychoanalysis, however, was, in many ways, misleading, similar in part to the revisionism of Freud found in Wilhelm Reich and others later in the century. See Mitchell's

reading of Reich in *Psychoanalysis and Feminism*, pp. 137–223.

33. For details of these relationships, see Feinstein, *Lawrence's Women*, pp. 44–59.

34. *D. H. Lawrence Miscellany*, ed. Moore, p. 132.

35. Frieda, letter to Aldington, *Frieda Lawrence and Her Circle*, p. 93.

36. West, *D. H. Lawrence*, p. 36; Miller, p. 40.

37. *Memoirs*, p. 353.

38. Bedford, *Aldous Huxley: The Apparent Stability*, pp. 263–4. In *The Genius and the Goddess*, p. 41, Huxley describes his Lawrence figure as 'on the loose . . . in search of some woman capable of meeting the demands of a symbiotic relationship, in which all the giving would be on her side, all the ravenous and infantile taking on his'.

39. Huxley, *The Genius and the Goddess*, p. 67, and Lucas, p. 203.

40. Lawrence to Ernest Collings, January 1913, *Letters of D. H. Lawrence*, ed. Huxley, p. 93.

41. Barr, *London Magazine*, Oct/Nov 1993, p. 16.

42. Letter to Edward Garnett, *Memoirs*, p. 202.

43. Frieda, *Memoirs*, p. 190. For all her ideas of free love, Frieda was determined to be loyal to Lawrence. She wrote to Edward Garnett in 1913: 'Yes, my theories have sadly altered; there are two sides to human love, one that wants to be faithful, the other wants to run; my running one was uppermost, but it's going to be faithful now'.

44. Rosalind Thornycroft, *Time Which Spaces us Apart*, pp. 78–9. These memoirs were completed by Rosalind Thornycroft's daughter, Chloë Baynes, and published for the first time by her in a limited private edition in Batcombe, Somerset, 1991. They include crucial extracts from Rosalind's notebooks, which cover the growing friendship with Lawrence from 1919 onwards, his stay with her in Fiesole in 1920, including their sexual encounter, and his subsequent correspondence. Their affair is presented as being short-lived, but entirely mutual and their correspondence continued until at least 1923.

45. Moore, *The Intelligent Heart*, p. 477: 'Frieda used to tell her intimates, "Lawrence has been impotent since 1926!" '

46. *Frieda Lawrence and Her Circle*, p. 100.

47. Frieda, letter to Murry, 1953, *Memoirs*, p. 333.

48. Tomalin, p. 118. Tomalin also discusses the complicated friendship

between the four of them in detail and has some sensitive insights into Lawrence, Frieda and their relationship.

49. Murry, letters to Frieda, 1946 and 1953, *Memoirs* pp. 282 and 330.
50. *Memoirs*, p. 311.
51. *Memoirs*, p. 368.
52. Bedford, *Aldous Huxley: The Apparent Stability*, p. 263.
53. *Memoirs*, p. 367.
54. See Tomalin, especially pages 126–54, for one of the best discussions of the complicated friendship between Murry, Mansfield, Lawrence and Frieda.
55. Lea, *The Life of John Middleton Murry*, p. 119.
56. Barr, *London Magazine*, Oct/Nov 1993, p. 16.
57. Frieda, letter to Martha Gordon Crotch, 1930, *Frieda Lawrence and Her Circle*, p. 43.
58. Maria Huxley, quoted in Bedford, *Aldous Huxley: The Apparent Stability*, p. 346.
59. Moore, *The Intelligent Heart*, p. 162.
60. My own book, *Mothers Who Leave*, which looks at this subject in more depth, devotes a chapter to this aspect of Frieda's history.
61. Frieda, letter to Edward Garnett, January 1913, *Memoirs*, pp. 189–90. All the following extracts from her letters are from these *Memoirs*.
62. Frieda, *Memoirs*, p. 360.
63. Quoted by Lucas, p. 100.
64. Garnett, *The Golden Echo*.
65. Lawrence, *Selected Poems*, p. 65.
66. Tomalin, p. 117.
67. Moore, *The Intelligent Heart*, p.199.
68. Lawrence to Edward Garnett, 17 July 1914, quoted in Sagar, p. 73.
69. Thornycroft, p. 58.
70. Barr, *London Magazine*, Aug/Sept 1993, p. 28.
71. Letter from Frieda, August 1923, in *Letters to Thomas and Adele Seltzer*, ed. Lacy, p. 105.
72. Frieda, *Memoirs*, p. 167.
73. Frieda, letter to Edward Gilbert, *Memoirs*, p. 303.
74. Sagar, letter to the author, 21 October 1993, quoted with his permission.

75. Sagar, p. 127.
76. Lawrence, *Fantasia of the Unconscious*, pp. 188–9.
77. See Light, *Forever England*, especially p. 7, on this misogyny and the establishment of a masculine literary culture in the inter-war years: 'Britain is the place where it is no longer possible to be properly male – a country gelded, as Lawrence might have said, and emasculated by the aftermath of war'.
78. Faludi, *Backlash*, pp. 339–46, gives a brilliant analysis of the anti-feminist enterprise in Robert Bly's 'new age' and 'new man' work.
79. In a letter to Aldington, Frieda recalls the incident when Lawrence 'was worked up and finally had his hands on my throat and said fiercely: "I am the master, I am the master!" and I said in astonishment: "Is that all? I don't care, you can be the master as much as you like." And then he was astonished all right'. *Frieda Lawrence and Her Circle*, pp. 98–9.
80. Mailer, *The Prisoner of Sex*, pp. 154–6.
81. *Memoirs*, p. 14.
82. The term 'apartheid of gender' is from MacLeod's *Lawrence's Men and Women*, p. 129. For an extended discussion of Bachofen and Lawrence, see Green, *The von Richthofen Sisters*, pp. 81–4.
83. Frieda, letter to Koteliansky, 1923, *Memoirs*, p. 231.
84. Letter from Katherine Mansfield to Beatrice Campbell, 4 May 1916, quoted in Tomalin, p. 147.
85. *Memoirs*, p. 119.
86. *Memoirs*, p. 137.
87. *Memoirs*, p. 186.
88. Letter to Aldington, 1956, in *Frieda Lawrence and Her Circle*, p. 134.
89. Huxley, *The Genius and the Goddess*, p. 40.
90. Frieda, Letter to Dorothy Brett, 1945, *Memoirs*, p. 411. One such reference to *Faust* is in the *Memoirs*, pp. 52–3.
91. Green, p. 154.
92. Light, p. 7, discusses this exapatriation in purely political terms: 'It is easy to read here the hysteria of the dispossessed, the fears of increasing egalitarianism, a reaction to the march of labour and working-class activism imagined as the onslaught of "barbarians" and vandals . . .'
93. *Memoirs*, p. 6.

94. *Memoirs*, p. 292.

95. *Memoirs*, p. 140.

96. Letter from Frieda to Mansfield, quoted in Tomalin, p. 143.

97. Caresse Crosby's autobiography describes Frieda as 'upholstered, petulant and full of pride', and that when she played the gramophone 'Lawrence in a fit of exasperation broke record after record over her head'. See Moore, *The Intelligent Heart*, p. 491.

98. Bertrand Russell, *Autobiography*

99. Green, p. 375.

100. Frieda, *Memoirs*, p. 135–6.

101. Frieda, letter to Aldington, 1949, *Frieda Lawrence and Her Circle*, p. 92.

102. Frieda, letter to Witter Bynner, 1942, *Memoirs*, p. 269.

103. Huxley, *The Genius and The Goddess*, pp. 98–9.

104. *Memoirs*, p. 16.

105. Letter to Edward Gilbert, 1944, *Memoirs*, p. 273.

106. Quoted in Sagar, p. 247.

107. *Frieda Lawrence and Her Circle*, p. 31.

108. All these extracts are from Frieda's *Memoirs*.

109. *Frieda Lawrence and Her Circle*, p. 55. Huxley, too, thought Frieda at a loss without Lawrence to restrain her.

110. *Frieda Lawrence and Her Circle*, pp. 90, 94.

111. Frieda, letter to Edward Gilbert, 1944, *Memoirs*, p. 274.

112. *Memoirs*, p. 150.

113. *Frieda Lawrence and Her Circle*, p. 94.

114. *Memoirs*, p. 5.

115. *Memoirs*, p. 202.

116. *Memoirs*, p. 17.